Shining Star B

Anna Uhl Chamot

Pamela Hartmann

Jann Huizenga

Longman

longman.com

Shining Star ★B

Pearson Education, 10 Bank Street, White Plains, NY 10606

Vice president, director of instructional design: Allen Ascher
Editorial director: Ed Lamprich
Acquisitions editor: Amanda Rappaport Dobbins
Project manager: Susan Saslow
Senior development editors: Susan Clarke Ball, Bill Preston
Vice president, director of design and production: Rhea Banker
Executive managing editor: Linda Moser
Production manager: Ray Keating
Senior production editor: Sylvia Dare
Production editor: Patricia W. Nelson
Director of manufacturing: Patrice Fraccio
Senior manufacturing buyer: Edith Pullman
Photo research: Kirchoff/Wohlberg, Inc.
Design and production: Kirchoff/Wohlberg, Inc.
Cover design: Rhea Banker, Tara Mayer
Text font: 12.5/16 Minion
Acknowledgments: See page 282.
Illustration and photo credits: See page 283.

Library of Congress Cataloging-in-Publication Data
Chamot, Anna Uhl.
    Shining star / Anna Uhl Chamot, Pamela Hartmann, Jann Huizenga.
        p. cm.
    Includes index.
    Contents: A. Level 1. — B. Level 2. — C. Level 3.
    ISBN 0-13-093931-5 (pt. A) — ISBN 0-13-093933-1 (pt. B) — ISBN
0-13-093934-X (pt. C)
    1. English language—Textbooks for foreign speakers.   [1. English
language—Textbooks for foreign speakers. 2. Readers.]   I. Hartmann,
Pamela.   II Huizenga, Jann. III. Title.

PE1128.C48 2003
428.2'4—dc21

2002043460

ISBN: 0-13-093933-1

Printed in the United States of America
6 7 8 9 10–RRD–08 07 06 05

About the Authors

Anna Uhl Chamot is professor of secondary education and faculty adviser for ESL in George Washington University's Department of Teacher Preparation. She has been a researcher and teacher trainer in content-based second-language learning and language-learning strategies. She codesigned and has written extensively about the  Cognitive Academic Language Learning Approach (CALLA) and spent seven years implementing the CALLA model in the Arlington Public Schools in Virginia.

Pamela Hartmann is a teacher and writer in the field of Teaching English to Speakers of Other Languages (TESOL). She has taught ESL and EFL in California and overseas since 1973. In addition, she has authored several books in the fields of TESOL and cross-cultural communication.

Jann Huizenga is an educator and consultant in the field of TESOL, with a special interest in teaching reading. She has worked as a teacher trainer at Hunter College in New York City, at the University of New Mexico at Los Alamos, and overseas. She has written numerous books for ESL students.

Consultants and Reviewers

Jennifer Alexander
Houston ISD
Houston, Texas

Heidi Ballard
University of California at Berkeley
Henry M. Gunn High School
Palo Alto, California

Susan Benz
Balboa High School
San Francisco, California

Lynore M. Carnuccio
esl, etc Educational Consultants
Yukon, Oklahoma

Wes Clarkson
El Paso ISD
El Paso, Texas

Lynn Clausen
Pajaro Valley USD
Watsonville, California

Brigitte Deyle
Northside ISD
San Antonio, Texas

Janet L. Downey
Riverside Unified School District
Riverside, California

Elvira Estrada
Socorro ISD
El Paso County, Texas

Virginia L. Flanagin
University of California at Berkeley
Berkeley, California

Leanna Harrison
Stinson Middle School
San Antonio, Texas

Gloria Henllan-Jones
Amundsen High School
Chicago, Illinois

Ann Hilborn
Educational Consultant
Houston, Texas

Terry Hirsch
Waukegan High School
Waukegan, Illinois

Kevin Kubota
Freeman High School
Richmond, Virginia

Betsy Lewis-Moreno
Thomas Edison High School
San Antonio, Texas

Caroline LoBuglio
Lower East Side Preparatory High
   School
New York, New York

Jean McConochie
Pace University
New York, New York

James McGuinness
National Faculty – Lesley University
Yarmouthport, Massachusetts

Kaye Wiley Maggart
New Haven Public Schools
New Haven, Connecticut

Maria Malagon
Montgomery County Public Schools
Rockville, Maryland

Elva Ramirez Mellor
Chula Vista Elementary School
   District
Chula Vista, California

Wendy Meyers
Casey Middle School
Boulder, Colorado

Linda Nelson
Century High School
Santa Ana, California

Jessica O'Donovan
Bilingual/ESL Technical Assistance
   Center (BETAC)
Elmsford, New York

Patrizia Panella
Isaac E. Young Middle School
New Rochelle, New York

Kathy Privrat
Lower East Side Preparatory
   High School
New York, New York

Jan Reed
Garden Grove USD
Garden Grove, California

Leslie S. Remington
Hermitage High School
Richmond, Virginia

Linda Riehl
Grady Middle School
Houston, Texas

Michael Ringler
Hialeah-Miami Lakes Senior
   High School
Hialeah, Florida

Alma Rodriguez
Bowie High School
El Paso, Texas

Marjorie Bandler Rosenberg
Malrose Associates
Annandale, Virginia

Sandra Salas
Rayburn Middle School
San Antonio, Texas

Carrie Schreiber
International Newcomer
   Academy
Fort Worth, Texas

Angela Seale
Independent Consultant
Houston, Texas

Penny Shanihan
Pearland High School
Houston, Texas

Katherine Silva
Holmes High School
San Antonio, Texas

Kathleen Anderson Steeves
The George Washington
   University
Washington, D.C.

Trudy Todd
Fairfax Public Schools,
   Emeritus
Fairfax County, Virginia

Sylvia Velasquez
Braddock Senior High School
Miami, Florida

Sharon Weiss
Educational Consultant
Glenview, Illinois

Ruth White
Washington High School
Cedar Rapids, Iowa

To the Student

Welcome to

Shining Star

This program will help you develop the English skills you need for different school subjects. Each unit has selections about a variety of topics, including science, social studies, and math. There are also literary selections. These selections will help you understand the vocabulary and organization of different types of texts such as stories, poems, and nonfiction articles. They will give you the tools you need to approach the content of the different subjects you take in school.

Before starting to read a selection, you will do activities that help you relate your background knowledge to the new information in the text. You will also study some of the new words in the text to give you a head start as you begin to read. Finally, you will learn a reading strategy that will help you read with greater understanding.

While you read, ask yourself, "Am I understanding this? Does it make sense to me?" Remember to use the reading strategy! Your teacher may also play a recording of the selection so that you can listen to it as you read.

After you read, you will check your understanding of the text. Then you will work on activities to help improve your English skills in grammar, phonics, and spelling.

To extend your ability in English, you will participate in several types of activities related to the selections in each unit. Some of these activities involve listening and speaking, while in others you will produce different kinds of writing. Each unit also has a number of projects in which you can practice your artistic, musical, dramatic, scientific, mathematical, language, social, and thinking talents. You'll also see some suggestions for further reading related to the theme of the unit.

We hope that you enjoy *Shining Star* as much as we enjoyed writing it for you!

Anna Uhl Chamot
Pamela Hartmann
Jann Huizenga

Contents

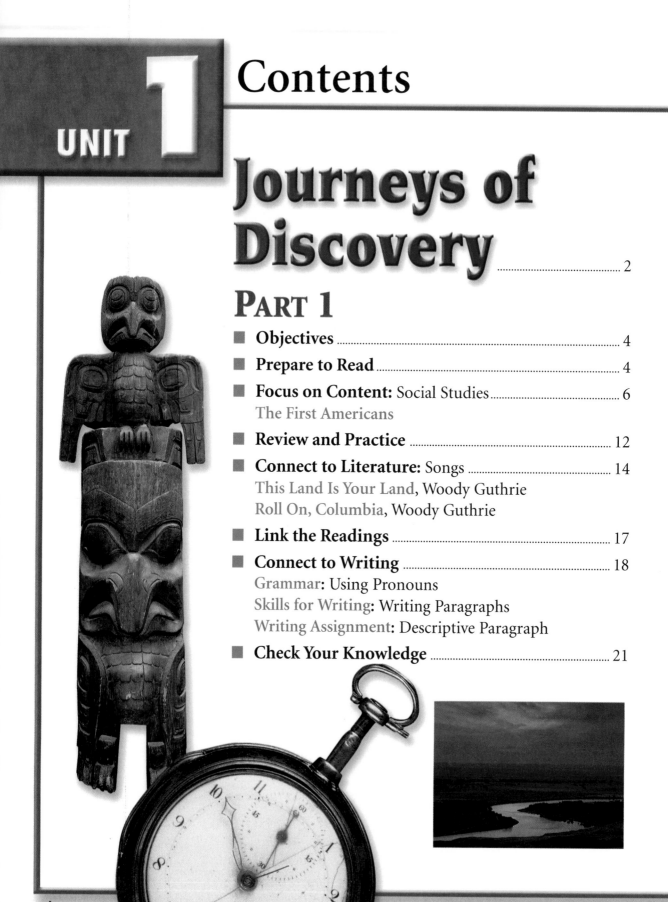

PART 2

PUT IT ALL TOGETHER

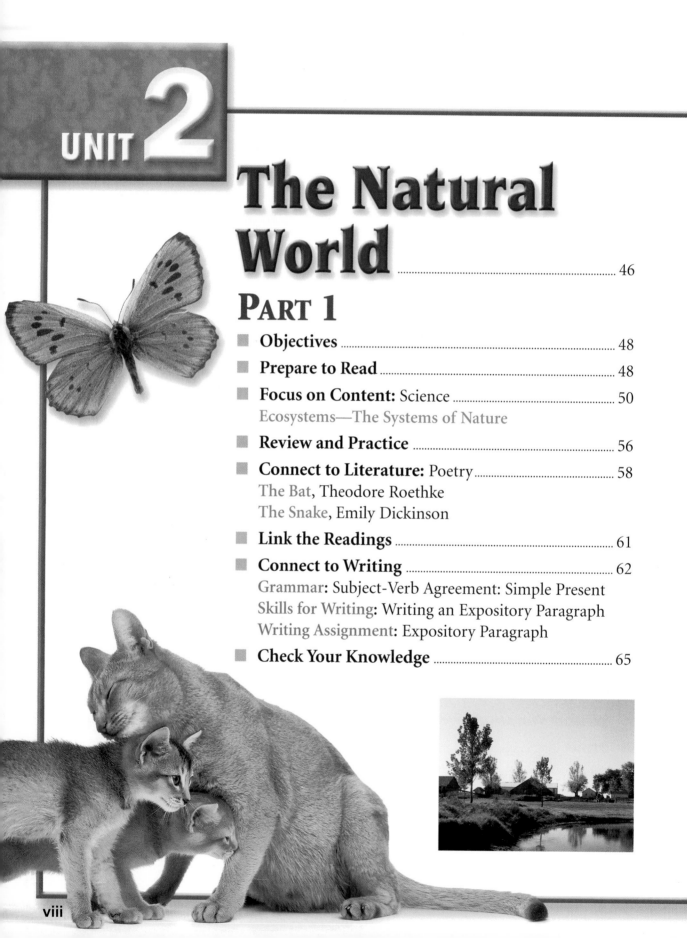

UNIT 2

The Natural World

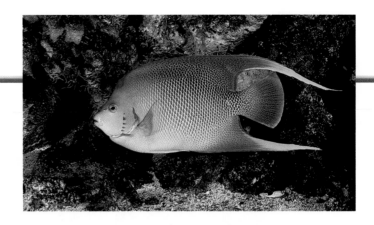

PART 2

PUT IT ALL TOGETHER

UNIT 3

Striving for Success

PART 2

PUT IT ALL TOGETHER

UNIT 4

Change 134

PART 1

PART 2

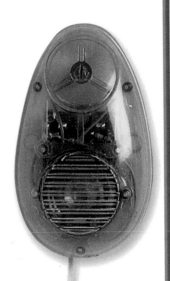

PUT IT ALL TOGETHER

UNIT 5

The Frontier 178

PART 1

PART 2

PUT IT ALL TOGETHER

UNIT 6

Observing the Universe

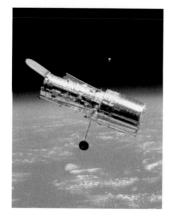

Part 2

Put It All Together

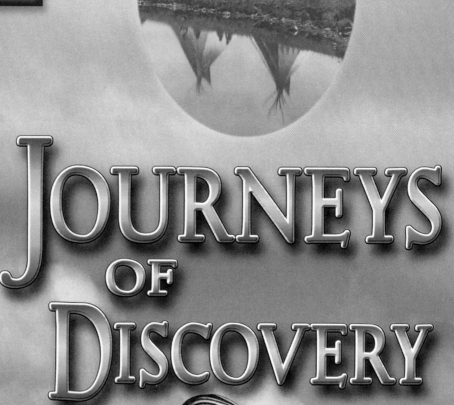

UNIT 1

JOURNEYS OF DISCOVERY

PART 1

- "The First Americans"
- "This Land Is Your Land," Woody Guthrie
- "Roll On, Columbia," Woody Guthrie

PART 2

- From *River to Tomorrow*, Ellen Levine
- "Reading a Relief Map"

A journey usually means a trip from one place to another. However, a journey can also take place in our own minds. For instance, our thoughts can take us on a journey into the past. All of our travels help us discover new things. In this unit, you will go on several journeys of discovery.

In Part 1, you will read a social studies article about the first people to discover and settle some regions of the land that we now call the Americas. Then you will hear two folk songs that describe places in the United States.

In Part 2, you will read about the American explorers Lewis and Clark and their journey to the West Coast of the United States. You will also meet the Native American woman who helped make their journey possible. Finally, you will examine and learn about relief maps.

Prepare to Read

OBJECTIVES

LANGUAGE
DEVELOPMENT

Reading:
- Vocabulary building: *Context, dictionary skills*
- Reading strategies: *Previewing, predicting*
- Text types: *Social studies article, songs*
- Literary element: *Alliteration*

Writing:
- Word web
- Descriptive paragraphs
- Self-evaluation
- Editing checklist

Listening/Speaking:
- Appreciation: *Songs*
- Culture: *Connecting experiences*
- Critical listening

Grammar:
- Pronouns
- Mechanics

Viewing/Representing:
- Maps, charts, illustrations

ACADEMIC CONTENT

- Social studies vocabulary
- Native American groups
- Geographical features and regions of the United States

BACKGROUND

"The First Americans" is an informational text about the first people to inhabit the Americas. It is nonfiction, which means it is about real events or facts.

The first Americans probably came here from northern Asia many thousands of years ago. They may have crossed a land bridge that is now underwater. The movement of large groups of people from one place to another is called migration.

Make connections Look at the map. The arrows show possible migration routes of those early peoples. Answer the questions.

1. Where is Asia?
2. Where is North America?
3. Why do you think early peoples followed these routes?

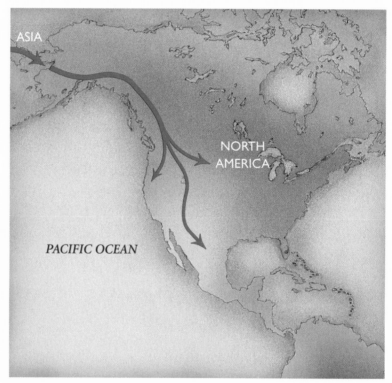

▲ Migration routes of early peoples

LEARN KEY WORDS

arid
climate
environment
irrigate
nomads
region
tribe

VOCABULARY

Read these sentences. Use the context to figure out the meaning of the **red** words. Use a dictionary to check your answers. Write each word and its meaning in your notebook.

1. The desert is **arid** because there is very little rainfall.
2. In the winter, the **climate** in the Northeast is cold and wet.
3. Land, water, and air are important parts of the **environment**.
4. Some tribes had to **irrigate** their crops because the climate was so dry.
5. Some Native Americans settled in one place, but others were **nomads**.
6. Some Native Americans settled in the Southwest **region** of the United States.
7. The Choctaw **tribe** is a group of Native Americans from the Southeast.

READING STRATEGY

Previewing and Predicting

Previewing a text helps you understand it better. Good readers always look at the text to get some ideas about it before they read. They also keep in mind their purpose for reading the text.

When you preview a text, follow these steps.

*   Think about what you already know about the subject.

*   Look at the title and headings.

*   Look at any pictures, photographs, graphs, charts, or maps.

*   Use this information to **predict** what the text is about.

*   As you read, predict what will happen next.

*   Think about your purpose for reading the text.

Preview the text. Look at the title and headings. What is the main topic? What five regions of the United States will you read about? What do you already know about these regions? As you read, predict what will come next in the text. For what purpose are you reading the text?

THE

FIRST
AMERICANS

Where Did the First Americans Come from?

According to one popular **theory**, the first Americans came from northern Asia. Some scientists believe that they crossed a land bridge between northern Asia and North America between 15,000 and 30,000 years ago. Some of those **peoples** stayed in North America, and others traveled into Central and South America. In the 1970s, a scientist found a **campsite** in southern Chile that is one of the oldest known human **dwelling** places in the Americas. It is at least 12,500 years old and contains remains of people's homes and tools.

▲ Stone tools found at Monte Verde, a very old campsite in Chile, include items for chopping, scraping, and pounding.

theory, idea that tries to explain something
peoples, groups of people who have the same way of life
campsite, place to set up a shelter where people can live for a
    short time
dwelling, where people live

Native Americans in the United States

By 1500 C.E., about 1 million people lived in the different regions of North America that are now the United States. Each tribe lived in a specific region and developed its own **customs** and language. The climate and **geographical features** of the different regions affected how the tribes lived. Several of the major regions are described below.

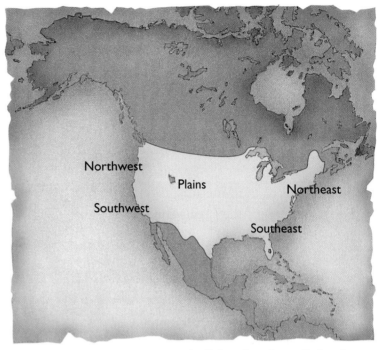

▲ Cultural regions of what is now the continental United States

The Northeast

The Northeast had great forests and many rivers and lakes. It was rich in **game** and fish. Many native peoples, including the Iroquois, the Penobscot, and the Malecite, lived in the eastern forests. These tribes made tools and canoes. They hunted deer and birds and fished in the lakes, rivers, and ocean. They also grew corn, squash, and beans.

---

customs, special ways that a group of people does things
geographical features, important parts of Earth, such as oceans and mountains
game, animals that people hunt for food

BEFORE YOU GO ON . . .

1 What did a scientist find in Chile?

2 What did people in the Northeast do to get their food?

HOW ABOUT YOU?

- Describe the climate in your region. Is it hot or cold? Wet or arid?

A Malecite canoe ▶

7

The Plains

The Plains stretch north to south for 2,000 miles between the Rocky Mountains and the Mississippi River. They are **enormous**, flat, grassy lands. The first Americans in the Plains lived in villages. The women grew beans, corn, and squash, and the men hunted deer and some buffalo. After the Spanish brought horses to the Americas, the Native Americans of the Plains could ride horses when they hunted buffalo. Then they became nomads, following the buffalo **herds** from place to place. They ate buffalo meat, and they made clothes, **tepees**, tools, and drums from buffalo skins, hair, and horns. Native Americans of the Plains made medicines from plants. For example, they used skunk cabbage root as medicine for **asthma**.

By 1800, about 150,000 Native Americans, in thirty tribes, lived on the Plains. Among those tribes were the Pawnee and the Dakota (also called the Sioux).

▼ Sioux villages ▲

The Southwest

The hot, arid Southwest was home to many Native American tribes. The Pueblo tribes learned to irrigate crops with the little water that was available. The Pueblo also performed rituals, or special ceremonies. For example, they performed a nine-day Snake Ceremony to bring rain and a good **harvest**. The history of the Pueblo goes back 2,000 years. Today, some Pueblo people live in stone and clay villages that are more than 1,000 years old.

enormous, very large
herds, large groups of animals that eat grass
tepees, Native American cone-shaped tents
asthma, illness that causes difficulty in breathing
harvest, fruit and vegetables that farmers gather from the fields

The Southwest was also home to the Navajo and the Apache. The Navajo came to the Southwest in about the year 1400. They lived in the territory that is now northern Arizona and New Mexico and in part of southern Colorado and Utah. The Apache settled in modern-day Texas in the 1520s.

The Navajo and Apache were hunters. Later, they learned farming from the Pueblo. The Navajo also learned **weaving**, pottery making, and sand painting from the Pueblo.

When horses arrived in the Americas, the Navajo and Apache quickly learned to **breed** them.

---

weaving, making cloth
breed, help animals reproduce

BEFORE YOU GO ON . . .

1. What do we call the grassy lands between the Rocky Mountains and the Mississippi River?

2. What animals were very important to the Native Americans in the Plains? Why?

HOW ABOUT YOU?

- Why do you think that some tribes farmed and some tribes hunted?

▲ Painting of a herd of buffalo on the Upper Missouri River (Karl Bodmer, about 1834)

▲ Totem pole village

The Northwest

The thirty tribes that lived in the forests of the Northwest were **unique** in several ways.

First, unlike Native Americans in other regions, they didn't become farmers. Instead, they caught fish and game for their food.

Second, they had social classes. For example, some people were nobles, the highest social class. Others were commoners, and some were slaves.

Third, the Native Americans of this region were excellent builders and **architects**. Their huge houses were made of cedarwood.

Finally, members of many of these tribes made wooden totem poles to record their **family tree**. Every family chose a spirit in the form of an animal, such as a raven, wolf, bear, or eagle. They carved images of these spirits in their totem poles.

◄ A family's spirit images

---

unique, the only one of its type
architects, people who design buildings
family tree, treelike illustration of family members and relationships

The Makah people lived in what is now northwestern Washington. The Makah were very skilled at fishing. Traditionally, they built big canoes from red cedar and hunted whales in the ocean.

Like many northwestern tribes, the Makah had potlatches—large feasts where people gave away blankets and other property. By giving away property, people earned a high position in society. Potlatches were a way to pass on important cultural information from one **generation** to the next.

The Southeast

Native Americans who settled in the Southeast enjoyed a mild climate and an environment rich in **natural resources**. The first settlers, sometimes known as the Temple Mound Builders, were skilled builders and farmers. They built large towns. The mound builders have **vanished**, but you can still see the flat-topped **mounds** of their cities in parts of Louisiana today.

▲ Creek council house

By the late 1500s, the Choctaw, Cherokee, Chickasaw, Creek, and Seminole peoples had created a remarkable **civilization** in the Southeast. These tribes lived in planned villages and were good farmers and hunters. They started schools and had knowledge of diseases and medicines. European settlers called them the "Five Civilized Tribes."

Most of these southeastern peoples were forced to move west because European settlers wanted their land. Between 1830 and 1850, the government moved the Cherokee, the Choctaw, and other peoples to land west of the Mississippi River. Many died traveling there, and the journey of the Cherokee became known as the Trail of Tears.

---

generation, all the people who are about the same age
natural resources, things from the Earth that people use, such as trees and minerals
vanished, disappeared
mounds, hills
civilization, developed society

BEFORE YOU GO ON . . .

1 What is a potlatch?

2 Why did the tribes of the Northwest make totem poles?

HOW ABOUT YOU?

• What region of the United States do you live in? Which Native American tribes have lived there?

Review and Practice

Reread "The First Americans." Then copy this chart into your notebook.
Complete the chart with information from the text.

Region	Tribes	How They Got Food	Natural Resources	Other Information
Northeast	Penobscot Malecite Iroquois	hunted, fished, and farmed	forests, rivers, lakes, fish, deer, birds	made tools and canoes
Plains				
Southwest				
Northwest				
Southeast				

EXTENSION

If you could live with a Native American tribe, which one would you choose? Why? Draw a word web like this one in your notebook. Write the name of the tribe you chose in the center circle. Complete the other circles with information about the tribe. Share this information in small groups. Explain why you chose this tribe.

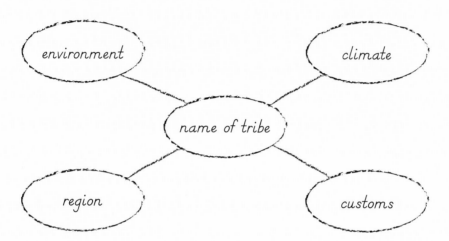

DISCUSSION

Discuss in pairs or small groups.

1. Where do some scientists think that the first Americans migrated from?

2. Why do you think they migrated? Why do you think some people continued to move south?

3. Why do you think European settlers called the Choctaw, Cherokee, Chickasaw, Creek, and Seminole tribes the "Five Civilized Tribes"?

4. Think about how you used the previewing and predicting strategies. What did you look at? Were your predictions correct? Which previewing strategy helped you the most?

▲ Traditional coiled basket

Songs

Read and listen to two folk songs by Woody Guthrie. Most folk songs are traditional to the people who live in a particular place. These songs describe places in the United States. Preview the songs. What do you think they are about?

This Land Is Your Land

Chorus:
This **land** is your land, this land is my land,
From California to the New York Island,
From the redwood forest to the gulfstream waters,
This land was made for you and me.

Verses:
As I went walking that **ribbon of highway**
I saw above me that **endless** skyway,
I saw below me that golden valley,
This land was made for you and me.

I've **roamed and rambled**, and I followed my footsteps,
To the sparkling sands of her diamond deserts,
All around me a voice was sounding,
This land was made for you and me.

When the sun came shining, then I was **strolling**,
And the wheat fields waving, and the dust clouds rolling,
A voice was **chanting** as the fog was lifting,
This land was made for you and me.

"This Land Is Your Land," words and music by Woody Guthrie. TRO-© 1956 (Renewed) 1958 (Renewed) 1970 (Renewed) Ludlow Music, Inc., New York, NY. Used by permission.

---

land, country
ribbon of highway, long, narrow road, like a ribbon
endless, continuing; without end
roamed and rambled, moved freely through a wide area without any
    special purpose or goal
strolling, walking without a purpose (like *rambling*)
chanting, repeating a word or phrase again and again

LITERARY ELEMENT

Alliteration is the poetic use of two or more words that begin with the same sound: "I've roamed and rambled . . . ."

BEFORE YOU GO ON . . .

1 What states does Woody Guthrie mention in this song?

2 What geographical features does Guthrie describe?

HOW ABOUT YOU?
● How do you think Guthrie feels about this country? Explain.

Roll On, Columbia

Chorus:
Roll on, Columbia, roll on,
Roll on, Columbia, roll on,
Your **power** is turning our darkness to **dawn**,
So roll on, Columbia, roll on.

Verses:
Green Douglas firs where the waters break through,
Down the wild mountains and valleys she flew,
Canadian Northwest to the ocean so blue,
So roll on, Columbia, roll on.

Many great rivers add power to you
The Yakima, Snake, and the Klickitat too,
Sandy Willamette and Hood River too,
So roll on, Columbia, roll on.

Tom Jefferson's **vision** would not let him rest,
An **empire** he saw in the Pacific Northwest,
Sent Lewis and Clark and they did the rest,
So roll on, Columbia, roll on.

At Bonneville now there are ships in the **locks**
The waters have risen and cleared all the rocks,
Shiploads of plenty will steam past the **docks**,
So roll on, Columbia, roll on.

And on up the river is Grand Coulee Dam,
The **mightiest** thing ever built by a man,
To run the great factories and water the land,
So roll on, Columbia, roll on.

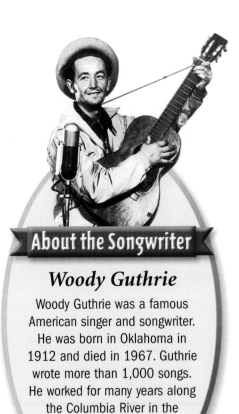

About the Songwriter

Woody Guthrie

Woody Guthrie was a famous American singer and songwriter. He was born in Oklahoma in 1912 and died in 1967. Guthrie wrote more than 1,000 songs. He worked for many years along the Columbia River in the northwestern region of the United States.

---

roll on, continue to move
power, energy
dawn, sunrise; daybreak
vision, idea or plan for the future
empire, group of countries or peoples ruled by one government
locks, parts of a river enclosed by gates on either end so that the water level can be increased or decreased to raise or lower boats
docks, places where ships stop and people can get on or off
mightiest, strongest

BEFORE YOU GO ON . . .

1 Where is the Columbia River? Find it on a map.

2 What rivers flow into the Columbia?

HOW ABOUT YOU?
• Which song do you like better? Why?

16

Link the Readings

REFLECTION

Look at the chart. Reread "The First Americans" and the two songs by Woody Guthrie. Then copy the chart into your notebook and complete it.

Title of Selection	Type of Text (Genre)	Fiction or Nonfiction	Purpose of Selection	Culture
"The First Americans"		nonfiction	to inform or instruct	Native American
"This Land Is Your Land"	song		to entertain	
"Roll On, Columbia"				

DISCUSSION

Discuss in pairs or small groups.

1. Geographical features include mountains, valleys, plains, and deserts (land features) and lakes, rivers, and oceans (water features). Copy the chart into your notebook and complete it with geographical features described in the texts.

	Land Features	Water Features
"The First Americans"		
"This Land Is Your Land"		
"Roll On, Columbia"		

2. Which region do you think was the best place for the first Americans to settle? Why?

3. Which description in "The First Americans" is your favorite? Which descriptions in Woody Guthrie's songs are your favorites? Why?

Connect to Writing

GRAMMAR

Using Pronouns

Pronouns can replace nouns.

> The **Columbia** is a river. **It** is very large.

The pronoun *it* replaces, or refers to, the noun *Columbia*.

Pronouns can be subjects or objects. They can be singular or plural.

	Subject Pronouns	Object Pronouns
Singular	I, you, he, she, it	me, you, him, her, it
Plural	we, you, they	us, you, them

Singular pronouns refer to singular nouns, and plural pronouns refer to plural nouns.

> singular noun   singular pronoun
> The **Northeast** had great forests. **It** was a region rich in game.
>
> plural noun   plural pronoun
> Some **tribes** lived in the eastern forests. **They** used the wood to make tools.

Object pronouns are used as objects in sentences.

> object noun   object pronoun
> The Spanish brought **horses** to the Americas. The Navajo rode **them**.

Practice

Copy these sentences into your notebook. Circle the noun that each underlined pronoun refers to. Then check your answers in pairs.

1. The Plains are large, grassy lands. <u>They</u> extend 2,000 miles.
2. Totem poles are beautiful. Tribes carved images of animals into <u>them</u>.
3. A potlatch was a large feast. <u>It</u> was a way to pass on cultural information.
4. Woody Guthrie wrote many songs. Some of <u>them</u> are about the land around <u>him</u>.

SKILLS FOR WRITING

Writing Paragraphs

A paragraph is a group of sentences about one idea in a piece of writing. Read this paragraph. Then answer the questions.

Indent the first sentence.

Write the title in the middle of the first line.

Begin each sentence with a capital letter.

Use a period at the end of each sentence.

> Thomas José Harding
>
> The Northeast
>
> I love the northeastern part of the United States. It is a great place to live in all seasons. In the summer, you can hike through open fields or swim in blue lakes. In the winter, you can ski down snow-covered mountains and go ice-skating on frozen lakes. The most beautiful season is the fall, when the leaves change color. They change from green to red, orange, gold, and yellow. Spring brings colorful flowers. The Northeast is my favorite part of the United States.

1. What is the title? Where is it?

2. Which sentence is indented?

3. What punctuation is at the end of each sentence?

4. What should each sentence begin with?

WRITING ASSIGNMENT

Descriptive Paragraph

You will write a descriptive paragraph about your region.

1. **Read** Reread "The First Americans" on pages 6–11 and "This Land Is Your Land" on page 14. What descriptive words do the author and songwriter use?

Writing Strategy: Word Web

A word web can help you organize your ideas before you write. First, write the main idea in a circle. Then write details that support the main idea in circles around it.

Here is the word web for the paragraph "The Northeast" on page 19. Look at the web. Then answer the questions.

summer—hike in open fields, swim in blue lakes

spring—colorful flowers

the Northeast—a great place to live

winter—ski on snow-covered mountains, ice-skate on frozen lakes

fall—leaves change color

1. What is the main idea?
2. What details support the main idea?
3. What words help you picture the region?

EDITING CHECKLIST

Did you . . .

▶ indent the first sentence?

▶ begin each sentence with a capital letter?

▶ end each sentence with a period?

▶ describe your region?

▶ use pronouns correctly?

2. **Make a word web** Draw a word web in your notebook. Include descriptive words.

3. **Write a paragraph** Use your word web to write a paragraph that describes your region.

Check Your Knowledge

Language Development

1. How can you figure out the meanings of new words?
2. How do you use previewing and predicting as reading strategies?
3. What is alliteration? Give an example.
4. What is a pronoun? Give an example of a sentence in which there is a pronoun.
5. How can a word web help you prepare to write?
6. What is a paragraph? A descriptive paragraph?

Academic Content

1. What new social studies vocabulary did you learn in Part 1? What do the words mean?
2. What are the names of three Native American tribes?
3. What are some geographical features of different regions of the United States?
4. What are three regions where different Native American peoples lived?

A North American tribe carved and painted this round face mask, which represents the sun, to wear in special dance ceremonies. ▶

Prepare to Read

OBJECTIVES

LANGUAGE DEVELOPMENT

Reading:
- Vocabulary building: *Context, dictionary skills*
- Reading strategy: *Visualizing*
- Text types: *Historical fiction, social studies article*
- Literary element: *Flashback*

Writing:
- Word web
- Descriptive essays

Listening/Speaking:
- Appreciation: *Story*
- Retell a story
- Major ideas
- Listen for chronology
- Compare and contrast characters

Grammar:
- Conjunctions

Viewing/Representing:
- Maps, illustrations

ACADEMIC CONTENT
- Social studies vocabulary
- Lewis and Clark, Sacagawea
- Geographical features
- Relief map

BACKGROUND

In this section, you will read an excerpt from *River to Tomorrow,* a historical novel. Historical fiction combines imaginary elements (fiction) with real people, events, and settings (history).

Make connections In 1803, the United States purchased the Louisiana Territory from France. President Thomas Jefferson wanted Americans to move there. He asked Meriwether Lewis and William Clark to explore the huge new territory.

Lewis and Clark had three main goals. The first goal was to find a water route to the Pacific Ocean. The second goal was to learn about the Native Americans who lived on the lands between the Mississippi River and the Pacific Ocean. The third goal was to draw detailed maps of the new territory.

Find the Louisiana Territory on the map. What is to the north of the territory? To the southwest? To the northwest?

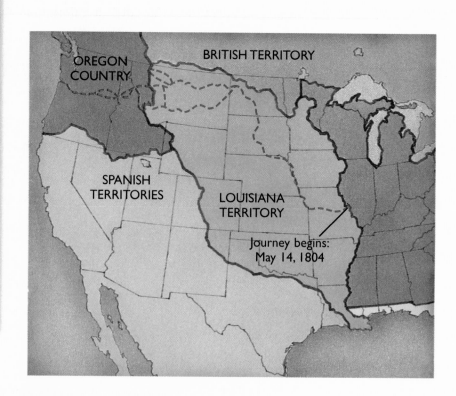

OREGON COUNTRY

BRITISH TERRITORY

SPANISH TERRITORIES

LOUISIANA TERRITORY

Journey begins: May 14, 1804

LEARN KEY WORDS

expedition
interpreter
kidnapped
moccasins
recognized
trade

VOCABULARY

Read these sentences. Use the context to figure out the meaning of the **red** words. Use a dictionary to check your answers. Write each word and its meaning in your notebook.

1. Their **expedition** to the Pacific Ocean was a long, difficult, and dangerous journey.
2. Sacagawea was the expedition's **interpreter** and translated some of the Native American languages for Lewis and Clark.
3. Some people **kidnapped** Sacagawea when she was a child and took her away from her tribe.
4. She wore beaded leather **moccasins** on her feet.
5. Sacagawea's brother hadn't changed much. She **recognized** him immediately.
6. Lewis and Clark wanted to **trade** some of their supplies for horses.

▲ Moccasins

READING STRATEGY

Visualizing

Visualizing means picturing something in your mind. Writers use adjectives and other words to help readers visualize, or see, what they read. For example, close your eyes and picture this: fluffy white clouds moving quickly across a deep-blue sky. As you read a story, pay attention to the adjectives and other descriptive words. Try to visualize the characters, places, and events.

Historical Fiction

Preview the text. Then, as you read, try to visualize. What people, places, and things can you "see" most clearly? What do they look like? What words help you visualize them?

from River to Tomorrow

Ellen Levine

On their journey west, Lewis and Clark and their "Corps of Discovery" met Sacagawea. Sacagawea was a young Native American woman from the Shoshone tribe who joined Lewis and Clark and acted as their interpreter. This excerpt starts with a conversation between Captain Clark and Sacagawea.

"Quick!" said Captain Clark to his aide. "Bring the **Indian** woman." George Drewyer ran through the **brush** to the **clearing** at the river's edge.

"Sacagawea . . . over here!" he motioned. Sacagawea followed Drewyer through the brush.

"Could your people have camped here?" Captain Clark asked.

"I am not certain," she said slowly, walking the distance between the **ash piles**. "Perhaps." Five winters had passed since she had been kidnapped from her people. "Perhaps," she repeated.

---

corps, group of people who do a particular job
Indian, Native American
brush, small bushes and trees
clearing, area of forest without trees
ash piles, powder left from burned-out campfires

John Shields, another of Clark's men, asked, "What do you **make of this**, sir? I found it by a log at the edge of the clearing." He handed a well-worn moccasin to Clark. The captain looked at it and passed it to Sacagawea.

This time there was no question. "No," she said firmly. Her people did not **stitch** this way. This was definitely not a Shoshone moccasin.

She turned back to the river. Sadness filled her. Perhaps these white men would never find her people. And if they did, would there be anyone left who knew her? Her mother and many others had been killed in the Minnetaree enemy raid five winters ago. The Minnetaree had taken her to live in a village far away in the east.

---

make of this, think this is
stitch, sew

LITERARY ELEMENT

A *flashback* is an interruption of the sequence of events in a story to tell about something that happened in the past.

For so many winters, so many summers, Sacagawea had thought about tomorrow. *Tomorrow* everything would be better, she told herself. At first she had thought about escaping. Then the Minnetaree warrior who had **captured** her lost her in a gambling game to a French-Canadian trader named Charbonneau. He took her as one of his wives. That's when Sacagawea stopped thinking about tomorrow. That's when she gave up hope of ever seeing her people again.

Then one day some white men had come to the Minnetaree village in long boats. They came, they said, with orders from the white Chief of the United States. They planned to travel up the great river until they reached the Shining Mountains where the snow never melted. They would cross the mountains and travel down another river to the Great Stinking Lake the whites called the Pacific Ocean.

---

captured, took as a prisoner

BEFORE YOU GO ON . . .

1 When was Sacagawea kidnapped?

2 How does Sacagawea know that the moccasin is not Shoshone?

HOW ABOUT YOU?

- Who do you think the white men are?

The captains had hired Charbonneau as an interpreter. When Charbonneau told Sacagawea about the trip, she had turned away. Her heart had pounded so loudly, she was certain he would see and hear it. The Shining Mountains, he had said. They were her mountains! And her people were there.

Several nights later, she had stood with Charbonneau in the Minnetaree chief's **lodge**, listening to the white men talk about their trip.

"The Missouri River will take us to the Rocky Mountains," Captain Clark had said, as the chief drew a map in the dust.

"This is where the waters flow to the setting sun." The chief pointed as he drew the line of another river to the ocean.

"We must have horses for the **portage** across the mountains from the Missouri to the Columbia River," Captain Lewis said. "We cannot get across on foot with all our supplies."

---

lodge, North American Indian home
portage, act of carrying boats and canoes
    over land from one river to another

"The Shoshone people have herds of horses," the chief answered. "They might be willing to trade." He paused. "And the Frenchman's wife is Shoshone," he said, pointing to Sacagawea.

With excitement in his voice, Lewis turned to Clark. "She will be important to us. When they see her, maybe the Shoshone will be more willing to trade with us!"

And so Sacagawea, her two-month-old baby, Pomp, and Charbonneau joined thirty others in the Lewis and Clark expedition to the Pacific. That had been in the spring.

It was midsummer now, and the canoes and flat-bottomed boats had traveled upriver for many miles. Some days the men rowed, or even put up a sail if the wind was right. Often they walked along the shoreline, pulling long ropes attached to the **bow**.

The men had **blistered** and cut their feet on the sharp stones on the river bottom. They ached from the piercing prickly pear thorns that tore their clothes and flesh. They had lost supplies and canoes crossing **treacherous rapids**. They had faced rattlesnakes and grizzly bears, and still they traveled on.

---

bow, front of a boat
blistered, wounded, or hurt, by continual rubbing
treacherous rapids, very dangerous part of a river
  where water moves quickly over rocks

The canoes traveled upriver. Then the men stopped to hunt for food. As the group walked to a clearing on shore, Sacagawea gasped and pointed to a **grove** of pine trees. The bark had been stripped from many of them.

"My people," she said. "They have been here."

"How do you know?" asked Captain Clark, as the men gathered around.

"When food is **scarce**, we eat the soft wood under the bark. It is filling," she said as she touched the torn edge.

They traveled on through the hot day. Sacagawea felt a nervous excitement. She **scanned** the riverbank.

---

grove, small group of trees that are close together
scarce, rare; not enough
scanned, looked at

BEFORE YOU GO ON . . .

1 Who did the captains hire as an interpreter?

2 What do the explorers need to be able to cross the mountains?

HOW ABOUT YOU?
- What do you think will happen next?

Suddenly, she motioned to the bank. "I have been here! We used that white earth for paint. The place where the water parts in three is not far!"

That night she told Captain Clark that her people often camped at the three forks. It was there that she had been kidnapped by the Minnetarees.

Captain Lewis immediately planned a **search party**. "We *must* find the Shoshone and get horses before the snows close the mountain passes. Everything **depends on** it," he said.

Sacagawea explained to Captain Lewis the Shoshone signs of peace. "Hold a blanket this way," she said, gripping two corners. Then she flung it over her head and down to the ground. "Three times you must do this. Then my people will know that you come in friendship."

A few days later, Captain Lewis set off on foot with Drewyer and three other men in search of Sacagawea's people. Captain Clark remained with the others, and they continued their **struggle** up the river in the boats.

To lighten the boat load, one day Sacagawea walked on the shore carrying Pomp. Suddenly, a small cloud of dust rose ahead.

A group of riders swept down to the river's edge. Sacagawea quickly scanned their faces. Their clothes and riding ways had told her they were Shoshone, but she recognized no one except Drewyer, who had ridden back with the warriors.

"The Indians feared Captain Lewis was **setting a trap for** them," Drewyer told Captain Clark.

---

search party, group of people who look for someone
depends on, is affected by

struggle, difficult journey
setting a trap for, trying to catch a person or animal

28

"But we were coming with supplies," said Clark.

"Yes, but not everyone believed that," answered Drewyer.

When they reached the camp, the Shoshone were gathered at the edge of the lodges. An old woman pointed at Sacagawea.

The chief of the Shoshone, standing next to Captain Lewis, stepped forward to greet Captain Clark. Then he led the two men and a group of Shoshone into a tent where they sat around a grass circle. The chief lit a long-stemmed pipe. He pointed the stem to the four corners of the earth, then to the sky and the earth below. He took three puffs and repeated the ceremony three times. Then he passed the pipe around to the group.

Drewyer explained in **sign language** that the Shoshone woman with them would act as interpreter. Captain Lewis then sent Drewyer to get Sacagawea. She came into the tent and sat near the captains. She scarcely looked at anyone.

The chief began to speak. Sacagawea slowly looked up. She paid no attention to the words. All she could hear was the tone, the voice, the way the man spoke. She leaned forward. The chief **gestured** as he spoke. She knew that gesture. She knew that voice. She swayed forward and caught herself before she fell. Then she leapt up and ran to him. She took the blanket from off her shoulders and threw it around him.

---

sign language, communication using signs, such as
   hand movements
gestured, used hands, head, or arms to communicate
   without words

"Cameahwait! Cameahwait!" Tears ran down her cheeks as she hugged her brother. He, too, wept. Then, straightening up, he placed his hands on her shoulders.

"We must hear what the white men have to say, little sister," he said in a low voice. "Later we will talk."

Sacagawea returned to her seat. She was filled with a peace. She sang a silent song to the river, for the river had brought her home. The river had brought her tomorrow.

About the Author

Ellen Levine

Ellen Levine enjoys writing fiction, but she is best known for her nonfiction books for young readers. She also enjoys telling students about different ways of getting interesting information. She wants students to understand that research can be exciting.

BEFORE YOU GO ON . . .

1 What place does Sacagawea recognize?

2 How does Sacagawea feel at the end of the story? Why?

HOW ABOUT YOU?
- How do you feel about the ending?

Review and Practice

Reread the passage from *River to Tomorrow*. Then copy the flowchart into your notebook. Think about the events in the story. What happens first? Second? After that? Write the events in the boxes. Use chronological (time) order.

Events

- Sacagawea joins the expedition.
- Sacagawea recognizes her brother.
- John Shields finds a moccasin.
- Sacagawea lives with the Shoshone.
- Sacagawea is kidnapped.

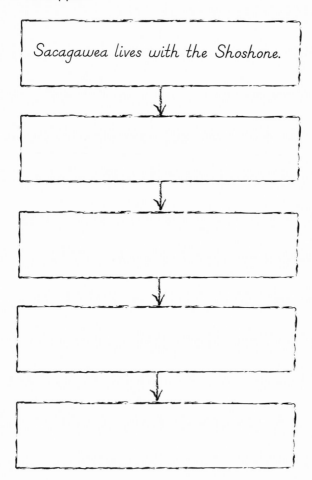

Compare your charts in pairs or small groups. Revise your chart if necessary. Take turns using your charts to retell the story.

1. How are Sacagawea and Charbonneau similar? How are they different? Copy the Venn diagram into your notebook. Then use the reading on pages 24–29 to complete the diagram. Write things about Sacagawea in the left part of the diagram. Write things about Charbonneau in the right part. Write things about both of them in the middle of the diagram.

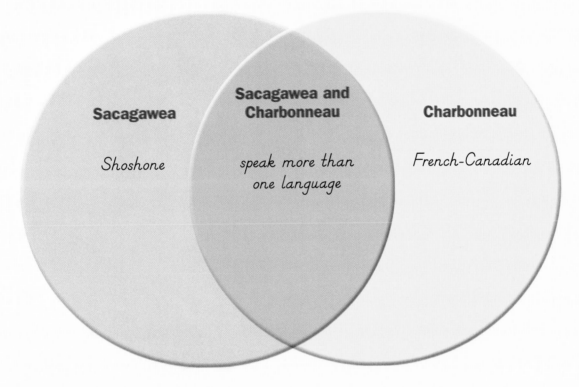

Sacagawea

Shoshone

Sacagawea and Charbonneau

speak more than one language

Charbonneau

French-Canadian

2. Compare your Venn diagrams in pairs or small groups. Which qualities did you find in the story? Which qualities did you imagine?

DISCUSSION

Discuss in pairs or small groups.

1. What parts of the story do you think are factual?
2. What parts of the story do you think are fictional?
3. How do you think writers of historical fiction get their ideas?

This is an informational text. It gives information about how to use relief maps. Preview the text before you read it. Read the title and look at the pictures. What do you already know about maps?

Reading a Relief Map

A relief map shows the geographical features of a region. It shows the differences in a region's elevation, or height. For example, by looking at a relief map, you can see whether the land in a region has plains, hills, or mountains.

Relief maps have a key—a box with different colors that tell how high the land is above sea level. Sea level is the level of the surface of the sea where it meets the land. We **measure** sea level in meters and in feet.

Maps have scales. The scale on a map looks like a ruler. It shows how many kilometers or miles equal a certain **distance** on the map. You can use the scale to figure out the distance between places on the map.

measure, find the size, weight, or amount of
    something
distance, amount of space between two places

HEIGHT OF LAND

Meters		Feet
Over 4,000		Over 13,000
2,000–4,000		6,600–13,000
1,000–2,000		3,300–6,600
500–1,000		1,650–3,300
200–500		650–1,650
0–200		0–650
Below sea level		

0   150   300 miles

0   150   300 kilometers

▲ Western United States, Canada, and Mexico (relief map)

BEFORE YOU GO ON . . .

1. What do the colors in the key tell you?

2. Which color on this map represents 610 meters (2,000 ft.)?

HOW ABOUT YOU?

• Does your region have plains, hills, or mountains?

33

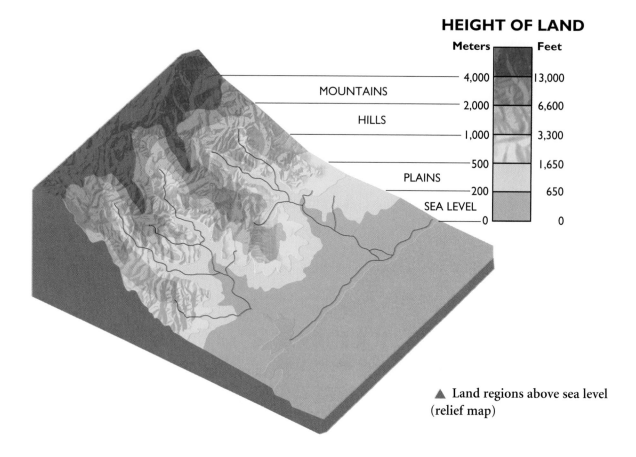

HEIGHT OF LAND

MOUNTAINS

HILLS

PLAINS

SEA LEVEL

Meters	Feet
4,000	13,000
2,000	6,600
1,000	3,300
500	1,650
200	650
0	0

▲ Land regions above sea level (relief map)

Sea level is always 0 on a relief map. Most land in the United States is above—higher than—sea level. For example, the city of Denver, Colorado, is about 1,609 meters (5,280 ft.) above sea level. Dallas, Texas, is about 141 meters (463 ft.) above sea level. Cities that are on a seacoast, such as San Francisco, California, and Boston, Massachusetts, have some land that is at sea level and some land that is higher. San Francisco, for example, is about 20 meters (65 ft.) above sea level in some places. Some land is below—lower than—sea level. For example, Death Valley in California is 86 meters (282 ft.) below sea level.

BEFORE YOU GO ON . . .

1. What color on the map above shows the highest land? What color shows the lowest land?

2. What is the height of sea level on a relief map?

HOW ABOUT YOU?

- When would you use a relief map?

Link the Readings

1. What geographical features did Lewis and Clark see on their way to the Pacific Ocean? Copy this chart into your notebook. Complete the chart with information from *River to Tomorrow* on pages 24–29 and the relief map on page 33.

Mountains and Hills	Plains	Rivers
Rocky Mountains		

2. Lewis and Clark kept a record, or log, of their trip. Imagine that you were a member of their corps. Use the information from the chart to write a log entry for one day of the journey. Write the date. Then describe what you saw that day. (See example below.) Share your log entries in small groups.

> May 29, 1805
>
> Today I found a beautiful stream. The water was very clear. I named the stream Judith River.

DISCUSSION

Discuss in pairs or small groups.

1. Do you think the Corps of Discovery found a water route from St. Louis to the Pacific Ocean? Explain.

2. The Lewis and Clark expedition was a difficult journey. What geographical features made this journey difficult?

Connect to Writing

GRAMMAR

Using the Conjunctions *and* and *or*

The words ***and*** and ***or*** are conjunctions.

Some sentences have more than one subject, verb, or object. Conjunctions combine these subjects, verbs, or objects.

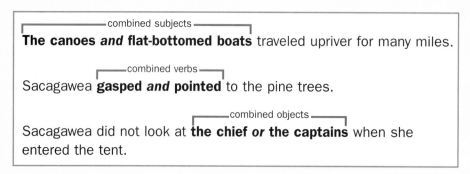

combined subjects

The canoes *and* flat-bottomed boats traveled upriver for many miles.

combined verbs

Sacagawea **gasped *and* pointed** to the pine trees.

combined objects

Sacagawea did not look at **the chief *or* the captains** when she entered the tent.

The word *or* combines two or more things in negative sentences:

Drewyer didn't speak Shoshone **or** Minnetaree.

The word *or* can also combine two or more choices:

The expedition can travel by boat **or** on foot.

Practice

Copy these sentences into your notebook. Circle the conjunctions. Then underline the subjects, verbs, or objects that the conjunctions combine.

1. Sacagawea didn't want to eat or drink.
2. The Shoshone and Minnetarees are two different Native American groups.
3. The explorers ate and slept before going any farther.
4. The thorns tore the explorers' clothes and flesh.
5. On some days, the travelers chose fish or meat for supper.
6. Lewis called for Sacagawea or Charbonneau to interpret.

SKILLS FOR WRITING

Writing Essays

An essay is a group of paragraphs about one topic. All the information in an essay supports one main idea.

Read the essay. Then answer the questions.

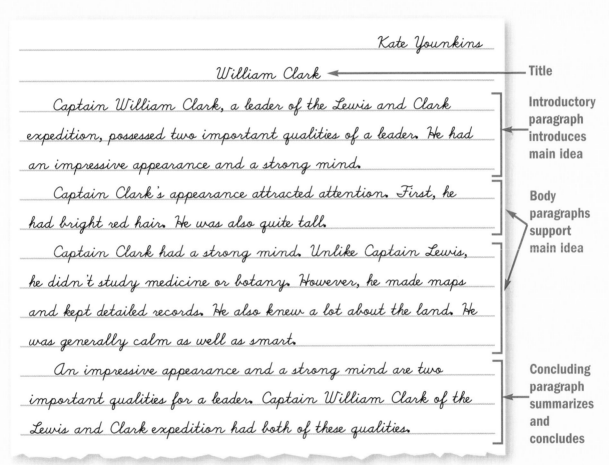

Kate Younkins

William Clark ← ————————— Title

Captain William Clark, a leader of the Lewis and Clark expedition, possessed two important qualities of a leader. He had an impressive appearance and a strong mind.

— Introductory paragraph introduces main idea

Captain Clark's appearance attracted attention. First, he had bright red hair. He was also quite tall.

Captain Clark had a strong mind. Unlike Captain Lewis, he didn't study medicine or botany. However, he made maps and kept detailed records. He also knew a lot about the land. He was generally calm as well as smart.

— Body paragraphs support main idea

An impressive appearance and a strong mind are two important qualities for a leader. Captain William Clark of the Lewis and Clark expedition had both of these qualities.

— Concluding paragraph summarizes and concludes

1. How many paragraphs are in this essay?
2. What is the writer's main idea?
3. Which paragraph introduces the main idea?
4. Which paragraph or paragraphs give details supporting the main idea?
5. Which paragraph gives the writer's concluding thoughts?

WRITING ASSIGNMENT

Descriptive Essay
You will write a descriptive essay about someone you knew when you were younger.

1. **Read** Reread the essay on page 37. What details describe William Clark?

Writing Strategy: Word Web
A word web can help you organize information. Look at the word web the writer used to organize information about William Clark.

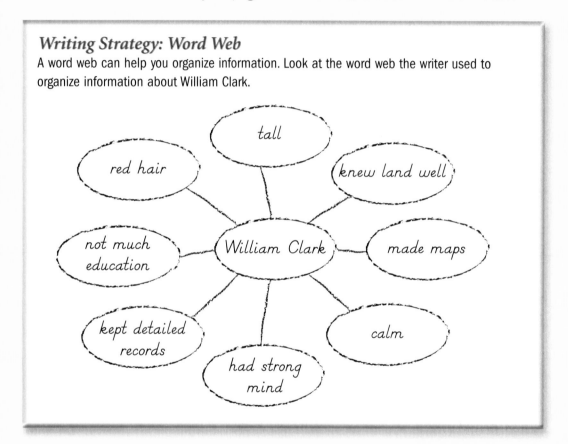

2. **Make a word web** Think of a person you knew when you were younger. Draw a word web. Write details about the person in the circles.

3. **Write an essay** Using your word web, write an essay about the person. Include an introductory paragraph, two body paragraphs, and a concluding paragraph. Write about the person's appearance and personality in the body paragraphs. Use conjunctions to combine ideas.

EDITING CHECKLIST
Did you . . .
▶ include an introductory paragraph?
▶ write about the person's appearance and personality in the body paragraphs?
▶ include a concluding paragraph?
▶ use conjunctions?

Check Your Knowledge

Language Development

1. Describe visualizing as a reading strategy.

2. What is a flashback? Why do writers use flashbacks?

3. What is historical fiction? Explain why the excerpt from *River to Tomorrow* is historical fiction.

4. What kind of words are *or* and *and*? Use each in a sentence.

5. How can a word web help you organize your writing?

6. What kinds of words can be used to describe a person's feelings, appearance, and personality? Give examples.

Academic Content

1. What new social studies vocabulary did you learn in Part 2? What do the words mean?

2. What was the Lewis and Clark expedition?

3. What does a relief map show?

▲ This bag that early Native Americans made is decorated with porcupine quills. The quills were dyed and sewn on bags and clothing.

Put It All Together

LISTENING and SPEAKING WORKSHOP

GROUP PRESENTATION

You will give a group presentation that describes an ideal vacation place.

1 **Think about it** Answer these questions in your notebook.

What kind of weather do you like? What geographical areas do you like? What activities do you enjoy? What vacation places have these features?

Compare your answers in small groups. Choose an ideal vacation place.

2 **Organize** Make a list of reasons that the vacation place is ideal. Decide which features of the place each group member will present.

3 **Practice** Practice your part of the presentation. Use adjectives and other words to help listeners visualize your group's ideal vacation place.

4 **Present and evaluate** Give your group presentation to the class. As each group finishes, evaluate the presentation. Did you understand the speakers? What did you like best about the presentation? Do you have suggestions for improvement?

SPEAKING TIPS
- Look at the audience as you speak.
- Speak slowly and clearly so that the audience can understand you.

LISTENING TIPS
- Listen carefully to other people's ideas.
- Ask questions after the presentation if you want more information.

◄ The Eiffel Tower in Paris, France, is a popular place for travelers to visit.

WRITING WORKSHOP

DESCRIPTIVE ESSAY

In a descriptive essay, the writer uses descriptive details to help the reader visualize what a person, place, or thing is like.

A good descriptive essay includes the following characteristics:

- several important ideas supported by specific details
- adjectives and other words that help the reader visualize the scene
- clear organization

You will write an essay describing a special place. Use the following steps and the model on page 42 to help you.

 Prewrite Brainstorm a list of places that are special to you. Choose one place to write about. Why is this place so special? Make a word web to organize your ideas. Add as many ideas to your web as you can.

Organize ideas Review your ideas. Circle the three most important or interesting ideas about your place. Then decide which idea you will describe first, next, and last. Number your ideas.

WRITING TIPS

- Use adjectives and other words to help the reader visualize what you are describing. For example, the word *snowy* helps a reader "see" a mountain. The word *salty* helps a reader "taste" a fish.
- Freewriting can sometimes help you think of ideas. When you freewrite, write down your ideas quickly. Don't worry about grammar, spelling, or punctuation. Then underline your best ideas and use them in your essay.

Before you write a first draft of your essay, read the following model. Notice the characteristics of a descriptive essay.

Jennifer Rosario

My Special Place

People need a special place where they can relax and feel good or just be alone. For me, that special place is my room. It is the only place I can call my own.

My room has everything that I need. I believe it is a reflection of my unique personality. I love to decorate my room with colorful posters and photos. It's a way to express myself.

I spend a lot of my free time in my room. I read, draw, and listen to my favorite music. I like to keep my room neat and clean.

The best thing about my room is its large window. It lets warm, golden sunlight into my room during the day, and it frames the moon and stars in the dark night sky. Sometimes I like to pretend it is my window to the rest of the world.

My room is a place where I can be myself and express my individuality. For these reasons, it is the most special place to me.

The writer introduces her topic.

She presents one important idea about her room and gives supporting details.

She gives another important idea and supporting details.

She presents a third important idea and supporting details.

She summarizes and concludes her essay.

2 **Draft** Use your word web to write an essay about your special place.

- Give one idea about why the place is special in each paragraph. Then give specific details to support each of your ideas. Remember to include adjectives and other words to help your reader visualize the place.

- Present your ideas so that they will be clear to your reader. For example, you might present your most important idea first and then present your other ideas in the other body paragraphs. Or you might present your most important idea last, after presenting your other ideas.

- Reread the model essay. In which paragraph does the student say what is the best feature in her room?

3 **Edit** Work in pairs. Trade papers and read each other's essays. Use the questions in the editing checklist to evaluate each other's work.

EDITING CHECKLIST

Did you . . .

- ▶ use adjectives and other words to help your reader visualize?
- ▶ begin each sentence with a capital letter?
- ▶ indent the first sentence of each paragraph?
- ▶ use pronouns correctly?
- ▶ use conjunctions correctly to combine subjects, verbs, or objects?

4 **Revise** Revise your essay. Add details and correct any mistakes.

5 **Publish** Share your essay with your teacher and classmates.

PROJECTS

Work in pairs or small groups. Choose one of these projects.

1 Write a poem or song about the United States (or another country). Then read or sing it to the class.

2 Write a poem that describes a person. Try to use alliteration. Then read your poem to the class.

3 Use the library or Internet to find a relief map of your state. Make a poster-size relief map. Use colored pencils, pens, or crayons to show different elevations. Be sure to include a key. Then present the map to the class.

4 Use the library or Internet to research a Native American tribe. Then share the information with the class.

5 Obtain a copy of the home video *Lewis & Clark: The Journey of the Corps of Discovery*. It is a TV film that historian Ken Burns created for PBS (Public Broadcasting Service). The film tells the story of explorers Lewis and Clark, the young men in the Corps of Discovery, and Sacagawea. After you have watched the film, write a paragraph about the character you liked best in the film. Share your paragraph with the class.

6 Find the sheet music for "This Land Is Your Land," "Roll On, Columbia," or another folk song. Practice singing it as a group. If possible, have one group member play the song on the guitar or piano. Then perform the song for the class.

Further Reading

To find out more about the theme of this unit, choose from these reading suggestions.

***The Last of the Mohicans,* James Fenimore Cooper** It is 1757, and the British are fighting the French in North America. The two young daughters of a British colonel are trying to reach their father safely. This story is about their journey and the discovery that their destiny is linked to the lives of the Native Americans who are helping them.

***Heidi,* Johanna Spyri** Heidi lives with her grandfather high in the mountains in Switzerland. Suddenly, Aunt Dete arrives to take her to the city to live with a little girl named Clara. Heidi likes Clara and learns many things in the city, but she misses her grandfather and the outdoor life she loves. Heidi travels back to her mountain home and discovers what is important in life.

***The Swiss Family Robinson*, Johann Wyss** A Swiss family of six—a pastor, his wife, and their four sons—survive a shipwreck and struggle ashore on a remote island. They use the plants and animals they find there for farming, food, shelter, and clothing and build machines and tools. Each day brings exciting discoveries, as well as disagreements and disappointments.

***Round the World in Eighty Days,* Jules Verne** Phileas Fogg bets some members of London's Reform Club that he can travel around the world in eighty days. So Fogg and Passepartout, who works for him, cross three continents and two oceans by train, steamer, elephant, and whatever else is handy, facing wild adventures along the way.

***Girl of the Shining Mountains: Sacagawea's Story,* Peter and Connie Roop** Sacagawea joins the Lewis and Clark expedition as the group searches for a water route to the Pacific Ocean. She tells of her desire to find her people, from whom she was kidnapped years earlier. Through her eyes we explore the vast territory between the Mississippi River and the Pacific Ocean.

The Natural World

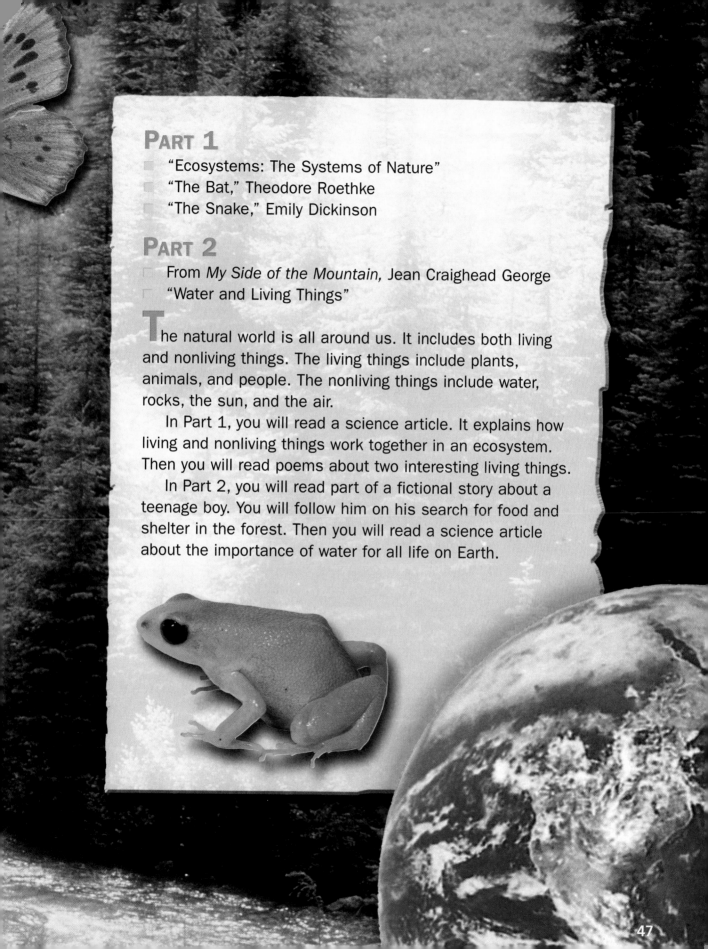

Part 1

- "Ecosystems: The Systems of Nature"
- "The Bat," Theodore Roethke
- "The Snake," Emily Dickinson

Part 2

- From *My Side of the Mountain,* Jean Craighead George
- "Water and Living Things"

The natural world is all around us. It includes both living and nonliving things. The living things include plants, animals, and people. The nonliving things include water, rocks, the sun, and the air.

In Part 1, you will read a science article. It explains how living and nonliving things work together in an ecosystem. Then you will read poems about two interesting living things.

In Part 2, you will read part of a fictional story about a teenage boy. You will follow him on his search for food and shelter in the forest. Then you will read a science article about the importance of water for all life on Earth.

Prepare to Read

OBJECTIVES
LANGUAGE DEVELOPMENT

Reading:
- Vocabulary building: *Greek and Latin roots*
- Reading strategy: *Skimming*
- Text types: *Science article, poetry*
- Literary element: *Rhyme*

Writing:
- Organizational diagram
- Expository paragraph

Listening/Speaking:
- Poetry
- Comparing experiences
- Asking for and giving information

Grammar:
- Subject-verb agreement

Viewing/Representing:
- Diagrams

ACADEMIC CONTENT
- Science vocabulary
- Natural systems and the environment
- Nature poetry

BACKGROUND

"Ecosystems: The Systems of Nature" is an informational science text. It contains facts about living and nonliving things.

Make connections What do you know about your environment—that is, the air, water, and land around you? Are there rivers or lakes? Plants or trees? Birds, fish, or other animals? What is the weather like?

Earth has several major kinds of environments. Tundra regions—treeless, nearly flat plains—cover much of the Arctic and other cold areas. Rain forests—very tall trees growing close together in places where it rains a lot—are found both in hot regions, such as Brazil, and in cooler areas, such as Washington state. Forests of trees that stay green or lose their leaves in the fall grow in regions with moderate temperatures and rainfall. Other major environments are deserts and grasslands, as well as water environments—oceans, lakes, rivers, streams, and wetlands. Which major environment do you live in?

Tropical rain forest

Tundra with ice

Savanna (grassland)

Ocean

LEARN KEY WORDS

carnivore
herbivore
omnivore
interact
organism
ecosystem

VOCABULARY

Many English words, especially science words, have Greek or Latin roots. Learning the roots and their meanings can help you figure out the meanings of many new words.

Look at the chart. Use your understanding of the Greek or Latin roots and words to figure out the meaning of the **red** words. Write each word and its meaning in your notebook.

Greek or Latin Root	Greek or Latin Word	New Word
carn- (flesh; meat)	*vorare* (to eat)	**carnivore**
herba- (plant)	*vorare* (to eat)	**herbivore**
omni- (everything)	*vorare* (to eat)	**omnivore**
inter- (between; together)	*actus* (to do)	**interact**
organ- (tool; part of the body; activity)	*-ism* (condition of)	**organism**
eco- (house; natural environment)	*systema* (placing together)	**ecosystem**

READING STRATEGY

Skimming

Skimming a text means reading it very quickly to get a general understanding of what it's about. Skimming can also help you establish your purpose for reading the text.

When you skim a text, follow these steps:

- Read the first and second paragraphs quickly.
- Read only the first sentences of the following paragraphs.
- Read the last paragraph quickly.

When you have finished skimming, you can read the whole text more carefully.

First, preview the text. Then skim it. Read the first and second paragraphs. Then read only the first sentences of the paragraphs that follow. Finally, read the last paragraph. When you've finished skimming, read the text more carefully. Be aware of your purpose for reading it.

Ecosystems
THE SYSTEMS OF NATURE

Organisms and Species

An organism is a living thing. A huge redwood tree is an organism. A small mouse is an organism. A tiny insect is an organism. You are an organism, too. Millions of organisms are so small that you cannot see them. Bacteria and viruses are examples of very small organisms.

A group of very similar organisms is a species. The organisms in a species are so similar that they can reproduce—have offspring, or babies—together, and their offspring can reproduce, too. Horses and cows, for example, cannot have offspring together because they are different species.

▲ Insect (water strider)

◀ A cat and its offspring

▲ Birds tend their nest.

Habitats

A habitat is the place where an organism lives—its surroundings or environment. A habitat provides the things an organism needs to **survive**, such as food, water, a livable temperature, and **shelter**. A habitat can be as large as an ocean or as small as a drop of water. It can be a forest or one tree. Several species may live in the same habitat, such as a river.

Different organisms live in different habitats because they have different **requirements** for survival. For example, a river or lake can be the habitat of some species of freshwater fish, such as trout. Freshwater trout cannot survive in the ocean, which contains salt water. An ocean and a lake are very different habitats. Similarly, the desert in the southwestern United States and northern Mexico is the habitat of the saguaro cactus. The saguaro cactus cannot survive in a **tropical** rain forest.

▲ Saguaro cacti

Sometimes animals move to different places within their habitats. For example, many kinds of frogs are born in water. However, they live mostly on land when they grow up. During very cold weather, some frogs go under the ground or bury themselves in mud at the bottom of **ponds** to stay warm.

---

survive, live
shelter, protected place to live
requirements, needs
tropical, having a hot and wet climate
ponds, small lakes

BEFORE YOU GO ON . . .

1 What is an organism? Give an example.

2 What does an organism's habitat provide?

HOW ABOUT YOU?
• What is your habitat?

Populations and Communities

All the members of one species in the same area are a population. For example, all the frogs in a lake are a population. All the pine trees in a forest are a population. All the people in a city, state, or country are a population. Some populations do not stay in one place. Monarch butterflies travel south each year from parts of western Canada and the United States to Mexico. Some species of whales travel around many oceans.

A community is all the populations that live together in one place, such as all the plants and animals in a desert. In a community, the different populations live close together, so they interact with one another. One way populations interact in a community is by using the same resources, such as food and shelter. In a desert, for example, snakes, lizards, and spiders may all use rocks and holes for shelter. They may eat insects, other animals, or their own kind for food.

▲ A population of pine trees

▲ Two frogs on a mossy stone

The Parts of an Ecosystem

An ecosystem is made up of both the living and
nonliving things in an area. Nonliving things include air,
sunlight, water, rocks, and **soil**. All parts of an ecosystem,
living and nonliving, interact. Plants take water from the
soil, and they produce **oxygen**. Animals **breathe** in oxygen
from the air. They eat plants and other animals.

---

soil, earth
oxygen, gas in the air that animals breathe in
breathe, take in air through the nose and mouth

▲ Oak tree ecosystem

BEFORE YOU GO ON . . .

1 What is a population?

2 What is an ecosystem?

HOW ABOUT YOU?
- What parts of the
  ecosystem do you
  interact with?

53

Three Kinds of Organisms

In an ecosystem, there are three kinds of organisms: producers, consumers, and decomposers. Each kind of organism is important.

Most producers are plants. They use **energy** from sunlight to make their own food from water and carbon dioxide. (Carbon dioxide is a gas in the air. People and animals breathe it out.) This **process** of making food is called photosynthesis.

▲ Vulture (scavenger)

Consumers cannot make their own food. They eat, or consume, other organisms. All animals are consumers. Consumers are **classified** by what they eat. Some consumers, such as deer, horses, and many birds, are herbivores: They eat only plants. Other consumers, such as lions, spiders, and snakes, are carnivores: They eat only animals. Some consumers, such as crows and bears, eat plants *and* animals: They are called omnivores. Some carnivores are scavengers. A scavenger eats dead organisms. Scavengers include vultures and catfish.

▲ Bear (omnivore)

Some consumers are also decomposers. Decomposers break down dead plants and animals. The dead plants and animals are changed into **nutrients**, which go back into the soil. Producers—plants—consume these nutrients. Decomposers are very important in the ecosystem because plants need nutrients to grow.

The two main kinds of decomposers are bacteria and fungi. Bacteria are very small living things. We cannot see bacteria, but they live in soil, air, and water and on other organisms. Fungi are plantlike organisms without leaves that grow in dark, warm, wet places. Mushrooms are one kind of fungus.

▲ Fungi (decomposers)

---

energy, power that produces heat
process, steps needed for something to happen
classified, put into groups
nutrients, substances that help plants or animals grow

▲ Food chain of grass (a producer), a mouse (a small consumer), and a hawk (a larger consumer)

Food Chains

The **movement** of food through a community is called a food chain. A food chain always begins with producers—plants. In the ocean, a food chain begins with algae, which are very small plantlike organisms. Small fish eat the algae. Medium-size fish eat the small fish. Big fish eat the medium-size fish.

On land, a food chain is similar. It begins with a plant. A consumer, such as an insect, eats the plant. Then another consumer, such as a bat, eats the insect. Next, a bigger consumer, such as an owl, eats the bat. Finally, the owl dies, and decomposers break it down into nutrients.

Every part of the food chain is necessary to every other part. Without water, plants die. Without plants, animals cannot live.

movement, change in position or place

BEFORE YOU GO ON . . .

1 Name the three kinds of organisms in an ecosystem.

2 What are three kinds of consumers?

HOW ABOUT YOU?

• Are you a herbivore, a carnivore, or an omnivore? Explain.

Review and Practice

Reread "Ecosystems: The Systems of Nature." Think about an ecosystem near your home, such as a river, a vacant lot, a marshy area, or a backyard. Next, copy this chart into your notebook. Complete the chart by listing all the living and nonliving things in the ecosystem you selected. Then pick one living thing and one nonliving thing in the ecosystem and, in the space below the two columns, describe how they interact.

Ecosystem	
Living Things	*Nonliving Things*
Interaction	

Deer (herbivore) ▶

Match the words in the box with their definitions. Write the words and their definitions in your notebook.

bacteria	carnivore	community
ecosystem	food chain	habitat
organism	population	

1. a living thing
2. an animal that eats only animals
3. all the populations that live together in one place
4. all the members of one species in the same area
5. the movement of food through a community
6. a place where an organism lives
7. all the communities of living and nonliving things in an area
8. a type of decomposer

DISCUSSION

Discuss in pairs or small groups.

1. How do living things in the natural world affect you? How do you affect them? Give examples.
2. How do you affect nonliving things in the natural world? How do they affect you?
3. What would happen if something destroyed a part of an ecosystem? For example, what would happen if someone cut down the trees in a forest? How would that affect other living and nonliving things?

A poem expresses emotions, experiences, and ideas. The lines of a poem are often short. Groups of these lines are called stanzas, or verses. Poets—people who write poems—may choose words for the way they sound. You will read two poems, one about a bat and the other about a snake.

The Bat

By day the bat is cousin to the mouse.
He likes the attic of an **aging** house.

His fingers make a hat about his head.
His **pulse beat** is so slow we think him dead.

He **loops** in crazy **figures** half the night
Among the trees that face the corner light.

But when he **brushes up** against a **screen**,
We are afraid of what our eyes have seen:

For something is **amiss** or **out of place**
When mice with wings can wear a human face.

Theodore Roethke

LITERARY ELEMENT

Sometimes words in a poem *rhyme*. Two words that rhyme have the same ending sounds but different beginning sounds. For example, in "The Bat," the words *mouse* and *house* rhyme. What other words in the poem rhyme?

aging, becoming older
pulse beat, heartbeat
loops, flies in circles
figures, patterns
brushes up, touches lightly
screen, wire net that covers a window
amiss, wrong
out of place, strange or unusual

Theodore Roethke

Theodore Roethke (1908–1963) was an American poet who often wrote about the natural world. He spent much of his youth working in a greenhouse, where he developed a lifelong love of nature. He won the Pulitzer Prize in 1954 for his collection of poetry *The Waking: Poems 1933–1953*. He was a professor of English at the University of Washington.

BEFORE YOU GO ON . . .

1. How many stanzas are there in "The Bat"?
2. What does the poet mean by saying the bat "can wear a human face"?

HOW ABOUT YOU?

- How do you feel about bats? Why?

The Snake

A narrow fellow in the grass
Occasionally rides;
You may have met him,—did you not,
His notice sudden is.

The grass divides as with a comb,
A spotted **shaft** is seen;
And then it closes at your feet
And opens further on.

He likes a **boggy acre**,
A floor too cool for corn.
Yet when a child, and **barefoot**,
I more than once, **at morn**,

Have passed, I thought, a whip-lash
Unbraiding in the sun,—
When, stooping to secure it,
It wrinkled, and was gone.

Several of nature's people
I know, and they know me;
I feel for them a transport
Of **cordiality**;

But never met this fellow,
Attended or alone,
Without a tighter breathing,
And zero at the bone.

Emily Dickinson

---

shaft, long, thin object
boggy acre, wet and muddy ground
barefoot, without shoes
at morn, in the morning
unbraiding, becoming straight
cordiality, friendliness

About the Poet

Emily Dickinson

Emily Dickinson (1830–1886) was an American poet. She was a quiet, shy person, and she spent much of her time writing at home. Although she wrote almost 2,000 poems, only seven of them were published during her lifetime. Most of Dickinson's poems are about serious themes, such as death, love, and eternity.

BEFORE YOU GO ON . . .

1 What words does the poet use to describe the snake?
2 How does she describe how it moves?

HOW ABOUT YOU?

- How do you feel about snakes? Why?

Link the Readings

"Ecosystems: The Systems of Nature" and the two poems describe organisms that live in different habitats. Copy the chart into your notebook. Reread "Ecosystems" and the poems. Then complete the chart.

Title of Selection	Type of Text (Genre)	Fiction or Nonfiction	Purpose of Selection	One Idea from the Text
"Ecosystems: The Systems of Nature"				
"The Bat"				
"The Snake"				Snakes scare the poet.

DISCUSSION

Discuss in pairs or small groups.

1. Compare how the two poets use rhyme.

2. Which poem do you think better describes how the animal actually looks? Which poem better describes how the animal moves? Discuss how the poets help you visualize the animals.

3. List ten animals in your notebook. What type of consumer is each animal? Is it a herbivore, a carnivore, or an omnivore?

Connect to Writing

GRAMMAR

Subject-Verb Agreement: Simple Present

In the **simple present**, the subject and the verb must agree in number (singular or plural).

Add **-s** or **-es** to verbs with a subject that is a singular noun or with the subject pronouns *he, she,* and *it.*

> The owl **hunts** for food at night.
> It **catches** bats, insects, and mice to eat.
> He **likes** a boggy acre.
> She **writes** poetry.

Do not add **-s** or **-es** to verbs with a subject that is a plural noun or with the subject pronouns *I, we, you,* and *they.*

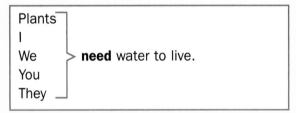

Plants
I
We   } **need** water to live.
You
They

Practice

Copy this paragraph into your notebook. Use the correct simple present form of the verbs in parentheses.

My brothers (1. spend / spends) a lot of time at the pond near our house. They (2. watch / watches) the animals in and near the pond. My sister (3. feed / feeds) the ducks. She (4. chase / chases) frogs. I (5. love / loves) to watch the frogs hop from plant to plant. We (6. think / thinks) the pond is very peaceful. You (7. come / comes) to the pond, too, don't you?

▲ Pond

SKILLS FOR WRITING

Writing an Expository Paragraph

Expository writing explains something. "Ecosystems: The Systems of Nature" is an example of expository writing. It gives factual information about the natural world.

Here are some rules for writing an expository paragraph.

- Make sure that your paragraph has one main idea about the topic. The main idea should be stated in the topic sentence.

- Use facts to support your main idea.

- Make your explanations simple and clear.

Read the paragraph. Then discuss the questions.

Drew Newgent

The Chipmunk in Its Food Chain

The chipmunk is an important consumer in the middle of —Topic sentence
the food chain. The chipmunk is an omnivore. It eats parts of plants, such as nuts, grains, seeds, and berries. It also eats small animals, such as insects. Many larger carnivores eat chipmunks. When the larger carnivores die, decomposers return the nutrients to the soil. Plants use the nutrients in the soil to grow. Therefore, the chipmunk plays an important part in the food chain.

1. What kind of paragraph is it?
2. What is the topic? What is the main idea about the topic?
3. What facts support the main idea?
4. Find the simple present verbs. What is the subject of each verb? Is there subject-verb agreement?

WRITING ASSIGNMENT

Expository Paragraph
You will write an expository paragraph. Choose an animal. Explain its place in the food chain.

1. **Read** Reread the paragraph about the chipmunk in its food chain on page 63.

2. **Look for information** Research the place of the animal you chose in the food chain. Look for information in the library or on the Internet.

Writing Strategy: Organizational Diagram

An organizational diagram can help you put your ideas in order for a paragraph. First, draw several boxes, as below. Write the main idea in the first box. Write supporting facts in the other boxes. Look at this organizational diagram for the paragraph on page 63.

The chipmunk is in the middle of the food chain.

▼

The chipmunk eats nuts, grains, seeds, and insects.

▼

Chipmunks are food for many larger carnivores.

▼

When the larger carnivores die, decomposers return the nutrients to the soil.

▼

Plants use the nutrients in the soil to grow.

1. What is the topic?
2. What is the main idea about the topic?
3. How many facts support the main idea? What are the facts?

---

3. **Make a diagram** Draw an organizational diagram in your notebook. Write the main idea about the animal you chose in the first box. Write each supporting fact in another box.

4. **Write a paragraph** Use your diagram to write a paragraph about the place of your animal in the food chain.

EDITING CHECKLIST

Did you . . .

▶ include a topic sentence stating the main idea?

▶ include facts that support your main idea?

▶ write sentences that make your ideas clear?

▶ check subject-verb agreement?

Check Your Knowledge

Language Development

1. Describe how to use skimming as a reading strategy.

2. What are some Greek and Latin roots? How can you use them to find out what a word means?

3. What is rhyme? Give an example of two words that rhyme.

4. What type of writing often uses rhyme? Why?

5. What is the purpose of expository writing?

6. What is subject-verb agreement? Give examples.

7. How can an organizational diagram help you put ideas in order for a paragraph?

Academic Content

1. What new science vocabulary did you learn in Part 1? What do the words mean?

2. What is a food chain?

3. What is a species?

4. What are some populations that live in a desert ecosystem?

Prepare to Read

OBJECTIVES

LANGUAGE DEVELOPMENT

Reading:
- Vocabulary building: *Context, dictionary skills*
- Reading strategy: *Identifying with a character*
- Text types: *Novel, science article*
- Literary elements: *Personification, characterization*

Writing:
- Sequence-of-events chart
- Describing a process

Listening/Speaking:
- Hearing about a process
- Explaining a process

Grammar:
- Adverbs

Viewing/Representing:
- Illustrations

ACADEMIC CONTENT
- Science vocabulary
- The natural world
- The water cycle

BACKGROUND

In this section, you will read an excerpt, or small section, from the novel *My Side of the Mountain.* The novel is about a boy who tries to survive in a mountain forest.

Make connections Work in pairs or small groups. Imagine that you are going to a mountain forest for three days. The climate is dry but cool. Make a list of the things you will need. Think about food, clothing, and shelter. The pictures below show some of the things you might need. Some national and state parks do not allow campers to burn firewood. Do you know why?

LEARN KEY WORDS

bank
bark
bite
game
grub
line

VOCABULARY

Many English words have more than one meaning. For example, the word *bat* can mean a small animal or a long wooden stick used for playing baseball.

Read each sentence. Look up the red word in the dictionary. Read all the meanings of the word. Use the context to figure out the correct meaning in the sentence. Write each word and its meaning in your notebook.

1. Plants grew along the bank of the river.
2. I cut a strip of bark from the tree.
3. I felt something pull my fishing rod and knew I had a bite.
4. My uncle went to the forest to catch game.
5. I saw a grub moving under the rock.
6. I tied a line to the end of the fishing rod.

READING STRATEGY

Identifying with a Character

Identifying with a character can help you enjoy and understand what you read.

As you read, ask yourself these questions:

* What does the main character do?
* How does the main character feel?
* Would I do the same things?
* Would I feel the same way?

As you read, try to identify with the main character. What does the boy do? How does he feel? Would you do the same things? Would you feel the same way?

from

MY SIDE OF THE MOUNTAIN

Jean Craighead George

Sam Gribley is a young city boy who runs away from home and heads for his great-grandparents' land in the Catskill Mountains of New York. Sam gets a ride to the edge of a dark forest, where he decides to start out on his own.

I must have walked a mile into the woods until I found a **stream**. It was a clear **athletic** stream that rushed and ran and jumped and splashed. Ferns grew along its bank, and its rocks were **upholstered** with moss.

I sat down, smelled the piney air, and took out my penknife. I cut off a green twig and began to **whittle**. I have always been good at whittling. I carved a ship once that my teacher **exhibited** for parents' night at school.

---

stream, small river
athletic, strong and active
upholstered, covered
whittle, cut wood into a shape
exhibited, displayed

Personification is the giving of human qualities to animals or things. One example of personification is the description of the stream on page 68. What words does the author use to personify the stream? Does the personification make you see it in a different way?

First I whittled an angle on one end of the twig. Then I cut a smaller twig and sharpened it to a point. I whittled an angle on that twig, and bound the two angles face to face with a strip of green bark. It was supposed to be a fishhook.

According to a book on how to survive on the land that I read in the New York Public Library, this was the way to make your own hooks. I then dug for worms. I had hardly chopped the moss away with my ax before I hit frost. **It had not occurred to me** that there would be frost in the ground in May, but then, I had not been on a mountain before.

This did worry me, because I was depending on fish to keep me alive until I got to my great-grandfather's mountain, where I was going to make traps and catch game.

I looked into the stream to see what else I could eat, and as I did, my hand knocked a rotten log apart. I remembered about old logs and all the sleeping stages of insects that are in it. I chopped away until I found a cold white grub.

I swiftly tied a string to my hook, put the grub on, and walked up the stream looking for a good place to fish. All the **manuals** I had read were very **emphatic** about where fish lived, and so I had memorized this: "In streams, fish usually **congregate** in pools and deep calm water.

It had not occurred to me, I had not realized

---

manuals, instruction books
emphatic, sure; forceful
congregate, gather

BEFORE YOU GO ON . . .

1 Where is Sam going? What does he plan to do there?

2 How does Sam make a fishhook?

HOW ABOUT YOU?

• Do you know how to find food in the woods? If so, what kind?

The heads of **riffles**, small rapids, the tail of a pool, **eddies** below rocks or logs, deep undercut banks, in the shade of overhanging bushes—all are very likely places to fish."

This stream did not seem to have any calm water, and I must have walked a thousand miles before I found a pool by a deep undercut bank in the shade of overhanging bushes. Actually, it wasn't far, it just seemed that way because as I went looking and finding nothing, I was sure I was going to **starve** to death.

I **squatted** on this bank and dropped in my line. I did so want to catch a fish. One fish would set me upon my way, because I had read how much you can learn from one fish. By examining the contents of its stomach you can find what the other fish are eating or you can use the **internal organs** as **bait**.

The grub went down to the bottom of the stream. It swirled around and hung still. Suddenly the string came to life, and rode back and forth and around in a circle. I pulled with a powerful jerk. The hook came apart, and whatever I had went circling back to its bed.

LITERARY ELEMENT

Characterization is the creation and development of a character in a story. Writers sometimes show what a character is like by describing what the character says and does. How does the author show what Sam is like?

Well, that almost made me cry. My bait was gone, my hook was broken, and I was getting cold, frightened, and mad. I whittled another hook, but this time I cheated and used string to wind it together instead of bark. I walked back to the log and luckily found another grub. I hurried to the pool, and I flipped a **trout** out of the water before I knew I had a bite.

The fish **flopped**, and I threw my whole body over it. I could not bear to think of it flopping itself back into the stream.

I cleaned it like I had seen the man at the fish market do, **examined** its stomach, and found it empty. This horrified me. What I didn't know was that an empty stomach means the fish are hungry and will eat about anything. However, I thought at the time that I was a **goner**. Sadly, I put some of the internal organs on my hook, and before I could get my line to the bottom I had another bite. I lost that one,

BEFORE YOU GO ON . . .

1 How does Sam feel when he loses his bait? Why?

2 How does Sam catch the trout?

HOW ABOUT YOU?

● How would you feel if you were alone in a woods without food? Explain.

71

but got the next one. I stopped when I had five nice little trout and looked around for a place to build a camp and make a fire.

It wasn't hard to find a pretty spot along that stream. I selected a place beside a mossy rock in a circle of **hemlocks**.

I decided to make a bed before I cooked. I cut off some **boughs** for a mattress, then I leaned some dead limbs against the **boulder** and covered them with hemlock limbs. This made a kind of tent. I crawled in, lay down, and felt alone and **secret** and very excited.

But ah, the rest of this story! I was on the northeast side of the mountain. It grew dark and cold early. Seeing **the shadows** slide down on me, I **frantically** ran around gathering firewood. This is about the only thing I did right from that moment until dawn, because I remembered that the driest wood in the forest is the dead limbs that are still on the trees, and I gathered an enormous pile of them. That pile must still be there, for I never got a fire going.

I got **sparks**, sparks, sparks. I even hit the **tinder** with the sparks. The tinder burned all right, but that was as far as I got. I blew on it, I breathed on it, I cupped it in my hands, but no sooner did I add twigs than the whole thing went black.

---

hemlocks, trees belonging to the pine family
boughs, large branches
boulder, large rock
secret, hidden from other people
the shadows, the darkness following sunset
frantically, in a hurried way
sparks, bits of fire
tinder, material that burns easily

Then it got too dark to see. I clicked steel and **flint** together, even though I couldn't see the tinder. Finally, I gave up and crawled into my hemlock tent, hungry, cold, and miserable. . . .

---

flint, stone used to make fire

About the Author

Jean Craighead George

Jean Craighead George has been a newspaper reporter as well as an award-winning novelist. She has written more than sixty books, including *My Side of the Mountain* and *Julie of the Wolves.* She loves nature and is interested in protecting the environment.

BEFORE YOU GO ON . . .

1 What does Sam use to make a bed?

2 How does he feel when it starts to grow dark? Why?

HOW ABOUT YOU?
- How would you feel if you were Sam? What would you do?

Review and Practice

COMPREHENSION

Reread the excerpt from *My Side of the Mountain*. Think about the order of events. Copy the sequence-of-events chart into your notebook. Complete the chart with important events from the story in chronological order. Add boxes if needed.

In pairs or small groups, compare your charts. Add or change information if needed. Take turns retelling the events of the story.

EXTENSION

Have you ever been to a forest, a desert, an ocean, or a mountain? If so, compare your experience to Sam's experience. Copy the chart into your notebook. Complete the middle column with information from the story. Then complete the right column with information from your experience. Share your charts in small groups.

	Boy in Story	Me
Place	forest	
Reason for being there		
Who was there		
Activities		
Problems		

DISCUSSION

Discuss in pairs or small groups.

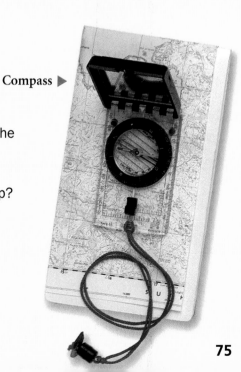

Compass ▶

1. Have you ever caught an animal, such as a fish or a bird? Have you ever made a shelter? If so, describe the experience. How did you feel?

2. If you were in a forest, how would you survive? How would you find and cook food? Where would you sleep?

3. What do you think will happen next in *My Side of the Mountain*?

This science article is expository nonfiction. It explains the importance of water to living things. It also explains the process of the water cycle. As you read, use the pictures to help you understand the process.

Water and Living Things

▲ Watery Earth

What do Earth's surface and **human beings** have in common? Answer: They both consist mostly of water. Water covers about three-quarters of Earth's surface. Water makes up about two-thirds of the human body. In fact, water is a large part of *every* living thing.

Water is **essential** for living things to grow, reproduce, and **carry out** other important life processes. For example, plants use water, plus carbon dioxide and sunlight, to make their food in the process of photosynthesis. Animals and other organisms eat plants or eat other organisms that eat plants. Water is also essential as an environment for living things. Both fresh water and salt water provide habitats for many kinds of living things.

---

human beings, people
essential, necessary
carry out, complete

▲ A tropical fish swims past rocks near the ocean floor.

Distribution of Water on Earth

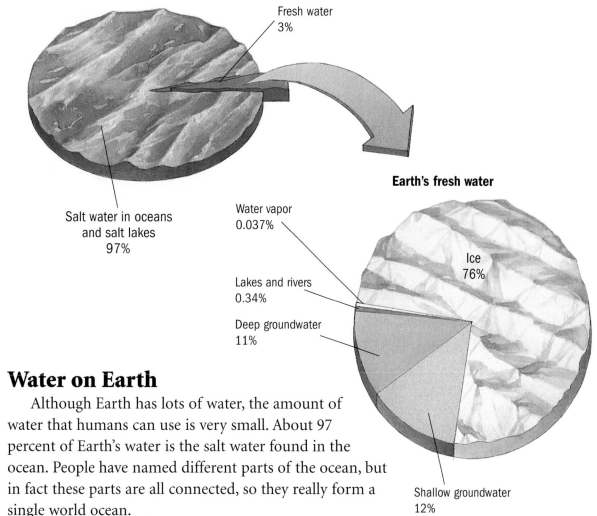

Total water on Earth

Fresh water
3%

Salt water in oceans
and salt lakes
97%

Earth's fresh water

Water vapor
0.037%

Lakes and rivers
0.34%

Deep groundwater
11%

Ice
76%

Shallow groundwater
12%

Water on Earth

Although Earth has lots of water, the amount of water that humans can use is very small. About 97 percent of Earth's water is the salt water found in the ocean. People have named different parts of the ocean, but in fact these parts are all connected, so they really form a single world ocean.

Only about 3 percent of Earth's water is fresh water. Most of that fresh water is found in the huge **masses** of ice near the North and South poles. Less than 1 percent of the water on Earth is **available** for humans to use. Some of this available fresh water is found in lakes, rivers, and streams. Other fresh water is located under the ground. This underground water is called groundwater. It fills the small cracks and spaces between underground soil and rocks.

masses, large amounts
available, obtainable; accessible

BEFORE YOU GO ON . . .

1 What do Earth's surface and human beings have in common?

2 Why is water essential for living things?

HOW ABOUT YOU?

● What are two ways that you use fresh water?

The water cycle ▶

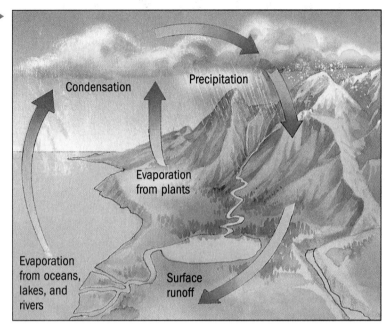

Condensation

Precipitation

Evaporation
from plants

Evaporation
from oceans,
lakes, and
rivers

Surface
runoff

The Water Cycle

Water is always moving
from one place to another. The
continuous process by which
water moves through the
living and nonliving parts of
the environment is called the water **cycle**. In the water
cycle, water moves from bodies of water (such as oceans,
rivers, lakes, and streams), land, and living things on
Earth's surface to the **atmosphere** and back to Earth's
surface.

The sun is the source of energy that creates the water
cycle. The sun's energy warms water in oceans, rivers, and
lakes. Some of this water evaporates—changes into a gas
called water **vapor**. Smaller amounts of water evaporate
from the soil, from plants, and from animals (through
their skin). Water vapor rises in the air and forms **clouds**.
As water vapor cools in the clouds, it condenses, or
changes into liquid water drops. When water drops in the
clouds become heavy, they fall back to Earth as
precipitation—rain, snow, sleet, or hail.

Precipitation is the source of all fresh water on or
under Earth's surface. The water cycle renews the supply of
usable fresh water on Earth.

Evaporation
Most evaporation happens over
oceans, lakes, and rivers. During
evaporation, the sun heats the
water and changes it to water
vapor.

Condensation
Clouds form as the water vapor
cools. The cool vapor changes to
very small water drops.

Precipitation
When drops of water in clouds
become larger and heavier, they
fall back to Earth.

BEFORE YOU GO ON . . .

❶ What is the water cycle?

❷ What happens when
water evaporates?

HOW ABOUT YOU?
• What kinds of
precipitation do you have
in your region?

---

continuous, without stopping
cycle, group of events that happen in the same order over and over
atmosphere, the air that surrounds Earth
vapor, tiny drops of fluid in the air
clouds, tiny drops of water that collect in the air
usable, able to be used

Link the Readings

Reread the excerpt from *My Side of the Mountain* and "Water and Living Things." Then copy the chart into your notebook and complete it with information from the readings. Compare your charts in pairs or small groups.

Title of Selection	Type of Text (Genre)	Fiction or Nonfiction	Purpose of Selection	What I Learned
From *My Side of the Mountain*			*to entertain*	
"Water and Living Things"				

DISCUSSION

Discuss in pairs or small groups.

1. What are the steps in the water cycle? Why is each step in this process important?

2. Where are some of the places that fish live in a stream?

3. Think about the stream in the excerpt from *My Side of the Mountain*. Then reread the first two paragraphs of "Water and Living Things." How is the mountain stream essential to the boy and the trout?

This fishhook, decorated to look like an insect, is called a fly. ▶

Connect to Writing

GRAMMAR

Using Adverbs to Describe

Writers often use adverbs to describe. An **adverb** usually describes the action of a verb, such as how an action happens. An adverb that describes a verb can be put in various places in a sentence. For example, an adverb can appear at the beginning or end of a sentence or before or after the verb.

> adverb   verb
> He **frantically** searched for firewood. [tells how]
>
> verb   adverb
> The stream flowed **rapidly**.

Many adverbs are formed by adding -ly to an adjective.

adjective	adverb
rapid	rapidly
careless	carelessly
careful	carefully
loud	loudly

Several adverbs are called **frequency adverbs**. Some frequency adverbs are *always*, *usually*, *often*, *sometimes*, and *never*. Frequency adverbs come between the subject and the verb.

> subject adverb   verb
>   Sam **never** started a fire.

Practice

Complete these sentences by using the adjective or adverb.

1. *clear, clearly*   Sam hoped for _____ weather.

2. *quiet, quietly*   The stream flowed _____.

3. *easy, easily*   Sam caught the fish _____.

4. *safe, safely*   He hoped to find a _____ place to camp.

Use a frequency adverb in each sentence.

5. The grub _____ sank to the bottom.

6. It _____ grows dark early on the mountain's northeast side.

SKILLS FOR WRITING

Describing a Process

A process is an event or activity with steps in a particular order. Examples are the water cycle (an event) and how to catch a fish (an activity). When you write about a process, remember that the steps must be clear and in the correct order. You can use sequence words to help make the order of the steps clear. Common sequence words are *first, second, next, then, after that,* and *finally.*

Practice

The following are the steps in the water cycle. However, they are mixed up. Write them in the correct order in your notebook. Start with "Energy from the sun warms bodies of water." Add sequence words to help make the order of the other steps clear.

- The vapor in the clouds cools.
- Some of the water becomes water vapor and rises in the air.
- The water vapor condenses into liquid water drops, which become heavy.
- The heavy drops fall to Earth as rain, snow, sleet, or hail.
- Energy from the sun warms bodies of water.
- The water vapor in the air forms clouds.

Writers sometimes use a thesaurus to vary their descriptions and make them more interesting. A thesaurus is a book of words and their synonyms (words with the same meaning). Using a thesaurus, find as many words as you can to describe falling water. (Hint: Look under the verb *fall* and the verb *flow.)*

WRITING ASSIGNMENT

Process Paragraph

You will write a paragraph about a survival skill.

1. **Read** Reread the part of *My Side of the Mountain* in which Sam catches a fish. Notice the order of the steps and the sequence words.

2. **Look for information** Choose a survival skill (for example, how to start a fire, hunt, find fresh water, or stay warm).

Writing Strategy: Sequence-of-Events Chart

A sequence-of-events chart can help you organize the steps in a process. Use it to put the steps in order before you write.

This sequence-of-events chart shows the steps Sam took to make a fishhook. (See pages 68–69.)

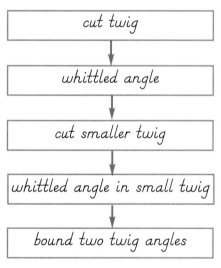

```
┌─────────────────────────────┐
│          cut twig           │
└─────────────────────────────┘
              │
              ▼
┌─────────────────────────────┐
│       whittled angle        │
└─────────────────────────────┘
              │
              ▼
┌─────────────────────────────┐
│       cut smaller twig      │
└─────────────────────────────┘
              │
              ▼
┌─────────────────────────────┐
│  whittled angle in small twig │
└─────────────────────────────┘
              │
              ▼
┌─────────────────────────────┐
│      bound two twig angles  │
└─────────────────────────────┘
```

---

3. **Make a sequence-of-events chart** In your notebook, organize the steps of the survival skill in a sequence-of-events chart.

4. **Write** Use your chart to help you write a paragraph about the survival skill you selected.

EDITING CHECKLIST

Did you . . .

▶ introduce your topic in the first sentence?

▶ write clear steps?

▶ put the steps in the correct order?

▶ use sequence words correctly?

Check Your Knowledge

Language Development

1. Did you identify with Sam in the passage from *My Side of the Mountain*? If so, how?

2. Describe how you use a dictionary to choose the correct meaning of a word.

3. What is the purpose of a science article? Of a novel?

4. What is personification? Give an example.

5. What is characterization? Give an example.

6. What is an adverb? Use an adverb in a sentence.

7. What is a process paragraph?

8. What is the purpose of a sequence-of-events chart?

9. How can pictures help you understand a text?

Academic Content

1. What new science vocabulary did you learn in Part 2? What do the words mean?

2. Describe the water cycle.

Put It All Together

OBJECTIVES

Integrate Skills
- **Listening/ Speaking:** *Individual presentation*
- **Writing:** *Expository essay*

Investigate Themes
- **Projects**
- **Further reading**

INDIVIDUAL PRESENTATION

You will give an individual presentation that explains how to make or do something.

1 **Think about it** Reread the part of *My Side of the Mountain* that tells how Sam makes a fishhook. Then reread the part of "Water and Living Things" that explains the process of the water cycle.

Work in groups. Brainstorm a list of topics for other natural processes, such as how a plant grows, how an egg becomes a butterfly, or how a forest develops from a pond or swamp. Each group member should choose a different process to explain.

2 **Organize** Use the Internet or a library to research your process. Then prepare your presentation: First, write each step of the process. Next, write a short introduction. Finally, make a poster to help explain the process.

3 **Practice** Practice your presentation within your group. Use your poster to help you explain your process.

4 **Present and evaluate** Give your presentation to your class. After each speaker finishes, evaluate the presentation. Did the speaker follow the speaking tips? Did the speaker answer your questions? What did you like best about the presentation? Do you have suggestions for improvement?

SPEAKING TIPS

- Speak clearly and slowly as you explain the process.
- Point to key ideas in the poster as you speak.
- Be ready to answer questions.

LISTENING TIPS

- Take notes as you listen.
- Write questions to ask after the presentation.

WRITING WORKSHOP

EXPOSITORY ESSAY

In an expository essay, the writer gives information about a topic. The writer includes details and examples to explain the information.

A good expository essay includes the following characteristics:

- an introductory paragraph that tells what the essay is about—the main idea
- details that explain and support the main idea
- clear organization
- a conclusion that summarizes the main idea about your topic

You will write a four-paragraph expository essay about your environment. Use the following steps and the model essay on page 86 to help you.

 Prewrite Make a list of some living things in your environment. Then make a list of some nonliving things.

Organize ideas Use a diagram—such as the organizational diagram on page 64—to put your ideas in order for a paragraph about living things in your environment. Then make another diagram to organize ideas for a paragraph about nonliving things.

WRITING TIP

Before you write an expository essay, think about your readers.
- What do they already know about your topic?
- What questions do you think they will have?

In your essay, try to answer the questions readers might have.

Before you write a first draft of your essay, read the following model. Notice the characteristics of an expository essay.

Jeremy Ng

My Environment

New York City is an interesting environment. It includes a surprising variety of living and nonliving things.

Nonliving things, such as tall buildings, cars, buses, and subways, are everywhere. Subways, bridges, and tunnels link the five boroughs of New York City.

Many people who live outside New York City don't know about the variety of living things there. Central Park has green grass, tall trees, and colorful flowers. Many small animals, such as chipmunks and squirrels, live in the park. So do many kinds of birds and insects. Of course, pests, such as rats, mice, and cockroaches, are also part of the environment.

New York has a great variety of living and nonliving things. Its unique environment includes buildings, cars, roads, and bridges as well as people and many other living things.

The introductory paragraph tells what the essay is about—the main idea.

The body paragraphs explain and support the main idea.

The conclusion summarizes the main idea.

2 **Draft** Use the model essay and your organizational diagrams to help you write your essay. Include an introductory paragraph, two body paragraphs, and a concluding paragraph.

- Introduce your main idea in an interesting way, so that your readers will want to know more and will read the rest of your essay. Reread the introductory paragraph of the model essay. How does the student get you interested in his topic?

- Use your organizational diagrams to write your two body paragraphs. These paragraphs should include details and examples that support your main idea. Be sure to include details about living and nonliving things.

- Conclude your essay by summarizing your main idea. Explain why your environment is special.

3 **Edit** Work in pairs. Trade papers and read each other's essays. Use the questions in the editing checklist to evaluate each other's work.

EDITING CHECKLIST

Did you . . .

▷ introduce your main idea clearly?

▷ include two body paragraphs?

▷ use details and examples to support your main idea?

▷ write a concluding paragraph?

▷ use correct subject-verb agreement?

4 **Revise** Revise your essay. Add information and correct mistakes, if necessary.

5 **Publish** Share your essay with your teacher and classmates.

A lake in Central Park, New York City ▶

PROJECTS

Work in pairs or small groups. Choose one of these projects.

1 Write a poem about a living or nonliving thing in your area. Use rhyme, if possible. Then read your poem to the class.

2 Walk around your school or neighborhood. List the living and nonliving things you see. Make a poster to show how the things in the ecosystem interact. Then share your poster with the class.

3 Use the library or Internet to research two animals in your area. Make a poster with a Venn diagram to show how the animals are similar and different. Then share your poster with the class.

4 What do you think happens when Sam, the boy in the passage from *My Side of the Mountain*, returns home? What does he tell his family and friends? Write a dialogue and practice it. Then perform it for the class.

5 Take photographs or find pictures of the different animals or plants in a habitat. Then make a display for the class.

6 Find a song about something in the natural world. Practice singing it. Then perform the song for the class.

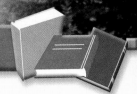

Further Reading

To find out more about the theme of this unit, choose from these reading suggestions.

***The Yearling,* Marjorie Kinnan Rawlings** Jody Baxter lives on a lonely farm in Florida with his poor, hardworking family. Jody longs for a friend to share his thoughts and feelings with, so when a young deer loses its mother, he takes it home. But as the deer, called Flag, grows up, he gets into so much trouble that Jody faces his hardest decision.

***Insectlopedia: Poems and Paintings,* Douglas Florian** Twenty-one poems and pictures about spiders and insects will make you laugh while you learn something about the bugs—and poetry. You'll read verses featuring a praying mantis, inchworms, moths, weevils, and other creepers and crawlers.

***The Beauty of the Beast: Poems from the Animal Kingdom,* Jack Prelutsky** More than 200 poems by poets all over the world are organized the way a zookeeper groups animals. Fish poems are grouped together, as are birds, snakes, and more. Some poems are long, some are short, some rhyme, some don't. There are watercolor pictures of the animals, too.

***The Call of the Wild,* Jack London** Kidnappers snatch Buck, a strong, smart dog, from his California home. He joins a sled dog team in Canada. Violence is everywhere: Dogs attack weaker dogs, and men beat and starve their dogs. Buck learns to be tough. He finally finds a kind master, but the attraction of the wilderness grows stronger.

***The River,* Gary Paulsen** Two years before this story begins, teenager Brian Robeson survived in the wilderness for fifty-four days with only a hatchet. Now he agrees to go back into the wilderness to teach a government worker ways to survive. Then things get tough. The man is injured, and Brian must build a raft to take him down a river to a doctor.

STRIVING for SUCCESS

PART 1

- "Success Stories"
- "An Interview with Naomi Shihab Nye," Rachel Barenblat

PART 2

- From *Seedfolks*, Paul Fleischman
- "How Seeds and Plants Grow"

Success means different things to different people. For some, success means having a good job. For others, it means achieving their dreams, helping others, or doing what makes them happy. Some people face physical challenges but still strive for—and achieve—success.

In Part 1, you will read about six people who strove for success in different lines of work—as a painter, a poet, an actor, a computer scientist, an astronaut, and an architect. Then you will read an interview with one of these people.

In Part 2, you will read about a father and son who strive to successfully grow lettuce in a city community garden. Finally, you will learn about some things plants need to grow successfully.

Prepare to Read

BACKGROUND

"Success Stories" is an informational text about six successful people. It contains their biographies, or stories about their lives.

Make connections Think of someone successful. What qualities or accomplishments of the person made you choose him or her? What makes or made this person successful?

Make a chart like the one below in your notebook. Complete it with information about the person you selected. Then compare your charts in small groups.

▲ Albert Einstein developed the theory of relativity and received the Nobel Prize in physics in 1921.

Einstein's Qualities	Einstein's Accomplishments
<ul><li>intelligence</li><li>creativity</li><li>perseverance (determination to keep trying)</li></ul>	<ul><li>developed important theories in physics</li><li>received more than eighteen honorary university degrees</li><li>won the Nobel Prize</li></ul>

LEARN KEY WORDS

astronaut
autobiography
distribute
ordinary
points of view
traditional

VOCABULARY

Read these sentences. Use vocabulary-building strategies (context, Greek and Latin roots) to figure out the meaning of the **red** words. Use a dictionary to check your answers. Write each word and its meaning in your notebook.

1. The **astronaut** made her third trip into space.
2. We know a lot about him from his description of his life in his **autobiography**.
3. Over the Internet, we can **distribute** information to all parts of the world.
4. She writes about **ordinary** people—the kind of people we meet every day.
5. Very often our **points of view** are determined by what we learned when we were young.
6. This **traditional** dance has been part of my culture for hundreds of years.

READING STRATEGY

Making Inferences

Writers don't always give information directly—sometimes they imply, or suggest, it. Readers must then infer, or figure out, what the writers mean. This is called **making inferences**. Read the statement below. What inferences can you make about Marta from what the writer tells you?

Statement: Marta is an A student.

We can infer that Marta is smart and that she probably studies hard, although the statement does not say this directly.

As you read, try to make inferences about what the writers mean.

U.S. rocket launch ▶

93

Social Studies

Preview and skim the text. Note how you are already making inferences. Then, as you read each biography more closely, ask yourself what the writer tells us directly and what we must infer.

SUCCESS STORIES

Frida Kahlo, painter

Frida Kahlo was born in 1907, in Coyoacán, which is now part of Mexico City, Mexico. When she was six years old, Kahlo got polio. Polio is a serious disease that often causes **paralysis**. As a result of her illness, Kahlo's right leg was always thinner and weaker than her left one.

When Kahlo was an art student, she met Diego Rivera, a very famous Mexican painter. They got married in 1929. They shared a love of Mexican art and culture. In some of her **self-portraits**, Kahlo is wearing traditional Mexican clothing and jewelry. In addition to her many self-portraits, Kahlo painted portraits of friends and made still-life paintings—pictures of arranged objects, such as flowers and fruit.

Frida Kahlo exhibited her work in New York City, Paris, and Mexico City. She died in 1954. Her house in Mexico City, called Casa Azul (Blue House), is now the Frida Kahlo Museum.

---

paralysis, the loss of the ability to move or feel part of your body
self-portraits, paintings or drawings of oneself

▲ *Self-Portrait with Monkey,* 1938

▲ *Watermelons,* Frida Kahlo

◄ Naomi Shihab Nye

Naomi Shihab Nye, poet

Naomi Shihab Nye is a poet, essayist, songwriter, and author of books for children and young adults. Born in 1952, in St. Louis, Missouri, she is the daughter of an American mother and a Palestinian father. Nye published her first poem when she was seven years old. At age fourteen, she and her family moved to Jerusalem, where she attended high school. A year later, her family moved to San Antonio, Texas. Nye now lives in San Antonio with her husband and son.

Naomi Shihab Nye's writing shows many **influences** and points of view. She writes about Arab Americans like herself, Mexican Americans who live near her, and other cultures in the United States. Because she is from a **multicultural** family and a multicultural community, her poetry often explores the similarities and differences between cultures. Her poems often describe ordinary people, events, and objects from a new **perspective**.

---

influences, things that have an effect on people or things
multicultural, made up of many cultures (people from different
    countries, races, or religions)
perspective, way of seeing something

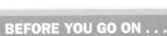

BEFORE YOU GO ON . . .

1 What disease did Frida Kahlo have as a child? How did it affect her?

2 At what age did Naomi Shihab Nye publish her first poem?

HOW ABOUT YOU?
- What kinds of paintings or poems interest you?

Christopher Reeve, actor

Christopher Reeve, who was born in 1952 in New York City, is a success in many ways. As a young man, he was a classical pianist, an expert pilot, a sailor, a skier, and a horseback rider. Of course, he was also a world-famous actor, especially known for his *Superman* films. In 1995, Reeve fell off a horse and seriously injured his head and spinal cord. He was paralyzed from the neck down and has been in a wheelchair since then.

Some people might have given up after such an accident, but not Reeve. Since 1995, he has been working to raise money to help people with spinal cord injuries. In 1996, he created the Christopher Reeve Foundation, which gives money to help people with disabilities. He returned to acting in TV films. He also wrote an autobiography, *Still Me*. And every day, Reeve exercised hard to keep his muscles strong. But doctors said he would never be able to move any part of his body below his shoulders.

Then Reeve discovered in 2000 that he could move one finger. Now he can move all his fingers. He can also move his joints while floating in water. Feeling has returned in much of his body, and he can breathe for two-hour periods without using a special machine. Reeve tells people in wheelchairs, "Do not give up. . . . Nothing is impossible."

▲ Christopher Reeve in a wheelchair

Reeve as Superman ▶

---

spinal cord, important part of the nervous system, located in the back

Tim Berners-Lee, computer scientist

Tim Berners-Lee was born in 1955. He graduated from Oxford University, England, in 1976.

In 1989, Berners-Lee invented the World Wide Web while working as a **software engineer.** He saw the Web as a way to share and distribute information around the world. Researchers and scholars had been using the Internet for many years before he invented the

▲ Tim Berners-Lee at his computer

Web. Before the invention of the Web, the Internet was a collection of computers that contained lots of information. However, it was difficult for people to get the information. The Web linked information across the Internet. The invention made it possible for people to get information with just one click of a **mouse** . The World Wide Web has created a communications **revolution** that some scientists compare to the invention of the printing press.

Computer scientist Berners-Lee now works in Boston at the Laboratory of Computer Science at the **Massachusetts Institute of Technology** (MIT). He also directs the World Wide Web **Consortium.** This is a group of companies and organizations working to discover all the possibilities of the World Wide Web.

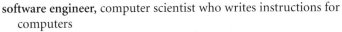

software engineer, computer scientist who writes instructions for computers
mouse, small object that you move when using a computer
revolution, time of great change
Massachusetts Institute of Technology, well-known research university
consortium, group of companies or organizations working together

BEFORE YOU GO ON . . .

1. What happened to Christopher Reeve when he fell off a horse in 1995?

2. How did Tim Berners-Lee's invention change our world?

HOW ABOUT YOU?

• If you met Christopher Reeve or Tim Berners-Lee, what would you say to them?

Dr. Mae Jemison, astronaut, physician, teacher

Mae Jemison was born in 1956 in Decatur, Alabama. She grew up in Chicago, Illinois. When she was growing up, Jemison watched spaceflights on television. After college, she went to medical school and also took graduate courses in engineering. What she really wanted, however, was to be a space traveler. In 1987, Dr. Jemison was one of fifteen people, out of almost 2,000 applicants, chosen for NASA's astronaut training program.

On September 12, 1992, Dr. Jemison and six other astronauts **went into orbit** aboard the **space shuttle** *Endeavour*. Dr. Jemison was the first African-American female astronaut. During her seven-day flight, she did experiments to understand the effects of weightlessness. She carried with her several small objects from West African countries. She did this to show her belief that space belongs to all nations.

Dr. Jemison is currently a professor in the Environmental Studies Program and director of the Jemison Institute for Advancing Technology in Developing Countries at Dartmouth College. People at the Jemison Institute study ways that modern technologies, such as satellite-based **telecommunications** and **solar** energy, can help developing countries around the world.

▲ Dr. Mae Jemison on the *Endeavour*

---

went into orbit, flew into space
space shuttle, space vehicle that can fly into space and
　　return to Earth
telecommunications, process of sending and receiving
　　information by telephone, radio, and so forth
solar, related to the sun

98

Maya Lin, architect

Maya Lin was born in 1959 in Athens, Ohio. Her parents, who were from China, were professors at Ohio University. Her father was an artist, and her mother is a poet.

In 1980, Lin was an **architecture** student at Yale University. The United States government held a contest to find a **designer** for a **memorial** to honor Vietnam veterans. These veterans were men and women who had fought and died during the Vietnam War (1957–1975). One of Lin's professors asked his students to send in their designs to the government. Altogether, more than 1,400 people entered the contest. In May 1981, the judges announced that Lin had won the contest. She was twenty-one years old at the time.

Maya Lin's design for the Vietnam Veterans Memorial is simple but powerful. It consists of two long, black stone walls that join to form a V. The names of more than 58,000 people who died in Vietnam are **engraved** on the memorial. People visiting the wall see their own **reflections** in the black stone, connecting them to the names of the veterans engraved there. It has become one of the most popular memorials in the United States.

Lin has also designed other projects, including a sculpture honoring the women of Yale University, a clock for Pennsylvania Station in New York City, and the Civil Rights Memorial in Montgomery, Alabama.

▲ Couple at the memorial making a copy of their son's name

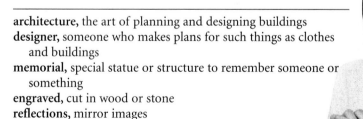

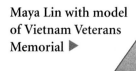

Maya Lin with model of Vietnam Veterans Memorial ▶

---

architecture, the art of planning and designing buildings
designer, someone who makes plans for such things as clothes and buildings
memorial, special statue or structure to remember someone or something
engraved, cut in wood or stone
reflections, mirror images

BEFORE YOU GO ON . . .

1 What kind of experiments did Dr. Jemison do in space?

2 What is engraved on the Vietnam Veterans Memorial?

HOW ABOUT YOU?

• Would you like to go on a space shuttle? Why or why not?

Review and Practice

COMPREHENSION

Reread "Success Stories." Think about the qualities and accomplishments of each person. Copy the chart into your notebook. Then complete it with information from the article.

Name	Qualities	Accomplishments
Frida Kahlo		
Naomi Shihab Nye		
Christopher Reeve		
Tim Berners-Lee		
Mae Jemison		
Maya Lin		

A photo collage of people from "Success Stories" ▼

EXTENSION

1. Look at the chart you prepared. Write a paragraph about each person's accomplishments. Then compare your paragraphs with a partner's. What similarities do you notice? What differences?

2. Work with a partner. Compare the qualities of the six people.

3. Did you make any inferences as you read and as you prepared the chart? If so, what are they?

DISCUSSION

Discuss in pairs or small groups.

1. Which person do you think had or has the easiest life? What inferences do you base this on? Explain.

2. Which person do you think had or has the most difficult life? What inferences do you base this on? Explain.

3. Which person do you admire most? Why?

4. Which would you prefer to be—an astronaut, a poet, a painter, an actor, a computer scientist, or an architect? Explain.

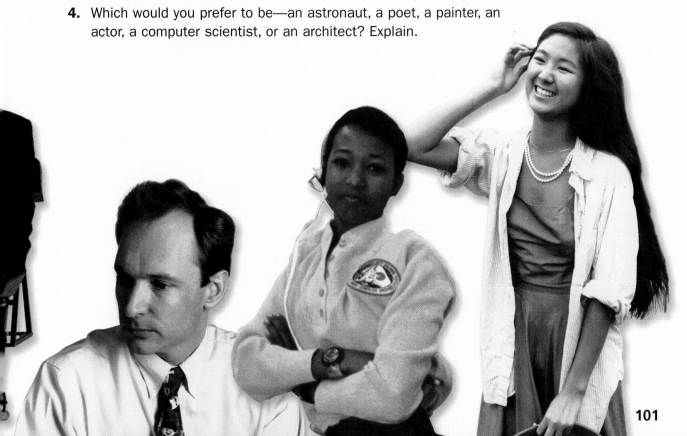

Interview

In this section, you will read an interview, led by Rachel Barenblat, with Palestinian-American poet Naomi Shihab Nye. Nye is one of the people in "Success Stories." In an interview, the interviewer asks someone about his or her life, ideas, and feelings. As you read the interview, note what new things you learn about Nye.

An Interview with

Naomi Shihab Nye

Rachel Barenblat

Rachel Barenblat (RB): *When did you start writing? Were you writing poems from the start?*

Naomi Shihab Nye (NSN): I started writing when I was six, immediately after learning *how* to write. Yes, I was writing poems from the start. Somehow—from hearing my mother read to me? from looking at books? from watching **Carl Sandburg** on 1950s black-and-white TV?— I knew what a poem was. I liked the **portable**, **comfortable** shape of poems. I liked the space around them and the way you could hold your words at arm's length and look at them. And especially the way they took you to a deeper, quieter place, almost immediately.

▲ Naomi Shihab Nye

Carl Sandburg, famous American poet (1878–1967)
portable, light and easy to carry
comfortable, pleasant and relaxed

▲ A 1950s black-and-white television set

COME WITH ME

To the quiet minute between two noisy minutes
It's always waiting ready to welcome us
Tucked under the wing of the day
I'll be there
Where will you be?

Naomi Shihab Nye

▲ Western Wall, Jerusalem

▲ The Alamo, San Antonio, Texas

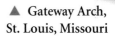
▲ Gateway Arch, St. Louis, Missouri

RB: *What did you write about, in the beginning? What provided your first* **inspiration**?

NSN: I wrote about all the little stuff a kid would write about: **amazement** over things, cats, wounded squirrels found in the street, my friend who moved away, trees, teachers, my funny grandma. At that time I wrote about my German grandma—I wouldn't meet my Palestinian grandma till I was fourteen.

RB: *Place plays an important role in your writing, especially the places you have lived and the places that hold your* **roots**. *Tell me about the places that have been important to you.*

NSN: The three main places I have lived—St. Louis, Jerusalem, San Antonio—are each deeply **precious** to me indeed, and I often find them weaving in and out of my writing. Each place has such **distinctive** neighborhoods and **flavors**. . . .

---

inspiration, something that gives you a good idea
amazement, great surprise
roots, connections with a place because you were born there or your family lived there
precious, much loved and very important
distinctive, clearly marking a person or thing as different
flavors, qualities or features

BEFORE YOU GO ON . . .

1 What did Nye like about poetry even as a child?
2 What topics did she write about as a child? What influences her poems today?

HOW ABOUT YOU?

• Do you like poetry? Why or why not? What are some poems you have read?

RB: *Where do you usually write? Do you have a desk, an office, a favorite chair, a favorite tree?*

NSN: I have a long wooden table where I write. Not a desk, really, as it doesn't have drawers. I wish it had drawers. I can write anywhere. Outside, of course, is always great. I am one of the few people I know who *loves* being in airports. Good thing. I can write and read well in them.

RB: *What is your advice to writers, especially young writers who are just starting out?*

NSN: Number one: Read, read, and then read some more. Always read. Find the voices that speak most to *you*. This is your **pleasure** and **blessing**, as well as **responsibility**!

It is **crucial** to make one's own writing circle—friends, either close or far, with whom you trade work and discuss it—as a kind of support system, place of conversation and energy. Find those people, even a few, with whom you can share and discuss your works— then do it. Keep the papers **flowing** among you. Work does not get into the world by itself. We must help it. . . .

▲ A writing circle

---

pleasure, feeling of happiness or enjoyment
blessing, something that helps you
responsibility, something that you must do
crucial, very important
flowing, moving

BEFORE YOU GO ON . . .

1 Where does Nye like to write?

2 What is Nye's advice to young writers?

HOW ABOUT YOU?

● Have you ever shared your work in a writing circle? If so, describe the experience.

About the Interviewer

Rachel Barenblat

Rachel Barenblat is an associate editor of *Pif,* an online literary magazine. She has a master of fine arts degree in writing and literature. Her first book of poems, *the skies here,* was published in 1995. She is executive director of Inkberry, a literary arts center in Massachusetts.

Link the Readings

REFLECTION

Reread "Success Stories" and "An Interview with Naomi Shihab Nye." Then copy the chart into your notebook. Complete it with information from the readings. Compare your charts in small groups.

Title of Selection	Type of Text (Genre)	Fiction or Nonfiction	Purpose of Selection	Two Interesting Facts I Learned
"Success Stories"				
"An Interview with Naomi Shihab Nye"				

DISCUSSION

Discuss in pairs or small groups.

1. Think of one interview question that you would like to ask each person in "Success Stories." Use the questions from "An Interview with Naomi Shihab Nye" to help you.

2. In both of the texts in Part 1, you read biographical information about people. Discuss differences between the way the information is presented in "Success Stories" and in the Nye interview. Did you make more inferences in one? If so, which one? Why?

3. In Part 1, you read about success in many contexts. Think about the people you read about. With your group, make a list of those people. Then compare what success means in each of their stories.

Connect to Writing

GRAMMAR

Yes/No and *Wh-* Questions in the Simple Past

Yes/no questions in the simple past usually begin with the word *did* or *didn't*. The main verb is in its base form, not in the simple past.

		subject	verb	
Did	Tim Berners-Lee	**invent**	the World Wide Web?
Didn't	Maya Lin	**design**	the Vietnam Veterans Memorial?

***Wh-* questions** in the simple past begin with a *wh-* word (or *how*) + *did*. The main verb is in its base form, not in the simple past.

wh- word + *did*		subject	verb
What	did	Tim Berners-Lee	**invent**?
When	did	Naomi Shihab Nye	**live** in Jerusalem?
Why	did	Mae Jemison	**do** experiments on the *Endeavour*?
Where	did	Frida Kahlo	**exhibit** her work?
How	did	Christopher Reeve	**injure** his spinal cord?

When the subject of a *wh-* question is *who* or *what*, a simple past verb follows the *wh-* word. Do not use the word *did*.

subject	verb	
Who	**invented**	the World Wide Web?
What	**happened**	to Christopher Reeve in 1995?

Practice

Copy the interview into your notebook. Complete the questions. Make *yes/no* or *wh-* questions in the simple past. Then compare questions in pairs.

Q: _____ _____ you write your first book?
A: I wrote it two years ago, when I was twenty-five.

Q: _____ _____ you to write the book?
A: My friends encouraged me to write it. My parents did, too.

Q: _____ _____ you write the book?
A: I wrote part of it in the United States and part of it in Paris.

Q: _____ you enjoy writing the book?
A: Yes, I did. It was a wonderful experience.

Q: _____ _____ you enjoy the most?
A: I enjoyed finishing each chapter!

106

SKILLS FOR WRITING

Writing Narratives: Interview Questions

A narrative is a story. Biographies are nonfiction narratives, or true stories, of real people. Writers usually tell the events in a narrative in chronological order.

Before writing narratives about people, writers often interview them. Imagine that you want to interview astronaut Mae Jemison. You might ask her *wh-* questions such as the ones in the left column of the chart.

Wh- Questions	Way to Use
Where did you grow up?	Use **where** to ask questions about places.
Who encouraged you to be a doctor?	Use **who** to ask about people.
Why did you want to be an astronaut?	Use **why** to ask for reasons or explanations.
When did you fly on the *Endeavour*?	Use **when** to ask about time.
What did you do on the flight?	Use **what** to ask about things or actions.
How did you eat food in space?	Use **how** to ask about the way to do something.

Read the narrative paragraph. Then answer the questions.

Lauren Younkins

My Dad's Fear of Flying

My dad was claustrophobic. He always got scared in small places, like subways and airplanes. For many years our family didn't go on a vacation far from home. My dad refused to get on an airplane! Last year, he took a class to help with his claustrophobia. The teacher taught my father how to control his fear. Later that year, my father got on an airplane, and he wasn't afraid.

1. Who is the narrative about?

2. What questions do you think the interviewer asked to write this narrative?

WRITING ASSIGNMENT

Narrative Paragraph

You will write a narrative paragraph about a successful friend or family member.

1. **Read** Reread "Success Stories" (pages 94–99) and the Naomi Shihab Nye interview (pages 102–104). Does someone you know have a success story? Choose one person to interview.

2. **Write interview questions** Write *wh-* questions to ask the person. Look at the questions in Skills for Writing and in the interview with Nye for ideas.

3. **Interview the person** Use your questions to interview the person. Sometimes an answer to one question will make you think of another question. Listen carefully to the person's answers and take notes.

Writing Strategy: Word Web

Using a word web can help you organize your ideas. First, write the subject inside a circle. Next, write your ideas about the subject around the circle. Then circle the ideas that you want to include in your narrative.

Look at the diagram for the paragraph on page 107.

- family's vacations near home
- Dad feared small places, including planes
- Dad's fear of flying
- Dad learned to control his fear
- Dad took class for claustrophobics

---

4. **Make a word web** Make a word web in your notebook. Write the name of the person you interviewed in a circle. Write information you learned about him or her around the circle. What made this person a success? Circle the ideas you want to include in your paragraph.

5. **Write a narrative** Use your word web to help you write a narrative paragraph about the person. Remember to use chronological order.

EDITING CHECKLIST

Did you . . .

▶ give information that shows why the person is a success?

▶ use simple past verbs correctly?

▶ present the events in chronological order?

Check Your Knowledge

Language Development

1. What are three words with Greek or Latin roots that you learned in Part 1?

2. How do you use making inferences as a reading strategy?

3. What is a biography? An interview?

4. What is a narrative?

5. What are some questions you might ask when you interview someone?

6. How can a word web help you organize your ideas?

Academic Content

1. What new social studies vocabulary did you learn in Part 1? What do the words mean?

2. What are some qualities that successful scientists, artists, and writers all have?

3. Why is the World Wide Web important?

4. What is a self-portrait? What can you learn about a person from looking at that person's self-portrait?

A painter's palette, brush, and paint tube ▶

Prepare to Read

OBJECTIVES

LANGUAGE DEVELOPMENT

Reading:
- Vocabulary building: *Context, dictionary skills*
- Reading strategy: *Monitoring comprehension*
- Text types: *Short story, science article*
- Literary elements: *First-person point of view, plot*

Writing:
- Organizational chart
- Personal narrative

Listening/Speaking:
- State and support opinions

Grammar:
- Independent clauses
- Coordinating conjunctions
- Compound sentences

Viewing/Representing:
- Diagrams, photographs

ACADEMIC CONTENT

- Science vocabulary
- Plant growth

BACKGROUND

Seedfolks is a work of fiction about a vacant lot that becomes a community garden. In some neighborhoods in big cities, people plant such gardens on empty areas of land, or vacant lots. Each neighbor can plant flowers or vegetables in one part of the lot.

In *Seedfolks*, a different character narrates each chapter, telling about the garden from his or her point of view. Each chapter is like a short story. Short stories usually present a short sequence of events, and the main character usually experiences a problem or conflict. A boy named Virgil narrates the chapter you are about to read. Virgil tells how he and his father try to grow lettuce in a community garden.

Make connections Work in small groups. Imagine that you are planting part of a community garden. What plants do you want to grow? Brainstorm and list your ideas.

LEARN KEY WORDS

coincidence
ground
package
passengers
plantation
seeds
wilt

VOCABULARY

Read these sentences. Use the context to figure out the meaning of the **red** words. Use a dictionary to check your answers. Write each word and its meaning in your notebook.

1. It's a **coincidence** that all my neighbors have rose gardens; they didn't plan it.
2. The **ground** is too hard to plant flowers now.
3. I got a large **package** in the mail.
4. My mother drove the car, and my brother and I were **passengers**.
5. Farmer John's cotton **plantation** is the largest in the county.
6. We planted flower **seeds** last week, and we're waiting for them to grow.
7. A few days after we picked the flowers, they began to **wilt**.

READING STRATEGY

Monitoring Comprehension

Monitor, or check, your **comprehension** as you read. For example, ask yourself, "Did I understand that paragraph? What don't I understand?" Follow these steps when you don't understand a text:

- Reread the text.
- Try to paraphrase the text—put the information in your own words.
- Write questions about things that you don't understand.
- After you read, look for answers in the text, or ask your teacher.

First preview and skim Virgil's story. Then, as you read more thoroughly, stop at the end of each page. Monitor your comprehension. If you don't understand something, reread it and try to paraphrase it. Write questions to ask later.

from SEEDFOLKS

Paul Fleischman

. . . My father drove a bus back in Haiti. Here he drives a taxi. That night he drove himself way across town to borrow two shovels from a friend of his. The next morning was the first day without school. **I was done with** fifth grade forever. I'd planned on sleeping till noon to celebrate. But when it was still half dark my father shook my shoulder. School was over, but that garden was just starting.

We walked down and picked out a place to dig up. The ground was packed so hard, the tip of my shovel bounced off it like a **pogo stick**. We tried three **spots** till we found one we liked. Then we walked back and forth, picking out broken glass, like chickens pecking seeds. After that we **turned the soil**. We were always digging up more trash—bolts and screws and pieces of brick. That's how I found the **locket**. It was shaped like a heart and covered with rust, with a broken chain. I got it open. Inside was this tiny photo of a girl. She was white, with a sad-looking face. She had on this hat with flowers on it. I don't know why I kept it instead of **tossing** it on our **trash pile**.

---

locket, necklace with a small case for a picture
tossing, throwing
trash pile, garbage

I was done with, I had finished
pogo stick, a toy used for jumping
spots, places
turned the soil, broke up the earth to prepare it for planting

It seemed like hours and hours before we had the ground finished. We rested a while. Then my father asked if I was ready. I thought he meant ready to plant our seeds. But instead, we turned another square of ground. Then another after that. Then three more after that. My father hadn't been smiling to himself about some little garden. He was thinking of a farm, to make money. I'd seen a package of seeds for pole beans and hoped that's what we'd grow. They get so tall that the man in the picture was picking **'em** way at the top of a ladder. But my father said no. He was always asking people in his cab about how to get rich. One of 'em told him that fancy restaurants paid lots of money for this baby lettuce, smaller than the regular kind, to use in rich folks' salads. The fresher it was, the higher the price. My father planned to pick it and then race it over in his cab. **Running red lights** if he had to.

'em, them (slang)
running red lights, driving without stopping at the stoplights

LITERARY ELEMENT

When a story is told from the *first-person point of view*, the narrator (the person telling the story) is one of the characters. The narrator uses the first-person pronoun *I* and tells what he or she knows and observes.

BEFORE YOU GO ON . . .

1 What did Virgil plan to do on the first day after school ended?

2 What did Virgil find? What did he do with it?

HOW ABOUT YOU?

- Have you ever found something special? If so, what was it?

Lettuce seeds are smaller than sand. I felt embarrassed, planting so much ground. No one else's garden was a **quarter** the size of ours. Suddenly I saw Miss Fleck. I **hardly** recognized her in jeans. She was **the strictest** teacher in Ohio. I'd had her for third grade. She pronounced every letter in every word, and expected you to talk the same way. She was tall and even blacker than my father. No **slouching** in your seat in her class or any kind of rudeness. The other teachers seemed afraid of her too. She walked over just when we finished planting.

"Well, Virgil," she said. "You seem to have claimed quite a large *plantation* here."

That's just what I was afraid of hearing. I looked away from her, down at our sticks. We'd put 'em in the ground and run string around 'em, cutting our land up into six pieces. I didn't know why, till my father stepped forward.

"Actually, madam, only this very first area here is ours," he said. He had on his biggest smile. He must have remembered her. "The others we have planted at the

LITERARY ELEMENT

Plot is a sequence of connected events in a fictional story. In most stories, the plot has characters and a main problem or conflict. The plot usually begins by giving information to help you understand the story. Then something happens that introduces the main problem. The problem grows until there is a turning point, or climax, when a character tries to solve the problem. The events that follow the climax lead to the end of the story.

---

quarter, one of four parts; one-fourth
hardly, almost did not
the strictest, the most demanding
slouching, not sitting or standing up straight

request of relatives who have no tools or who live too far."

"Really, now," said Miss Fleck.

"Yes, madam," said my father. He pointed at the closest squares of land. "My brother Antoine. My auntie, Anne-Marie."

My eyes opened wide. They both lived in Haiti. I stared at my father, but he just kept smiling. His finger pointed farther to the left. "My Uncle Philippe." He lived in New York. "My wife's father." He died last year. "And her sister." My mother didn't have any sisters. I looked at my father's smiling face. I'd never watched an adult lie before.

"And what did your *extended* family of gardeners ask you to plant?" said Miss Fleck.

"Lettuce," said my father. "All lettuce."

"What a coincidence," she said back. She just stood, then walked over to her own garden. I'm pretty sure she didn't believe him. But what principal could she send him to?

That lettuce was like having a new baby in the family. And I was like its mother. I watered it in the morning if my father was still out driving. It was supposed to come up

---

extended family, family that includes parents, children, grandparents, aunts, uncles, etc.

BEFORE YOU GO ON . . .

1 Why is Virgil embarrassed?

2 How does Virgil's father lie to Miss Fleck?

HOW ABOUT YOU?
- Do you know anybody like Miss Fleck? Explain.

in seven days, but it didn't. My father couldn't figure out why. Neither of us knew anything about plants. This wrinkled old man in a straw hat tried to show me something when I poured out the water. He spoke some language, but it sure wasn't English. I didn't get what he was **babbling** about, till the lettuce finally came up in wavy lines and bunches instead of straight rows. I'd washed the seeds out of their places.

The minute it came up, it started to wilt. It was like a baby always crying for its milk. I got sick of **hauling** bottles of water in our shopping cart. . . . Then the heat came. The leaves **shriveled** up. Some turned yellow. That lettuce was dying.

My father practically cried, looking at it. He'd stop by in his cab when he could, with two five-gallon water containers riding in the back instead of passengers. Then bugs started eating big holes in the plants. I couldn't see anyone buying them from us. My father had promised we'd make enough money to buy me an eighteen-speed bike. I was counting on it. I'd already told my friends. My father asked all his passengers what to do. His cab was like a library for him. Finally, one of 'em told him that spring or fall was the time to grow lettuce, that the summer was too hot for it. My father wasn't smiling when he told us.

---

babbling, talking without making sense
hauling, carrying or pulling something heavy
shriveled, became smaller and wrinkled

I couldn't believe it. I **stomped** outside. I could feel that eighteen-speed slipping away. I was used to seeing kids lying and making mistakes, but not grown-ups. I was mad at my father. Then I sort of felt sorry for him.

That night I pulled out the locket. I opened it up and looked at the picture. We'd studied Greek myths in school that year. In our book, the **goddess** of crops and the earth had a sad mouth and flowers around her, just like the girl in the locket. I scraped off the rust with our dish scrubber and shined up that locket as bright as I could get it. Then I opened it up, just a crack. Then I whispered, "Save our lettuce," to the girl.

---

stomped, walked angrily
goddess, female god

About the Author

Paul Fleischman

Paul Fleischman was born in Monterey, California, and grew up in Santa Monica. He now lives on California's Monterey Peninsula. He is the author of many books about music and natural history.

116

BEFORE YOU GO ON . . .

1 Why did the lettuce wilt?

2 Why is Virgil angry with his father?

HOW ABOUT YOU?
- Have you ever felt angry toward a parent or other relative? Explain.

Review and Practice

Copy the chart below into your notebook. Then reread the excerpt from *Seedfolks*. As you read, complete each box with an important event from the story. Use chronological order. Add as many boxes as you need. Then think about the parts of the plot. (See the Literary Element box on page 114.) Which events provide the information that helped you understand the story? Write *Helpful Information* over those events on your chart. Then, over the box that introduces the story's main problem or conflict, write *Conflict Introduced*. Finally, write *Climax* over the event that is the story's turning point, or climax.

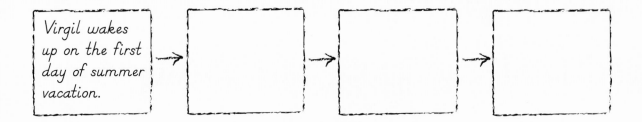

Virgil wakes up on the first day of summer vacation.

Work in pairs. Take turns using the chart to retell the story.

▲ A vegetable garden

118

EXTENSION

1. Work in pairs or small groups. Using the list of plants you would grow in a garden (see page 110), draw plans for a garden.

2. Does anyone in your family have a garden? If so, describe it.

3. Write about a time you tried to do something and didn't succeed. How does your experience compare with Virgil's experience with the lettuce? Write about your experience in your notebook.

DISCUSSION

Discuss in pairs or small groups.

1. Virgil's father lied to Miss Fleck. Was this wrong? Explain.

2. What do you think Virgil learned from his experience of planting lettuce?

3. What do you think Virgil's father learned from the experience?

4. What do you think Virgil and his father might do next?

This is an informational science article. It gives facts about how seeds and plants grow. Before you read, look at the diagrams, photographs, and captions. After you read each section, try to paraphrase what you read. If you don't understand something, write questions to ask later.

How Seeds and Plants Grow

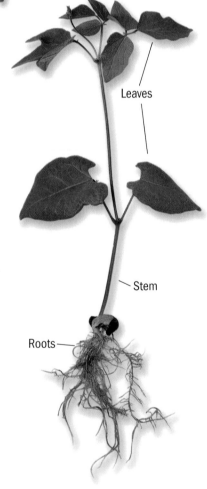

▲ A young plant

Leaves

Stem

Roots

Parts of a Seed

Most plants produce new plants from seeds. A seed is like a tiny package. It contains the beginning of a very young plant inside a **protective** covering.

A seed has three important parts—an embryo, stored food, and a seed coat. The embryo contains the basic parts from which a young plant will develop—**roots, stems,** and **leaves.** Stored food keeps the young plant alive until it can make its own food through photosynthesis. Seeds contain one or two seed leaves, called cotyledons. In some plants, food is stored in the cotyledons.

The outer protective covering of a seed is called the seed coat. The seed coat is like a plastic wrap, which protects the embryo and stored food from drying out. This protection is necessary because a seed may be inactive—may not begin to grow—for weeks, months, or even years. Then, when conditions are right, the embryo inside a seed suddenly becomes active and begins to grow. The time when the embryo first begins to grow is called germination.

---

protective, concerned with keeping something safe from danger
roots, parts of a tree or plant that grow underground
stems, long, thin parts of plants from which leaves or flowers grow
leaves, flat, green parts of plants or trees that grow from branches
    or stems

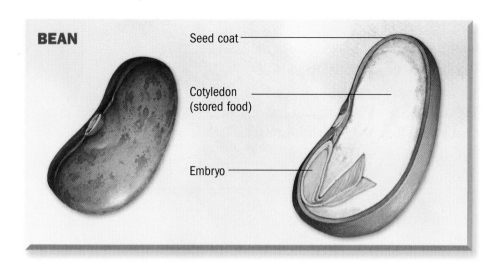

BEAN

Seed coat

Cotyledon
(stored food)

Embryo

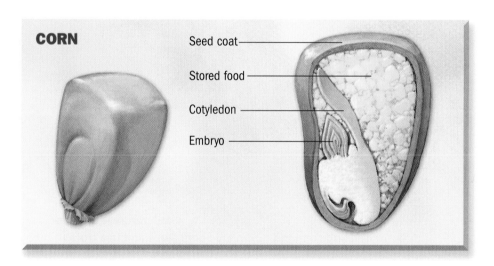

CORN

Seed coat

Stored food

Cotyledon

Embryo

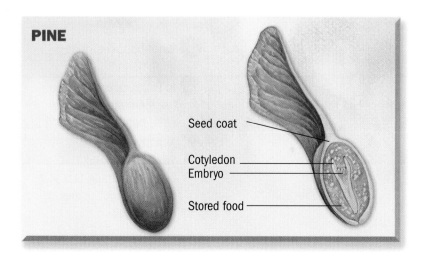

PINE

Seed coat

Cotyledon
Embryo

Stored food

BEFORE YOU GO ON . . .

1 What does a seed contain?

2 What does the seed coat do?

HOW ABOUT YOU?

- Do you understand everything on these pages? If not, write questions to ask later.

Germination

During germination, the seed **absorbs** water from the environment. Then the embryo uses its stored food to begin to grow. The seed coat breaks open, and the embryo's roots grow **downward**. Then its stem and leaves grow **upward**. As the stem grows longer, it breaks out of the ground. **Once** it is above the ground, the stem **straightens** up toward the sunlight, and the first leaves appear on the stem. When the young plant produces its first leaves, it can begin to make its own food by photosynthesis.

---

absorbs, takes in water slowly
downward, from a higher place to a lower place
upward, from a lower place to a higher place
once, when
straightens, becomes free of curves and bends

▲ Gardening tools: a hand fork (top) and two trowels for digging

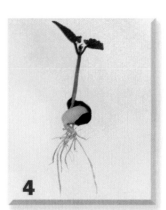

▲ Germination of a string bean

BEFORE YOU GO ON . . .

1 What happens during germination?

2 In which direction does the stem grow after the seed coat breaks open?

HOW ABOUT YOU?

- What is the most interesting thing that you learned about plants in this article?

Link the Readings

REFLECTION

The *Seedfolks* selection and "How Seeds and Plants Grow" both describe plant growth. Copy the chart into your notebook. Reread "How Seeds and Plants Grow." Then complete the chart. Compare your charts in pairs or small groups.

Title of Selection	Type of Text (Genre)	Fiction or Nonfiction	Purpose of Selection	What I Learned
From *Seedfolks*				
"How Seeds and Plants Grow"				

DISCUSSION

Discuss in pairs or small groups.

1. What facts about plants did you learn from these readings? Make a list.

2. Did the pictures and diagrams help you understand the readings? Explain.

3. Did monitoring your reading help you understand the readings? Explain.

Connect to Writing

GRAMMAR

Using Compound Sentences

A **compound sentence** contains two or more **independent clauses** (sentences) and a **coordinating conjunction**.

An independent clause is a complete sentence. It contains a subject and a verb, and it can be a simple sentence by itself.

> ┌─── subject ───┐ ┌─verb─┐
> **Virgil and his father planted** lettuce.

A coordinating conjunction joins two independent clauses. Common coordinating conjunctions are *and, but, so, for,* and *or*. Each coordinating conjunction has a different purpose. Be sure to use a comma after the first independent clause.

> Virgil and his father planted lettuce, **and** they shared it with their neighbors. (*addition*)
>
> The lettuce was supposed to come up in seven days, **but** it didn't. (*contrast*)
>
> Virgil's father didn't buy him a bike, **so** Virgil felt angry. (*effect*)
>
> Virgil was embarrassed, **for** his garden was bigger than all the others. (*cause*)
>
> A seed might grow right away, **or** it might not grow for several years. (*choice*)

Practice

Choose the correct coordinating conjunction to join the sentences. Then write the new sentences in your notebook.

1. Virgil wanted to sleep until noon. His father woke him up early. (but / or)
2. Virgil's father is planting lettuce. He thinks he can make a lot of money. (so / for)
3. Virgil found a locket. He decided to keep it. (and / but)
4. Miss Fleck is very strict. The students are afraid of her. (for / so)
5. Virgil's father might plant more lettuce. He might give up. (or / so)

SKILLS FOR WRITING

Writing a Personal Narrative

A **personal narrative** tells about an experience in the writer's life. The writer, or narrator, uses the first-person point of view and the pronoun *I* to describe his or her experience.

Read this personal narrative. Then answer the questions.

Thomas José Harding

My Marigold Plants

In the third grade, our teacher told us to plant flowers. My favorite color was yellow, so I chose marigolds. I followed the instructions on the packet, and I planted three seeds three inches apart and a quarter of an inch deep. I looked at different fertilizers that help plants grow, but I didn't know what to buy. Finally, I chose one called Grow Fast. My plants germinated in ten days, and they blossomed seven days later. I felt very successful, for my plants grew faster than my classmates' plants.

I learned two things from this experience. I learned to follow instructions, and I learned that some fertilizers can help plants grow.

1. What did the narrator do?
2. Was he successful?
3. What did he learn?
4. What point of view does the narrator use? How do you know?
5. What conjunctions does he use? What is the purpose of each one?

WRITING ASSIGNMENT

Personal Narrative

You will write a personal narrative about a successful or unsuccessful experience in your life.

1. Read Reread the personal narrative on page 125.

Writing Strategy: Organizational Chart

A chart can help you organize information. Look at the chart the writer used to organize information for the personal narrative on page 125.

> **Event**
> • planted marigolds in third grade

> **Outcome**
> • plants germinated in ten days
> • plants blossomed seven days later
> • plants grew faster than my classmates' plants

> **What I Learned**
> • to follow instructions
> • that fertilizers help plants grow

2. Complete a chart Think about a successful or unsuccessful experience in your life. Draw an organizational chart in your notebook. Write what the experience was in the first box. Write about the outcome in the second box. Describe what you learned in the third box.

3. Write a personal narrative Use your chart to write a personal narrative about your experience. Use the narrative on page 125 as a model.

EDITING CHECKLIST

Did you . . .

▶ use the pronoun *I*?

▶ include compound sentences?

▶ use coordinating conjunctions?

Check Your Knowledge

Language Development

1. How can monitoring your comprehension help your reading?
2. What is the first-person point of view? What is a narrator?
3. Describe how a personal narrative is different from a narrative.
4. What is a compound sentence? A coordinating conjunction?
5. How can diagrams help you understand a text?

Academic Content

1. What new science vocabulary did you learn in Part 2? What do the words mean?
2. What is germination?
3. What are the three basic parts of a plant? What does each do?

Separating plants with tangled roots ▶

Put It All Together

OBJECTIVES

Integrate Skills
- Listening/
  Speaking:
  *Group
  interview*
- Writing:
  *Biographical
  narrative*

**Investigate
Themes**
- Projects
- Further
  reading

LISTENING and SPEAKING WORKSHOP

GROUP INTERVIEW

You will work in groups. Each group will interview one of five students who have volunteered to talk about problems they have solved. For example, a student might have had trouble getting to school on time or might have been shy about speaking in front of a class.

1 **Think about it** Work in groups of three or four. Think about what your group wants to find out during the interview. What do you want to learn about the student's problem and his or her success in solving it? What questions will help you find out about the student's thoughts, feelings, and ideas? Write a list of questions to ask during the interview.

2 **Organize** Decide which questions each group member will ask and in what order to ask the questions. Be prepared to ask follow-up questions to get more information.

3 **Practice** Conduct a practice interview. Take turns asking and answering questions in your group. Take notes. Which questions help you get the most interesting information?

4 **Present and evaluate** While the rest of the class listens, interview one of the five students who volunteered. Ask questions from your group's practice interview. After each interview, evaluate: Did the group doing the interview ask good questions? Did any answers need to be explained?

SPEAKING TIPS

- Let the person finish answering a question before you ask the next question.
- If someone doesn't understand a question, ask the question again in a different way.

LISTENING TIP

If you don't understand an answer, ask the person to repeat or explain his or her answer.

WRITING WORKSHOP

BIOGRAPHICAL NARRATIVE

In a biographical narrative, the writer tells a story about another person's life. Usually, the writer describes the person's actions and feelings concerning a conflict, problem, or other situation.

A biographical narrative usually includes the following characteristics:

- The writer uses the third-person point of view and the pronoun *he* or *she*.

- The narrative has a clear sequence of events that includes a beginning, middle, and end.

- The narrative tells the person's actions and feelings concerning a conflict, problem, or other situation.

- The narrative's conclusion tells how the person felt about the experience or situation.

You will write a biographical narrative about a classmate's successful experience. Use information from your interview in the Listening and Speaking Workshop and the following steps to help you.

1 **Prewrite** Think about the classmate your group interviewed. How did your classmate succeed? How did he or she feel about this success? Make a chart like the one on page 126 to organize your information.

WRITING TIPS

- In a biographical narrative, you use the third-person point of view and the pronoun *he* or *she*.
- In a personal or autobiographical narrative, you use the first-person point of view and the pronoun *I*.

Before you write a first draft of your narrative, read the following model. Notice the characteristics of a biographical narrative.

Holly Sihombing

Practice Makes Perfect

To succeed at something, a person must practice a lot. Travis Lau learned this lesson from playing the piano.

Travis is thirteen years old. He started taking piano lessons when he was eight. At first, he didn't like playing the piano. He sometimes got frustrated, and he didn't have a lot of confidence. He wanted to play with his friends instead of playing the piano.

Travis's parents encouraged him to practice. His sister and brother took piano lessons, and they also encouraged him to practice. They played the piano well, and Travis wanted to be like them. So he continued to practice, and he played better and better.

Travis began to enjoy playing the piano. He started playing more difficult music and gained confidence in his ability. Last year, he played a difficult piece at a recital and received lots of applause.

Travis still practices every day, but now playing the piano well is fun for him. Making beautiful music makes him happy.

Beginning, or introduction

Third-person pronoun

Middle, or body (includes problem, conflict, or other situation and how it was solved)

End, or conclusion (includes how he felt about succeeding)

2 **Draft** Use the model and your chart to write your biographical narrative.

- Start your narrative in an interesting way, so that readers will want to read your story. For example, you might introduce the person and write something about what he or she learned from the experience. Notice how the student starts her narrative. How does she make you interested in the story?

- Give some details about the person's experience in the next paragraph. Describe a problem, conflict, or other situation that he or she faced.

- Describe how the person solved the problem and experienced success. Include examples of what helped him or her succeed.

- Conclude your narrative by describing how the person felt about his or her success. If possible, explain what he or she learned from the experience.

3 **Edit** Work in pairs. Trade papers and read each other's narratives. Use the questions in the editing checklist to evaluate each other's work.

EDITING CHECKLIST

Did you . . .

- ▶ use correct verb forms?
- ▶ include compound sentences?
- ▶ use coordinating conjunctions correctly?
- ▶ use the pronoun *he* or *she*?
- ▶ present a clear sequence of events, with an introduction, body paragraphs, and a conclusion?

4 **Revise** Revise your narrative. Add details and correct mistakes if necessary.

5 **Publish** As a class, publish the narratives in a collection called "Our Success Stories."

PROJECTS

Work in pairs or small groups. Choose one of these projects.

▲ *Two Breton Women on the Road,* Paul Gauguin

1 Interview someone you admire. Write a narrative using information from the interview. Then read the narrative to the class.

2 With a friend or family member, visit an art museum or the art section of the library. Find a biography of a favorite artist and copies of his or her work. Then share the biography and art with the class.

3 Use the Internet to find more information about one of the people in "Success Stories." Then share the information with the class.

4 What do you think happens after Virgil whispers to the locket? Continue the story. Then share your story with the class.

5 Use the library to find poetry by Naomi Shihab Nye. Choose a poem that you like. Make a poster with an illustration of the poem and a copy of it. Then share it with the class.

6 Make a collage illustrating various ideas you have about a successful person. You can use photographs, drawings, paintings, written words (poetry or just sentences), or anything else you can think of. Try to show things about the person and things about the success he or she has had. Display your collage and tell your classmates about it.

To find out more about the theme of this unit, choose from these reading suggestions.

Gloria Estefan: Queen of Latin Pop, **David Shirley** Born in Cuba in 1957, this future singing star arrived in the United States at age sixteen months. Gloria's family settled in Miami, Florida. In 1975, Gloria joined Emilio Estefan's Latin band. By the mid-1980s, Gloria and Emilio had married, and their band, Miami Sound Machine, was a big success. Then an accident almost ended Gloria's career.

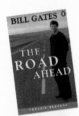

The Road Ahead, **Bill Gates** Bill Gates and a friend started Microsoft in 1975, when Gates was just nineteen. Microsoft was the first company to write computer programs for small computers. "A program tells a computer to do something," Gates explains. Now Microsoft is one of the most successful companies in the world. This book explains a lot about computers in a reader-friendly way.

What I Had Was Singing: The Story of Marian Anderson, **Jeri Ferris** Marian Anderson faced many hurdles to become one of the greatest singers of her time. Long before the civil rights struggles of the 1950s, she broke important racial barriers.

"Born Worker," a short story from *Petty Crimes,* **Gary Soto** People said José was born with dirt under his fingernails—a "born worker." José's cousin Arnie was lazy and spoiled. When Arnie and José teamed up to do yard work and other jobs, José did most of the work, while Arnie sat around watching. But then something happened that changed José's view of himself and others.

Extraordinary People with Disabilities, **Deborah Kent and Kathryn A. Quinlan** The men and women whose short biographies are in this book were chosen because they have earned lasting recognition for their accomplishments. All happen to have disabilities. The book tells about fifty-three people, from Louis Braille, who created a reading system for the blind, to Alicia Alonso, a famous ballet dancer, to Stevie Wonder, a popular musician.

UNIT 4

Change

PART 1

- "Changing Earth"
- "The Intersection," Dina Anastasio

PART 2

- "China's Little Ambassador,"
  Bette Bao Lord
- "Migration Patterns"

Everything changes. Our world changes. Our communities and towns change. And, of course, we change. We make changes to the outside world, and we make changes within ourselves. Some changes happen very slowly. Others happen very quickly.

In Part 1, you will read about Earth's growing human population and how population growth and changing technologies are affecting the environment. You will also read about some of the ways people are trying to protect the environment. Then you will read three fictional letters to the editor of a newspaper. These letters, written over a 100-year period, try to persuade people to change their driving habits so that there will be fewer accidents.

In Part 2, you will read about a Chinese immigrant girl's first day of school in the United States. The girl has to change to fit in at her new school. Then you will read an article about migration within the United States—about how often, how far, and why Americans move.

Prepare to Read

OBJECTIVES

LANGUAGE DEVELOPMENT

Reading:
- Vocabulary building: *Context, dictionary skills*
- Reading strategy: *Noting causes, effects, and solutions*
- Text types: *Science article, letters to the editor*

Writing:
- Cause-effect-solution diagram
- Persuasive writing
- Formal letter
- Editing checklist

Listening/Speaking:
- Opinions
- Persuading
- Compare and contrast

Grammar:
- Real conditional sentences

Viewing/Representing:
- Diagrams

ACADEMIC CONTENT
- Science vocabulary
- The environment
- Causes, effects, and solutions

BACKGROUND

"Changing Earth" is an informational science text. It describes the problems and challenges that population growth is causing on Earth. It also suggests some changes people can make to protect Earth.

Make connections Think about how Earth has changed in the last twenty-five years. Discuss these questions in small groups. Then compare answers as a class.

1. How has Earth's population changed?
2. How have cars changed?
3. How has food changed?
4. How have buildings changed?
5. How has energy changed?

▲ Electric power plant and transmission lines

LEARN KEY WORDS

chemicals
nuclear power
pollution
resources
technologies
waste

VOCABULARY

Read these sentences. Use the context to figure out the meaning of the red words. Use a dictionary to check your answers. Write each word and its meaning in your notebook.

1. People sometimes use **chemicals** to kill plant-eating insects.
2. Some people think **nuclear power** is a good source of energy.
3. When people throw garbage into the ocean, it causes **pollution**.
4. We have to be careful about how we use Earth's **resources**, such as oil, gas, and land.
5. Engineers are developing **technologies** to make cars safer and cleaner.
6. We shouldn't **waste** water. If we use more than we need, we won't have enough for everyone.

READING STRATEGY

Noting Causes, Effects, and Solutions

Science texts often have a **cause-and-effect organization**. The writer discusses **causes** and describes their **effects**. When the effect is a problem, such as pollution, the writer may also suggest a **solution**.

When you read a text with cause-and-effect organization, follow these steps.

- Look for words that signal cause, such as *because of, as a result of,* and *results from.*

- Look for words that signal effect, such as *so, therefore,* and *causes.*

- Read the text carefully to understand the relationships among causes, effects, and solutions.

- Copy this diagram into your notebook. Use it to note the causes, effects, and solutions you read about in the text.

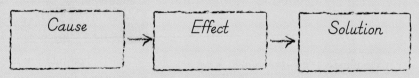

| Cause | Effect | Solution |

Preview and skim this science article. Then, as you read more carefully, look for words that signal cause, effect, and solution. Try to understand the relationships among them. Copy the diagram on page 137 into your notebook. Use it to note causes, effects, and solutions.

Changing Earth

▲ Earth's population is expected to increase to more than 9 billion by 2050.

Growth of Human Population

Earth has changed very quickly over the past 200 years. The human population has grown. Means of transportation have changed. Communication has exploded. People are experimenting with new sources of energy. Even food has changed. What are these changes, and what are their effects?

Until the early 1800s, there were fewer than 1 billion people living on Earth. But since then, improvements in medicine, agriculture, **living conditions**, and other areas have produced a longer **life expectancy** and a lower death rate. By 1900, Earth's population had doubled, to 2 billion people. The population had grown to 6 billion people by the year 2000. Today, 4.2 people are born and 1.8 people die every second, the United States Census Bureau reports. This means that every minute, 144 more people are alive and living on Earth.

This population growth is increasing the demand for Earth's limited natural resources, especially food, water, and **fossil fuels**. More fossil fuels are needed to power our means of transportation, more food is needed to feed hungry people, and more trees are needed for lumber and paper products.

---

living conditions, food, shelter, cleanliness of environment
life expectancy, length of time a person or animal is likely to live
fossil fuels, coal, natural gas, and oil

Society has had difficulty keeping up with the increased demand for resources. When fossil fuels were first used as an energy source, people did not know that burning them could affect the environment. This lack of knowledge, as well as limited technologies, led to air and water pollution. Now, thanks to government regulations and industry efforts, scientists have developed ways to reduce air and water pollution.

Our natural resources are extremely valuable, but they are being used up quickly. We must be careful not to run out of these resources. The choices we make as individuals, as a nation, and as citizens of Earth all affect the environment.

Food

To feed the world's growing population, scientists have been focusing on ways to increase the food supply. One way is through genetic engineering. In the United States, the government and scientists are working to safely regulate the genetic engineering of various plant and animal foods.

Genes are microscopic structures found in cells of every living thing. These genes **determine** the characteristics of an animal or a plant. In genetic engineering, scientists put genes from one organism, or living thing, into cells of another kind of organism. One way in which scientists are using genetic engineering is to try to make a plant or animal stronger, healthier, or larger. For example, scientists might insert genes from a certain organism into the cells of tomato plants to **enable** the plants to survive in very cold temperatures or poor soil. If scientists can produce a tomato that can grow in places where a typical tomato cannot survive, then both farmers and consumers will benefit.

Although genetic engineering seems like a good idea to some, others say that scientists can make mistakes when

Scientists have been working to increase the food supply. ▼

society, people in general
determine, control; decide
enable, make it possible for

BEFORE YOU GO ON . . .

1 How is Earth's population changing?

2 How is Earth's changing population affecting its natural resources?

HOW ABOUT YOU?
- What do you think Earth will be like in 200 years?

changing the characteristics of a plant or an animal. Because this is such a new technology, scientists are not sure yet how genetically engineered plants and animals will affect other living things.

Another way to increase the food supply is by using chemicals to produce bigger, stronger crops. The most common types of chemicals that farmers use are fertilizers, herbicides, and pesticides. Fertilizers add nutrients to the soil to help plants grow. Herbicides kill **weeds**. Pesticides kill insects and other organisms that harm plants.

Chemicals help foods grow and get rid of harmful insects and weeds, but some chemicals can hurt the environment if used carelessly or incorrectly. Certain pesticides, for example, may also kill insects that do not harm crops or may hurt the animals that eat the poisoned insects. Scientists test chemicals used in farming to ensure that they meet safety standards. And farmers are trying other ways of controlling insects, such as by adding an insect's natural enemies to fields where crops are growing.

Sometimes the exact source of chemical pollution is difficult to find. When rain or water from sprinklers falls on crops, the water washes away some of the chemicals on the plants. The chemically polluted water then enters the soil and runs off into streams, rivers, and lakes. Runoff also occurs in cities, where chemicals are carried as runoff to rivers and lakes, polluting them.

▲ Containers of chemicals

---

weeds, unwanted wild plants that harm more desirable plants

◀ A crop-duster plane spreads chemicals on a field.

Fuel Supply

We all use some form of energy in our everyday lives, whether by turning on bedroom lights, using a computer, or riding in a car. Whatever energy we use, the source of that energy is fuel. Oil, natural gas, and coal are Earth's most valuable fossil fuels. The cars we drive, the stoves we use for cooking, and many power plants that provide our electricity depend on these resources.

Fossil fuels are nonrenewable sources of energy, which means that once they're gone, they're gone forever. Fortunately, there are ways to **preserve** our natural resources. Everyday choices affect the environment in one way or another. Something as simple as riding a bicycle to school rather than riding in a car saves energy. Reusing valuable resources by recycling saves energy. Throwing an aluminum can into a recycling bin may not seem very important, but if we all do little things like that, it will help Earth.

Transportation Changes

Scientists are looking for new ways to power cars and other vehicles, such as by using **batteries**, **solar** power, and fuel cells. In an all-electric car, a large, heavy battery stores the electric energy that powers the car. When the battery runs low, the driver must **recharge** it by plugging it into a special electric outlet. Recharging the battery takes much longer than refilling a gasoline tank. Even so, electricity is a relatively clean source of energy for cars.

Some car manufacturers have developed **hybrid** cars, which run on a combination of electricity and gasoline.

---

preserve, keep and protect
batteries, objects that store electricity to power other objects
solar, relating to the sun
recharge, put more energy into a battery
hybrid, combination of two or more things

BEFORE YOU GO ON . . .

1. How do chemicals help increase the food supply? How might they harm the environment?

2. What are some new ways to power cars and other vehicles?

HOW ABOUT YOU?
- Do you participate in a recycling program in your community?

▲ Experimental solar car

Their batteries are small and can be recharged by the car's small gasoline **engine** while the car is being driven.

Scientists are also experimenting with solar energy and fuel cells for cars. Solar-powered cars use **solar cells** to change energy from the sun into electricity. Fuel cells combine two gases, hydrogen and oxygen, to produce electricity. Solar and fuel cells are clean energy sources.

Alternative Energy Sources

As the number of people on Earth grows, so does the need for energy to make things work. So scientists are searching for **alternative** sources of energy. One alternative is nuclear power, which does not cause air pollution. However, nuclear power must be handled carefully to prevent accidents that could have long-lasting negative effects on living things. That is why strict safety regulations at nuclear power stations are in place. In addition, much of the unwanted leftover material from nuclear plants is **radioactive**. It can be dangerous for a very long time if disposed of improperly.

Another alternative energy source is solar power. Some solar power stations have hundreds of large mirrors that collect and focus sunlight on a large container of water to make the water boil. The boiling water produces steam, which powers machines to produce electricity.

Wind is also an alternative source of power. People once used windmills to grind grains and pump water. Now wind farms use wind to **generate** electricity. A wind farm is a large area of land, usually a treeless hill or other windy spot, on which groups of modern windmills operate.

▲ **Wind-powered generators (windmills) on a wind farm**

In winter, warm air at the top heats cold air coming in at the bottom.

Hot, stale air is vented through louvers.

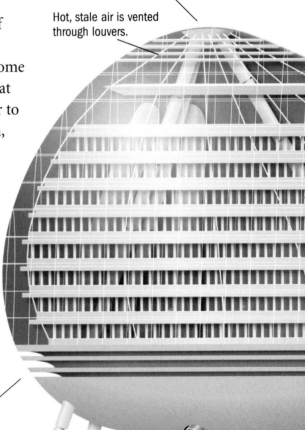

---

engine, machine that makes power from fuel and uses it to make something move
solar cells, small units that take in sunlight and change it into electricity
alternative, offering a choice
radioactive, containing or producing radiation
generate, produce; create

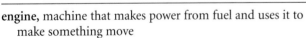

Streamlined shape allows wind to flow smoothly.

Both solar and wind power are clean sources of energy. They depend on natural forces, sunlight and wind, to work **effectively**. However, sunlight varies with the weather and the time of day, and wind also comes and goes. Therefore, solar and wind power are not always available to generate electricity.

Environmentally Friendly Buildings

Many buildings waste energy. They use oil, gas, or electricity for heat in the winter and for air-conditioning in the summer. To save energy, many architects and engineers are changing the way they design buildings. The model office building shown here is **environmentally friendly**. It uses sunlight and **ventilation** to heat and cool the building **efficiently**.

▲ A solar collector focuses sunlight on a single point to produce temperatures hot enough to power electric generators.

---

effectively, successfully
environmentally friendly, not harmful to the environment
ventilation, motion of fresh air into and out of a building
efficiently, without wasting energy or effort

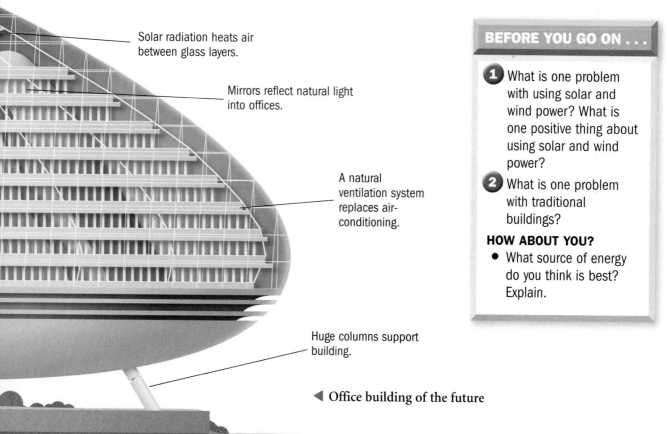

Solar radiation heats air between glass layers.

Mirrors reflect natural light into offices.

A natural ventilation system replaces air-conditioning.

Huge columns support building.

◀ Office building of the future

BEFORE YOU GO ON . . .

1 What is one problem with using solar and wind power? What is one positive thing about using solar and wind power?

2 What is one problem with traditional buildings?

HOW ABOUT YOU?
• What source of energy do you think is best? Explain.

Review and Practice

"Changing Earth" gives information about how various things have changed. The text describes problems and their causes. It also suggests solutions. Reread the text and your notes. Then answer the questions in small groups.

1. What has happened to Earth's population in the last 200 years? What problems has this caused?

2. How are scientists changing food? How do some people view these changes?

3. How do cars and other vehicles negatively affect the environment? What are some solutions to this problem?

4. How are architects and engineers changing buildings? Why are they making these changes?

5. What kinds of energy do people use? What are some good and bad points about each kind?

What do you notice about the people, cars, food, buildings, and sources of energy in your community? How are they changing? Copy this chart into your notebook. In small groups, complete the chart with your observations.

	Observations
People	
Cars	
Food	
Buildings	
Energy	

DISCUSSION

Discuss in pairs or small groups.

1. Look at the cause-effect-solution chart in your notebook. What might happen if you applied each solution? If you didn't apply it?

2. Look at the observation chart in your notebook. What problems did you notice? Can you suggest any solutions?

3. Compare and contrast a type of vehicle—an automobile, a truck, a train, a plane—of today with the same type of vehicle as it was fifty years ago. How has the vehicle changed? How has it stayed the same?

▲ Pickup trucks of the 1950s . . .

▲ . . . and today

*In most newspapers, you will see letters that people write to express their opinions. The letters are often about problems in the community. As you read "The **Intersection**," ask yourself these questions: When were these letters written? What stays the same in all these letters? What problems and solutions do the writers describe?*

THE INTERSECTION

Dina Anastasio

52 Main Street
January 2, 1900
To the Editor:

I am writing this letter to ask your readers for help. I live on the corner of Main and Third Streets. When it rains, this dirt road turns to mud. When it snows, it turns to **slush**.

From my sitting room window I see **carriages** race through the intersection. They are going too fast for such a slippery corner. The drivers do not look where they are going. Often another carriage is coming the other way. The horses **rear up**. The carriages turn over. Too many people are hurt.

Last night, I helped to pull a horse out of the mud again. The carriage had turned over. A woman broke her leg.

---

intersection, place where two roads or streets cross
slush, partly melted snow
carriages, vehicles that horses pull
rear up, rise on back legs

We have now moved into the twentieth century. The horseless carriage is about to change our lives. I hear that Mr. Henry Ford is trying to develop one right now. These motor cars will move people faster than we can imagine. Everyone says that they will solve all our traffic problems. But I'm not sure how. They will race past my house from morning to night. If we aren't careful, they will bang into each other on this corner. They will disturb my sleep. . . .

So please try and drive a little slower when you come to the corner of Main and Third.

Yours sincerely,
Jason Winthrop

52 Main Street
January 2, 1950
To the Editor:

Fifty years ago, my father wrote to your newspaper. He asked for his neighbors' help. At that time he was **concerned** about speeding. He was worried about the mud and slush on the road. He wanted people to slow down their horses and carriages.

Since that time, our city has changed. There are now 100,000 people instead of 10,000. Electric lights have replaced gas lights. Houses have been pulled down. Apartment and office buildings have replaced them.

I have watched these changes from my living room window ever since I was a child. I watched workers cover the road in front of my house with cobblestones. And after that I watched them pave it. I remember the day the first stop sign was put up on our corner.

I also remember the day, in 1929, when the first electric traffic light went up. Those lights were needed. Motor cars came speeding by, and they needed to be controlled.

This city is still getting larger. More and more people are moving here. That will mean more and more cars. Although there are **trolleys** and buses today, traffic is still a problem.

I cannot stop all the accidents. But I would like to stop the accidents that happen on my corner. And that is one reason that I am writing this letter.

Please slow down! I am tired of **dragging** injured people out of their cars.

I am writing for another reason, too. Cars are polluting our city. There may be nothing that we can do about our polluted air. But there is something that we can do about the noise.

So please stop blowing your horns! I need my sleep!

Best wishes,
Jason Winthrop Jr.

---

dragging, pulling

concerned, worried
trolleys, vehicles that use tracks and are powered by electric current from overhead wires

BEFORE YOU GO ON . . .

1 What problems does the writer of the first letter describe?

2 How do the problems in the second letter differ from those in the first letter?

HOW ABOUT YOU?

- Do you have any of these problems in your neighborhood? Explain.

52 Main Street
January 2, 2000
To the Editor:

One hundred years ago today, my grandfather wrote a letter to this newspaper. He asked your readers to slow down when they came to the corner of Main Street and Third. Fifty years later, my father wrote a letter, too. He asked your readers to slow down and stop blowing their horns.

Today, I too am asking for help. Our family still lives in the same house, and I have watched our city change over the past fifty years. This is now a big city. All around me are office buildings and parking lots. My home is the only house left in the whole downtown. Many people have **begged** me to sell it. But I will not sell.

This is not a **fancy** house. It is a small wooden house. It is not worth the money that people have offered me. But I do not care about the money. My family has lived here for over one hundred years. I hope we will live here for another hundred.

I would like to tell you what I see from my window. In some ways, the view is the same as my grandfather's view. I still see some of the things that my father saw, too. We have all seen traffic problems. Today, our street has been paved many times. The trolleys are gone. Traffic lights are now run by computers. Best of all, our street is now one-way.

Everyone said that a one-way street would cut the number of accidents in half. But it didn't.

begged, asked in an anxious way
fancy, elaborate and often expensive

People drive faster because it is one-way. Sometimes they even **drag-race** here. **Beating the light** is too often a game. So there are still accidents. People still get very badly hurt, because they go faster. . . .

So my family asks you again, for the third time, to slow down.

Sincerely,
Jason Winthrop III

---

drag-race, race from a standstill to a fast speed
beating the light, driving quickly through an intersection just as the traffic light turns red

About the Author

Dina Anastasio

Dina Anastasio has written many books for children. Her books for young adults include *The Case of the Grand Canyon Eagle, The Case of the Glacier Park Swallow,* and *The Torch Runner.* She was the editor of *Sesame Street Magazine* and has written several books about the TV show *Sesame Street* and the Muppets.

BEFORE YOU GO ON . . .

1 What problem does the writer of the third letter describe?

2 What solution does the writer of the letter suggest?

HOW ABOUT YOU?

- Do you think that beating a stoplight is dangerous? Explain.

Link the Readings

REFLECTION

"Changing Earth" and "The Intersection" both describe changes. Reread the texts. Copy the chart into your notebook and complete it. Then compare charts in pairs or small groups.

Title of Selection	Genre	Fiction or Nonfiction	Purpose of Selection	Types of Change
"Changing Earth"				
"The Intersection"				

DISCUSSION

Discuss in pairs or small groups.

1. "Changing Earth" and the letters suggest different solutions to problems caused by change. List the solutions in your notebook. Which ones do you think would work? Explain.

2. "Changing Earth" and the letters discuss problems, such as pollution and a dangerous intersection. Does your neighborhood have problems like these? Take turns describing a neighborhood problem. Talk about the cause, the effect, and possible solutions. Look back at the chart you made on page 145.

▲ A Canada goose in a polluted river

3. "Changing Earth" and "The Intersection" contain examples of fact and opinion. For example, on page 146, the statement "We have now moved into the twentieth century" is a fact, or something that can be proved. The next statement, "The horseless carriage is about to change our lives," is an opinion—a personal view that cannot be proved. Find other examples of fact and opinion in "The Intersection" and in "Changing Earth."

Connect to Writing

GRAMMAR

Using Real Conditionals: Sentences with *if*

A **real conditional sentence** includes an *if* clause and a main clause. Real conditional sentences tell facts. The *if* clause tells a condition, and the main clause tells the result or possible result of that condition.

Use a **simple present** verb in the *if* clause. Also use a **simple present** verb in the main clause if it tells something that is generally true.

> ┌─── *if* clause ───┐ ┌─main clause─┐
> If a building **uses** more natural light, it **saves** energy.

For events that *might* happen in the future, use a **simple future** verb in the main clause.

> ┌─── *if* clause ───┐ ┌─── main clause ───┐
> If we **use** our resources carefully, Earth **will survive** for many years.

The *if* clause can go before or after the main clause. Use a comma when the *if* clause is before the main clause.

> ┌─── *if* clause ───┐ ┌─── main clause ───┐
> If chemicals get into rivers, fish and animals will die.
> ┌─── main clause ───┐ ┌─── *if* clause ───┐
> Fish and animals will die if chemicals get into rivers.

Practice

Copy these sentences into your notebook. Circle the correct verbs. Then compare answers in pairs.

1. If oil burns, it (will make / makes) smoke.
2. If somebody (offers / will offer) to buy our house, we (say / will say) no.
3. We (will need / need) more food if there (will be / are) more people in 2050.
4. People (have / will have) fewer accidents if they (drive / will drive) more slowly.

SKILLS FOR WRITING

Writing a Formal Persuasive Letter

In persuasive writing, the writer tries to make readers change their beliefs, opinions, or behavior. Sometimes people write formal letters to newspapers to express their opinions and to persuade readers to support their positions.

Read the letter to the editor. Notice its parts. Then discuss the questions.

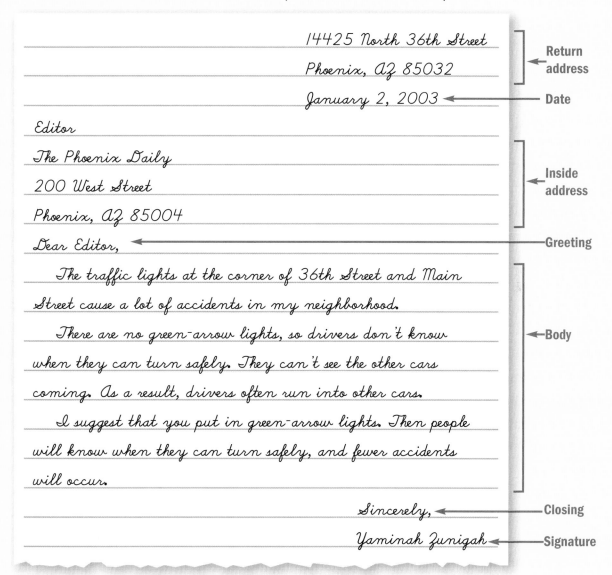

14425 North 36th Street
Phoenix, AZ 85032 — **Return address**
January 2, 2003 — **Date**

Editor
The Phoenix Daily
200 West Street
Phoenix, AZ 85004 — **Inside address**
Dear Editor, — **Greeting**

The traffic lights at the corner of 36th Street and Main Street cause a lot of accidents in my neighborhood.

There are no green-arrow lights, so drivers don't know when they can turn safely. They can't see the other cars coming. As a result, drivers often run into other cars.

I suggest that you put in green-arrow lights. Then people will know when they can turn safely, and fewer accidents will occur. — **Body**

Sincerely, — **Closing**
Yaminah Zunigah — **Signature**

1. What problem does the writer describe?

2. What solution does the writer suggest?

151

WRITING ASSIGNMENT

Formal Persuasive Letter

You will write a formal letter to the editor of a newspaper about a traffic problem in your neighborhood or community. You will explain the problem and suggest solutions.

1. **Read** Reread "The Intersection" on pages 146–148 and the letter in Skills for Writing on page 151. Notice how the writers state and support their opinions.

Writing Strategy: Cause-Effect-Solution Diagram

A cause-effect-solution diagram can help you organize your ideas to write a good persuasive letter. Look at the diagram that Jason Winthrop Jr. might have created before he wrote the letter on page 147.

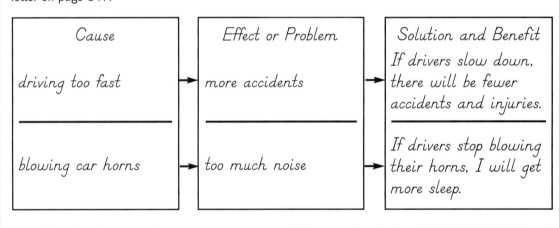

Cause	Effect or Problem	Solution and Benefit
driving too fast	more accidents	If drivers slow down, there will be fewer accidents and injuries.
blowing car horns	too much noise	If drivers stop blowing their horns, I will get more sleep.

---

2. **Make a cause-effect-solution diagram** Think about a traffic problem in your neighborhood or community. What are the causes of the problem? What solutions to the problem can you suggest? Make a cause-effect-solution diagram in your notebook. Write a problem in the middle box. Write the cause in the first box. Write a solution in the third box.

3. **Write a formal letter** Use the information in your diagram and the parts of the letter shown on page 151 to write a persuasive letter to the editor.

EDITING CHECKLIST

Did you . . .

▶ include your return address, the date, the address of the person you're writing to, a greeting, the body, a closing, and your signature?

▶ describe a problem?

▶ suggest a solution?

Check Your Knowledge

Language Development

1. Describe how to use the reading strategy of noting causes, effects, and solutions. How can a cause-effect-solution diagram help you organize ideas?

2. What words signal causes? Effects?

3. What is a fact? An opinion?

4. What is a real conditional sentence? Give an example.

5. What are the parts of a formal letter?

6. What is the purpose of persuasive writing?

Academic Content

1. What new science vocabulary did you learn in Part 1? What do the words mean?

2. What are three effects of the increasing human population?

3. How are people changing cars? Food? Energy sources?

4. What are three ways that cities have changed since 1900?

In 1922, this motorized carriage was the newest thing for babies. ▶

153

PART 2

Prepare to Read

OBJECTIVES

**LANGUAGE
DEVELOPMENT**

Reading:
- Vocabulary building: *Context, dictionary skills*
- Reading strategy: *Using your experience*
- Text types: *Novel, social studies article*
- Literary elements: *Dialogue, simile*

Writing:
- Word web
- Informal persuasive e-mail message

Listening/Speaking:
- Cultural differences
- Sharing memories

Grammar:
- Complex sentences
- Dependent and independent clauses
- Subordinating conjunctions

Viewing/Representing:
- Bar graphs
- Pie charts

ACADEMIC CONTENT
- Social studies vocabulary
- Cultural differences
- U.S. migration

BACKGROUND

"China's Little Ambassador" is a chapter from Bette Bao Lord's novel *In the Year of the Boar and Jackie Robinson*. The novel is about a young Chinese girl who moves to Brooklyn, which is part of New York City, with her family. This chapter is about her first day at school.

Make connections Think about your first day at the school you attend now. What was it like? Who did you meet? What happened? How did you feel? Copy this word web into your notebook. Complete it with memories of the first day at your school. Then compare your memories in pairs or small groups.

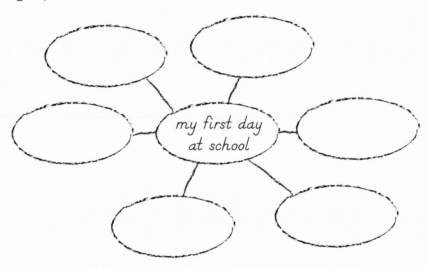

LEARN KEY WORDS

honor
principal
proof
reputation
trend
worthy

VOCABULARY

Read these sentences. Use the context to figure out the meaning of the **red** words. Use a dictionary to check your answers. Write each word and its meaning in your notebook.

1. Being asked to speak at graduation is a great **honor**.
2. The **principal** of our school let us leave school early.
3. To see that movie, you must have **proof** that you are eighteen.
4. Our teacher has the **reputation** of being strict but fair.
5. The **trend** now is that people in the United States are moving south.
6. She was **worthy** of the award because she worked hard all year.

READING STRATEGY

Using Your Experience to Understand a Story

Using your experience can help you understand a story. It can help you connect with the story and understand the main characters.
    As you read, ask yourself these questions.

- Who is the main character? How am I similar to this character?

- What happens to the main character? Have I had similar experiences?

- What does the main character think? How does he or she feel? Have I had similar thoughts or feelings? If so, what were they?

Brooklyn Bridge,
New York City ▶

As you read this chapter from the novel In the Year of the Boar and Jackie Robinson, *think about your own experiences. How are you similar to the main character? What happens to her on the first day of school in the United States? What does she think? How does she feel? Have you had any similar experiences, thoughts, or feelings?*

China's Little Ambassador

Bette Bao Lord

Nine o'clock sharp the very next morning, Shirley sat in the principal's office at **P.S.** 8. Her mother and the **schoolmistress** were talking. Shirley didn't understand a word. It was embarrassing. Why hadn't she, too, studied the English course on the records that Father had sent? But it was too late now. She stopped trying to understand. Suddenly, Mother **hissed**, in Chinese, "Stop that or else!"

Shirley snapped her head down. She had been **staring** at the stranger. But she could not keep her eyes from rolling up again. There was something more **foreign** about the principal than about any other foreigner she had seen so far. What was it? It was not the blue eyes. Many others had

them too. It was not the high nose. All foreign noses were higher than Chinese ones. It was not the blue hair. Hair came in all colors in America.

Yes, of course, naturally. The woman had no **eyelashes**. Other foreigners grew hair all over them, more than six Chinese together. This woman had none. Her skin was as bare as the **Happy Buddha's** belly, except for the neat rows of stiff curls that hugged her head.

She had no **eyebrows**, even. They were penciled on, and looked just like the character for man, 人. And every time she tilted her head, her hair moved all in one piece like a hat.

"Shirley."

Mother was trying to get her attention. "Tell the principal how old you are."

---

nine o'clock sharp, at exactly nine o'clock
P.S., public school (usually means a particular public school, such as P.S. 87)
schoolmistress, female principal
hissed, said in a loud whisper
staring, looking at for a long time without stopping
foreign, not from one's own country; not typical

eyelashes, short hairs on the eyelids
Happy Buddha, popular Chinese picture of a smiling Buddha with a round stomach
eyebrows, the hair above the eyes

Shirley put up ten fingers.

While the principal filled out a form, Mother argued excitedly. But why? Shirley had given the correct answer. She counted just to make sure. On the day she was born, she was one year old. That was the Year of the Rabbit. Then came the Dragon, Snake, Horse, Sheep, Monkey, Rooster, Dog and now it was the Year of the **Boar**, making ten. Proof she was ten.

Mother shook her head. Apparently, she had lost the argument. She announced in Chinese, "Shirley, you will enter fifth grade."

"Fifth? But, Mother, I don't speak

English. And besides, I only completed three grades in Chungking."

"I know. But the principal has explained that in America everyone is **assigned** according to age. Ten years old means fifth grade. And we must observe the American rules, mustn't we?"

---

boar, male pig; wild pig

assigned, given a particular place or job

Shirley nodded **obediently**. But she could not help thinking that only Shirley had to go to school, and only Shirley would be in trouble if she failed.

Mother stood up to leave. She took Shirley by the hand. "Remember, my daughter, you may be the only Chinese these Americans will ever meet. Do your best. Be extra good. Upon your shoulders rests the reputation of all Chinese."

All five hundred million? Shirley wondered.

"You are China's little **ambassador**."

"Yes, Mother." Shirley **squared her shoulders** and tried to feel worthy of this great honor. At the same time, she wished she could leave with Mother.

Alone, the headmistress and Shirley looked at each other. Suddenly the principal shut one eye, the right one, then opened it again.

Was this another foreign custom, like shaking hands? *It must be proper if a principal does it,* Shirley thought. She ought to return the gesture, but she didn't know how. So she shut and opened both eyes. Twice.

This brought a warm laugh.

The principal then led her to class. The room was large, with windows up to the ceiling. Row after row of students, each one unlike the next. Some faces were white, like

obediently, in the way her mother wanted
ambassador, someone who represents his or her country in another country
squared her shoulders, sat up tall with her shoulders straight

clean plates; others black like ebony. Some were in-between shades. A few were spotted all over. One boy was as big as a water jar. Several others were as thin as **chopsticks**. No one wore a **uniform** of blue, like hers. There were sweaters with animals on them, shirts with stripes and shirts with squares, dresses in colors as varied as Grand-grand Uncle's paints. Three girls even wore earrings.

While Shirley looked about, the principal had been making a speech. Suddenly it ended with "Shirley Temple Wong." The class stood up and waved.

Amitabha! They were all so tall. Even Water Jar was a head taller than she. For a **fleeting** moment she wondered if Mother would consider buying an ambassador a pair of high-heeled shoes.

"Hi, Shirley!" the class shouted.

Shirley **bowed** deeply. Then, taking a guess, she replied, "Hi!"

chopsticks, pair of thin sticks used to eat Chinese and other Asian food
uniform, clothing of one design worn by all members of a group
Amitabha, the Buddha of Immeasurable Light, used here to express amazement
fleeting, very quick
bowed, bent the head or top part of the body forward to show respect

BEFORE YOU GO ON . . .

1 How does Shirley's mother expect her to behave at school? How does Shirley feel?

2 What does Shirley notice when she first sees her classmates?

HOW ABOUT YOU?

• How do your parents expect you to behave at school? What was the first thing you noticed about your classmates?

The teacher introduced herself and showed the new **pupil** to a front-row seat.

Shirley liked her right away, although she had a most difficult name, Mrs. Rappaport. She was a tiny woman with **dainty** bones and fiery red hair brushed skyward. Shirley thought that in her **previous** life she must have been a bird, a cardinal perhaps. Yet she **commanded respect**, for no student talked **out of turn**. Or was it the long mean pole that hung on the wall behind the desk that commanded respect? It **dwarfed** the bamboo cane the teacher in Chungking had used to punish Four Hands whenever he stole a **trifle** from another.

Throughout the lessons, Shirley leaned forward, barely touching her seat, to catch the meaning, but the words sounded like gurgling water. Now and then, when Mrs. Rappaport looked her way, she opened and shut her eyes as the principal had done, to show friendship. . . .

The lessons continued. During arithmetic, Shirley raised her hand. She went to the blackboard and wrote the correct answer. Mrs. Rappaport rewarded her with a big smile. Shirley opened and shut her eyes to show her **pleasure**. Soon, she was dreaming about candy elephants and cookies the size of pancakes.

pupil, student
dainty, small and delicate
previous, earlier
commanded respect, had other people's admiration
out of turn, at the wrong time
dwarfed, made something else look much smaller
trifle, something unimportant
pleasure, happiness

Then school was over. As Shirley was putting on her coat, Mrs. Rappaport handed her a letter, obviously to be given to her parents. Fear returned. Round and round, this time like rocks.

She barely greeted her mother at the door.

"What happened?"

"Nothing."

"You look sick."

"I'm all right."

"Perhaps it was something you ate at lunch?"

"No," she said much too quickly. "Nothing at all to do with lunch."

"What then?"

"The job of ambassador is harder than I thought."

At bedtime, Shirley could no longer put off giving up the letter. Trembling, she handed it to Father. She imagined herself on a boat back to China.

He read it aloud to Mother. Then they both turned to her, a most quizzical look on their faces.

"Your teacher suggests we take you to a doctor. She thinks there is something wrong with your eyes."

---

trembling, shaking from nervousness or fear
quizzical, surprised; questioning

About the Author

Bette Bao Lord

Bette Bao Lord was born in China. She moved to the United States as a young girl. Lord used her own experiences growing up in Brooklyn to write *In the Year of the Boar and Jackie Robinson*, a chapter of which you just read. She has written several other books about China and Chinese people. Her husband was once U.S. ambassador to China.

BEFORE YOU GO ON . . .

1 Describe Shirley's teacher.

2 Was there something wrong with Shirley's eyes?

HOW ABOUT YOU?

- How did you feel when you got home after your first day of school?

Review and Practice

Reread the story. Think about the order of events. Copy the diagram into your notebook. Complete the diagram with important events in the correct order. Add boxes if you need to.

> *Shirley and her mother meet with the principal on Shirley's first day in a U.S. school.*

↓

↓

Compare your diagrams in pairs or small groups. Add or change information if needed. Take turns retelling the events of the story.

▲ Chinese New Year street parade with dancing dragon

Bette Bao Lord writes about Shirley's first day of school in the United States. Copy the Venn diagram into your notebook. Write about Shirley's first day of school in the United States in the left circle. Write about your first day of school in the right circle. Write about things that happened on both Shirley's first day and your first day in the middle circle. Then compare diagrams in pairs or small groups.

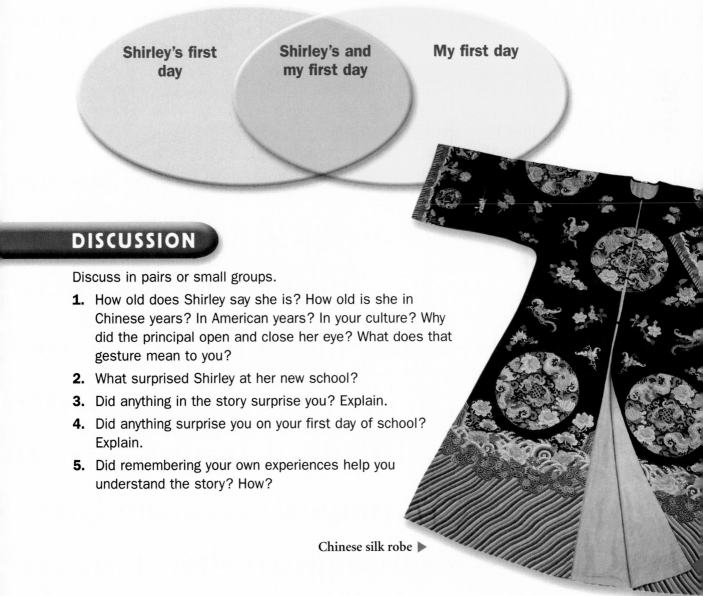

Shirley's first day

Shirley's and my first day

My first day

DISCUSSION

Discuss in pairs or small groups.

1. How old does Shirley say she is? How old is she in Chinese years? In American years? In your culture? Why did the principal open and close her eye? What does that gesture mean to you?

2. What surprised Shirley at her new school?

3. Did anything in the story surprise you? Explain.

4. Did anything surprise you on your first day of school? Explain.

5. Did remembering your own experiences help you understand the story? How?

Chinese silk robe ▶

This text contains factual information about how often, how far, and why people move in the United States. It also contains statistics, or groups of numbers that represent facts or measurements. Before you read, look at the graphs. What do they show? As you read, think about your own experiences. How often have you moved?

MIGRATION PATTERNS

People in the United States move often. According to the United States Census Bureau, 43.3 million Americans—more than 15 percent of the total population—changed **residence** between March 1999 and March 2000.

In that year, the people who moved didn't always move a long distance. This pie chart shows that about 56 percent of them stayed within the same **county**. About 20 percent moved from a different county within the same state. About 20 percent moved from a different state. Only 4 percent moved from another country. Although the overall moving **rate** hasn't changed much in the past **decade**, people have tended to move longer distances since 1998. In 1998, almost 65 percent of people who moved stayed within the same county. Only 15 percent of those who moved went to another state.

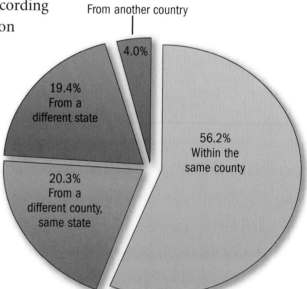

▲ Percent Distribution of Movers by Type of Move: March 1999 to 2000 (Source: U.S. Census Bureau)

---

residence, where a person lives
county, part of a state
rate, the number of times something happens in a period of time
decade, ten years

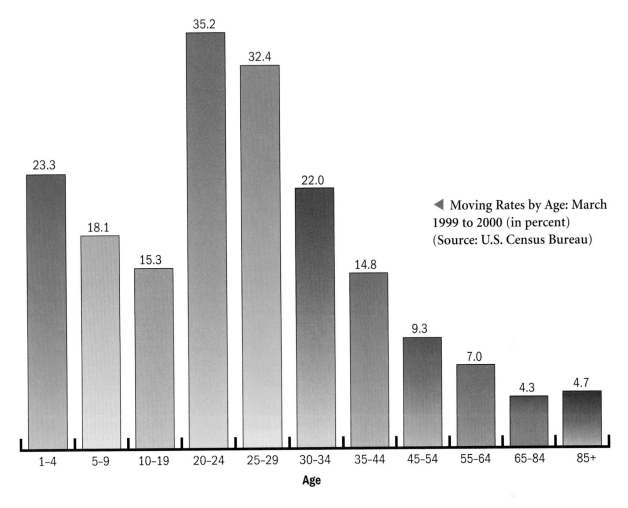

◀ Moving Rates by Age: March 1999 to 2000 (in percent) (Source: U.S. Census Bureau)

Moving rates vary according to such factors as age, **marital status**, property ownership, and **income**. The bar graph shows that in 1999–2000, about one-third of 25- to 29-year-olds moved, but less than 5 percent of people ages 65 to 84 moved. Younger people may have moved more often because they got married or because of new jobs. Single people and **divorced people** moved more often than married people. **Widowed people** moved least often, possibly because widowed people tend to be older. One-third of all renters moved in 1999–2000, compared with only 9 percent of homeowners. Finally, lower-income groups were more likely to move than higher-income groups.

---

marital status, being married or unmarried
income, money from your job; earnings
divorced people, people who have ended their marriage by law
widowed people, people whose husbands or wives have died

BEFORE YOU GO ON . . .

1 How many Americans moved between March 1999 and March 2000?

2 How far did most of them move?

HOW ABOUT YOU?
• When was the last time you moved? Why did you move?

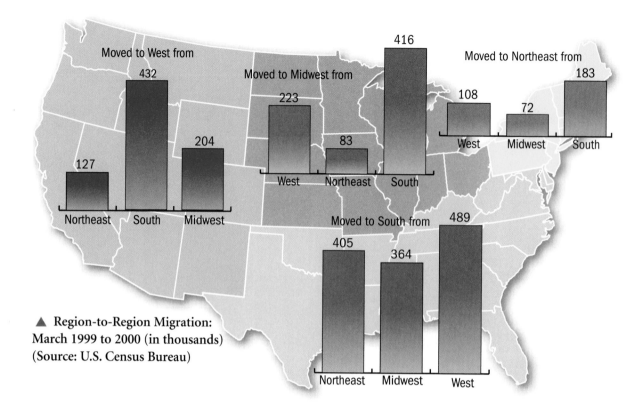

Moved to West from
432
204
127
Northeast   South   Midwest

Moved to Midwest from
223
83
416
West   Northeast   South

Moved to Northeast from
183
108
72
West   Midwest   South

Moved to South from
489
405
364
Northeast   Midwest   West

▲ Region-to-Region Migration:
March 1999 to 2000 (in thousands)
(Source: U.S. Census Bureau)

Moves to different regions in the United States have changed the country's **population distribution**. Look at the graphs above. As was true throughout the 1990s, more people moved from the Northeast to the South than from the South to the Northeast in 1999–2000. Many more people moved *from* the Northeast than *to* the Northeast. The number of people moving into and out of **urban** and **rural** areas remained about the same.

What will the future population distribution of the United States look like? If today's trends continue, more people may be moving to the South. In addition, the new residents there may be younger than those moving to the South today. The Northeast may become less populated, and more Southerners may migrate to the **less densely populated** areas of the West and Midwest.

population distribution, pattern of where people live in an area
urban, relating to a town or city
rural, relating to the country, especially farmland
less densely populated, having fewer people

BEFORE YOU GO ON . . .

1 How did the country's population distribution change during 1999–2000?

2 What might happen if these trends continue?

HOW ABOUT YOU?

• Would you prefer to live in an urban or rural area? In which region of the United States would you prefer to live?

Link the Readings

Reread "Migration Patterns." Copy the chart into your notebook and complete it. Then compare charts in small groups.

Title of Selection	Genre	Fiction or Nonfiction	Purpose of Selection	Three Interesting Facts I Learned
"China's Little Ambassador"				
"Migration Patterns"				

DISCUSSION

Discuss in pairs or small groups.

1. Look at the pie chart on page 164. Where would Shirley, the main character in "China's Little Ambassador," fit in the chart?

2. Look at the bar graph on page 165. Where do you fit in the graph? Where would Shirley fit?

3. What reading strategies helped you understand "China's Little Ambassador"? Did you use the same strategies or different ones to understand "Migration Patterns"?

A U.S. Census Bureau worker asks a woman questions about her age, job, residence, and similar things for Census 2000. ▶

Connect to Writing

GRAMMAR

Complex Sentences

A **complex sentence** contains an independent clause and a dependent clause.

An **independent clause** is a sentence. It has a subject and a verb and expresses a complete thought.

> ┌── subject ──┐ ┌─verb─┐
> The students waved.

A **dependent clause** has a subject and a verb, but it does not express a complete thought. A dependent clause usually begins with a **subordinating conjunction**. Examples of subordinating conjunctions are *because*, *before*, *after*, *when*, *while*, *although*, and *if*.

> ┌── subject ──┐ ┌── verb ──┐
> **after** the principal introduced Shirley

A dependent clause cannot stand alone. It combines with an independent clause to make a complex sentence. The dependent clause can come before or after the independent clause.

> ┌─independent clause─┐ ┌──────── dependent clause ────────┐
> The students waved after the principal introduced Shirley.

Use a comma when the dependent clause comes before the independent clause.

> ┌──────── dependent clause ────────┐ ┌── independent clause ──┐
> After the principal introduced Shirley, the students waved.

▲ Computer mouse

Practice

Copy these sentences into your notebook. Circle the subordinating conjunctions. Over the independent clauses, write IC, and over the dependent clauses, write DC.

1. Mrs. Rappaport smiled at Shirley when she wrote the correct answer.

2. Shirley's fingers trembled when she gave Father the letter.

3. Although some people moved to the Northeast, more people moved to the South.

4. Widowed people move less often because they tend to be older.

168

SKILLS FOR WRITING

Writing an Informal Persuasive E-Mail Message

People use persuasion in formal writing, such as in letters to the editor of a newspaper. They also use persuasion in informal writing, such as in e-mail messages to a teacher or to friends.

Read the student's informal e-mail message to her teacher. Then discuss the questions.

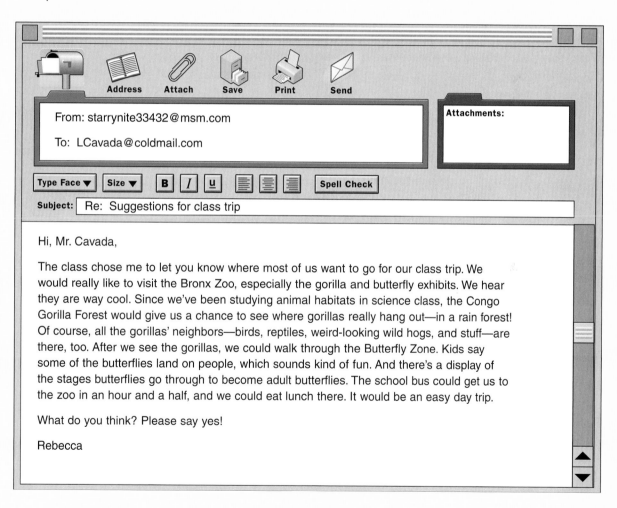

Address   Attach   Save   Print   Send

From: starrynite33432@msm.com

To: LCavada@coldmail.com

Attachments:

Type Face ▼   Size ▼   **B**   *I*   U   Spell Check

Subject: Re: Suggestions for class trip

Hi, Mr. Cavada,

The class chose me to let you know where most of us want to go for our class trip. We would really like to visit the Bronx Zoo, especially the gorilla and butterfly exhibits. We hear they are way cool. Since we've been studying animal habitats in science class, the Congo Gorilla Forest would give us a chance to see where gorillas really hang out—in a rain forest! Of course, all the gorillas' neighbors—birds, reptiles, weird-looking wild hogs, and stuff—are there, too. After we see the gorillas, we could walk through the Butterfly Zone. Kids say some of the butterflies land on people, which sounds kind of fun. And there's a display of the stages butterflies go through to become adult butterflies. The school bus could get us to the zoo in an hour and a half, and we could eat lunch there. It would be an easy day trip.

What do you think? Please say yes!

Rebecca

1. What is the writer's purpose in writing the message?
2. How does the writer try to persuade her teacher?
3. Does the writer use formal or informal language? Why do you think she does this?

WRITING ASSIGNMENT

Informal Persuasive E-Mail Message

You will write an informal persuasive e-mail message. Persuade a friend to join you in asking your school to form a soccer team.

1. Read Reread the e-mail message on page 169. How does the writer try to persuade her teacher?

Writing Strategy: Word Web

Before you write a persuasive message, use a word web to help you organize your ideas. First, write the purpose of your message in the center circle. Then write reasons that support your purpose in circles around it.

Here is the word web for the e-mail message on page 169. Look at the web. Then answer the questions.

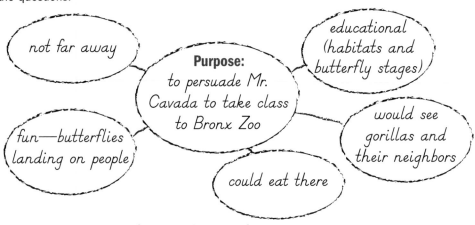

1. What is the purpose of the e-mail message?
2. What are the persuasive reasons?

---

2. Make a word web Draw a word web in your notebook. What is the purpose of your e-mail message? Write it in the center circle. Write persuasive reasons in circles around the main idea. Add as many circles as you need.

3. Write an e-mail message Use your word web to write a persuasive e-mail message to a friend.

PART REVIEW 2

Check Your Knowledge

Language Development

1. Describe how the reading strategy of using your experience can help you understand a story.

2. What is dialogue? What punctuation do you use to show dialogue?

3. What is a simile? Give an example.

4. What is a complex sentence? Give an example.

5. How are formal letters different from informal e-mail messages?

6. How can a word web help you organize ideas to write a persuasive message?

Academic Content

1. What new social studies vocabulary did you learn in Part 2? What do the words mean?

2. What are some of today's migration trends in the United States?

3. What is a pie chart? A bar graph? Give some examples of the kinds of things you can show with them.

Put It All Together

OBJECTIVES

Integrate Skills
- Listening/ Speaking: *Debate*
- Writing: *Travel brochure*

Investigate Themes
- Projects
- Further reading

LISTENING and SPEAKING WORKSHOP

DEBATE

You will debate the topic "Noise pollution should be a crime." In a debate, two teams present opposing arguments about an issue. Each team tries to persuade the audience that its arguments are better.

1 **Think about it** In "The Intersection," Jason Winthrop Jr. complained about noise pollution in his neighborhood. Do you think that causing noise pollution should be a crime? As a class, brainstorm a list of reasons, or arguments, for and against making noise pollution a crime. Write three arguments supporting each point of view.

Form two teams of three students each. Team A will argue that causing noise pollution should be a crime. Team B will argue that causing noise pollution shouldn't be a crime. The other students will be the audience.

2 **Organize** Each team researches facts to support its arguments. The students in the audience prepare questions to ask the teams.

3 **Practice** Teams A and B practice presenting their arguments. Team members listen to each other and take notes. They can modify their arguments if necessary.

4 **Present and evaluate** Team A presents its arguments to the audience. Then Team B presents its arguments. Next, Team A presents points opposing Team B's arguments. Then Team B presents points opposing Team A's arguments. Finally, the audience asks both teams questions. After the debate, the class votes for the more persuasive team.

SPEAKING TIP

You can use the following words to express disagreement politely.
- I'm not sure I agree with that.
- I don't completely agree with that.
- That's a good point. However, . . .

LISTENING TIP

When you listen to a debate, take notes. This will help you remember and evaluate each team's arguments.

TRAVEL BROCHURE

A brochure is a booklet that usually describes or advertises something. A travel brochure usually contains words and pictures that describe the special attractions and features of a place. Writers create brochures to persuade people to visit different places.

A travel brochure usually includes the following characteristics:

- a strong general reason that people should visit the place
- short descriptions of special or important attractions, organized by type of attraction
- interesting facts and details about the important attractions
- vivid adjectives and other words to help the reader visualize the attractions
- pictures or photographs of outstanding attractions

You will create a travel brochure persuading people to visit your city or town. Use the model brochure and the following steps to help you.

1 **Prewrite** Work in small groups. Ask yourselves these questions: How is your city or town unique or special? What are some interesting things to see and do there? Think about attractions, such as shopping areas, sports activities, natural features, famous places, and special events. Make a list of unique or interesting attractions.

Choose the best attractions from your group's list. Make a chart to organize your attractions in groups, such as natural scenery, historical places, arts and culture, sports, shopping, and special events.

WRITING TIP

Use a thesaurus or dictionary to find active or unusual verbs, adverbs, and adjectives to make your writing livelier. For example, the sentence *Boulder is an interesting town* tells readers very little about Boulder. Use a thesaurus to replace the adjective *interesting* with an adjective such as *colorful, exciting,* or *vibrant.* Perhaps find an active verb, too, such as *Boulder teems with exciting sports and cultural events,* to help persuade readers to visit Boulder.

Before you write a first draft of your brochure, read the following model. Notice the characteristics of a travel brochure.

Beautiful Boulder, Colorado

Holly Sihombing

Boulder teems with fun and exciting attractions.

▲▲ Natural Scenery

Boulder offers spectacular scenery. The majestic Flatirons and other gorgeous mountains tower over the town. Many fabulous hiking trails make it easy to explore the world-famous scenery.

▲▲ Sports Activities

Exciting sports events abound year-round. In the summer, you can go biking, boating, fishing, golfing, hang gliding, horseback riding, kayaking, mountain climbing, rock climbing, and swimming. In the winter, you can go cross-country skiing, ice-fishing, ice-skating, skiing, snowboarding, snowshoeing, and snow-tubing.

▲▲ Shopping

The Pearl Street Mall vibrates with cafes, restaurants, and shops. Walking around the mall, you might see amazing street performances: magicians, fire-eaters, dancers, musicians, jugglers, and more.

▲▲ Special Events

Boulder hosts a number of wonderful special events.

- The Boulder Bolder is a 10-kilometer race held on Memorial Day. World-famous runners participate in the professional race, while more than 40,000 people from the city and the neighboring area run in the separate Citizen's Race.

- The Boulder Creek Festival happens on the same weekend. You can munch tasty food, listen to music, and buy everything from art to clothes to toys at the festival.

- Summer brings the Colorado Shakespeare Festival, where you can watch William Shakespeare's plays performed outside at night.

- In the fall, don't miss the University of Colorado football games.

For a fun and exciting vacation, Boulder, Colorado, is the place to go!

2 **Draft** Use the model and your chart to write your travel brochure.

- State a strong general reason that readers should visit your city or town.

- Include some interesting facts and details to illustrate your city's attractions.

- Draw pictures of some of the attractions, or find photos in a newspaper or magazine.

- Use vivid adjectives, verbs, and adverbs to help persuade readers to visit your city or town.

3 **Edit** Trade brochures with another group. Use the questions in the editing checklist to evaluate your work.

> ### EDITING CHECKLIST
> **Did your group . . .**
> - state a strong general reason that readers should visit your city or town?
> - clearly organize the important attractions?
> - give facts and details about the attractions?
> - use vivid adjectives, verbs, and adverbs to persuade readers to visit your city or town?
> - use correct verb forms?
> - use correct capitalization and punctuation?

4 **Revise** Revise your brochure. Add information and correct mistakes, if necessary.

5 **Publish** Use a computer to create a final copy of your brochure. Add photographs or illustrations, if possible. Share your brochure with the class.

Work in pairs or small groups. Choose one of these projects.

1 Write a script for a television commercial to persuade people to change something (for example, their brand of toothpaste or shampoo). Role-play the commercial. Then perform it for the class.

2 Choose a topic from "Changing Earth" (for example, hybrid cars, solar power, or genetic engineering). Use the library or the Internet to research the topic. Then share the information with the class.

3 List places your family has lived. On a map, mark the places and the routes your family took from one place to another. Then share the information with the class.

4 Interview a family member, a friend, or a neighbor about a big change in his or her life. Ask the person to describe the reasons for the change and what impact it had on him or her. Write a story about the person's experience. Then share the story with the class.

5 Ask your classmates about where they have lived and whether they have moved. Report your findings. Show the results in a pie chart or bar graph. Then display the chart or graph in the class.

6 Write a skit or play of "China's Little Ambassador." Use the dialogue in the story or create your own dialogue. One student can be the narrator, and the others can be the main characters. Practice the play. Then perform it for the class.

To find out more about the theme of this unit, choose from these reading suggestions.

Rachel Carson, **Francene Sabin** The book *Silent Spring,* which Rachel Carson wrote in 1962, woke people up to the dangers of pollution. People began studying the effects of pesticides, such as DDT, on fish and wildlife, on food, and on health. Eventually, the U.S. government outlawed DDT. Carson called attention to the environment, ecology, and endangered animals. This biography tells of Carson's struggles to become a biologist.

The Circuit, **Francisco Jiménez** These twelve short stories are about the life of a migrant boy and his family as they move from farm to farm in California, picking crops and living in tents and old garages. The stories describe the strength, courage, poverty, and backbreaking work in a migrant family's life. In spite of never having a permanent home, the family stays together and doesn't give up hope.

Spider Boy, **Ralph Fletcher** Bobby is having trouble adjusting to his new home in northern New York. To keep his mind off missing his friends in Illinois, Bobby writes in his journal and takes care of his pet tarantula, Thelma. Because he knows a lot about spiders, the bully at his new school nicknames him "Spider Boy." But gradually, Bobby makes friends. Then the bully does something difficult to forgive.

Walking on the Boundaries of Change, **Sara Holbrook** These poems are about the problems young people struggle with as they and their worlds change: their difficult choices, new experiences, and search for what is true.

Zlata's Diary, **Zlata Filipović** Zlata started writing in her diary in September 1991 in Sarajevo, a city in Bosnia and Herzegovina, where she lived. At first, she writes gaily about the everyday events of a typical eleven-year-old. Then war crashes into Sarajevo, and Zlata becomes "a child without a childhood. A wartime child. I now realize that I am really living through a war, I am witnessing an ugly, disgusting war." She asks her diary, "Will I ever be a schoolgirl again, will I ever enjoy my childhood again?"

THE FRONTIER

PART 1

- "The Road to Texas Independence"
- From *A Line in the Sand*, Sherry Garland

PART 2

- From *Pecos Bill: The Greatest Cowboy of All Time,* James Cloyd Bowman
- "The Cowboy Era"

In the nineteenth century, people from the eastern United States were moving to the southern and western areas of North America. Most worked or settled there because they wanted to improve their lives. At that time, people called those wilder, less densely populated areas the frontier. In this unit, you will read about some of those people and the challenges they faced.

In Part 1, you will read a social studies article about why Americans settled in Texas, a part of the Spanish colony of Mexico. You will learn how Texas became an independent country and then a part of the United States. Then you will read excerpts from the fictional diary of a thirteen-year-old pioneer girl who lived on the Texas frontier at that time.

In Part 2, you will read a tall tale, or exaggerated story, about a young boy who gets lost during his family's travels across the country. Wild animals adopt him and teach him to survive on the frontier. Finally, you will read about the cowboys of the 1860s and 1870s and their life on the American frontier.

Prepare to Read

BACKGROUND

"The Road to Texas Independence" is an informational history text about how Texas became a state.

Make connections Work in small groups. Copy the chart into your notebook. Then discuss these questions.

1. What do you know about Texas history? Write your answer in the first box of the chart you copied into your notebook.
2. What do you want to know about Texas history? Write your questions in the second box of the chart.
3. After you have finished reading, write what you learned in the third box of the chart.

Know	Want to Know	Learned

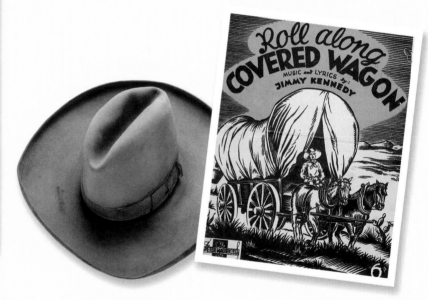

▲ Jimmy Kennedy's song "Roll Along Covered Wagon" was composed and became popular long after people stopped traveling west in wagons.

LEARN KEY WORDS

constitution
enforce
patriotism
political
republic
siege

VOCABULARY

Read these sentences. Use the context to figure out the meaning of the **red** words. Use a dictionary to check your answers. Write each word and its meaning in your notebook.

1. A country's **constitution** is a paper that describes how the government works.
2. The town had laws, but there were no police officers to **enforce** them.
3. Some citizens show their **patriotism** by displaying their country's flag.
4. The United States has two main **political** parties—the Democrats and the Republicans—which debate issues.
5. The United States is a **republic** because the people elect representatives to govern them.
6. The soldiers surrounded the city for ten days. During the **siege**, no one inside could get food or water.

READING STRATEGY

Taking Notes

Taking notes as you read can help you organize and remember information. A social studies text is often organized in chronological order. As you read, take notes on the main events and when they happened.

Use these steps to take notes on history texts.

- Divide your notebook page into two columns.
- As you read, write dates and time periods in the left column. Write events in the right column.
- Use your notes to review the chronology of events.

181

As you read, take notes about the important facts in the text. Note the important dates and events in your notebook. This will help you understand the chronology of the events.

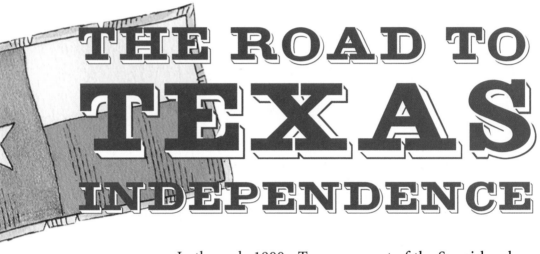

THE ROAD TO TEXAS INDEPENDENCE

Stephen F. Austin
(1793–1836) ▼

In the early 1800s, Texas was part of the Spanish colony of Mexico. Then, in 1821, Mexico won its independence from Spain.

The new government of Mexico claimed Texas as Mexican territory. Only about 4,000 Mexicans were living in Texas. In 1823, the Mexican government offered land at a low price to people who settled in Texas. The **settlers** also didn't have to pay taxes on the land for six years. The Mexican government hoped that more settlers would **strengthen** the Mexican **claim** to the land.

Americans in Mexican Texas

Many Americans wanted to move to Texas. In 1819, an American businessman named Moses Austin wanted to establish a colony there. However, he died in 1821. One of his sons, Stephen F. Austin, carried out his plan over the next few years. He **arranged for** several hundred Americans— mostly families—to move to southeastern Texas.

---

settlers, people who go to live in a new place
strengthen, make stronger
claim, request based on a right or entitlement
arranged for, made plans for

Many settlers were **cotton** farmers from the southern United States. Some were slaveholders, and they took enslaved African Americans with them. The colony of American settlers—Texians, as they called themselves—grew quickly under Austin's leadership. By the early 1830s, several thousand people lived in the colony.

In exchange for the cheap land, Austin and the other American settlers agreed to become Mexican citizens. They also agreed to **worship** in the Catholic Church and obey Mexican laws. However, most settlers still considered themselves Americans and felt no loyalty to Mexico. Most were Protestants, spoke little or no Spanish, and ignored Mexican laws. Soon there was conflict between the Americans in Texas and the Mexican government.

Conflict with Mexico

At the same time, the Mexican government made laws that affected the settlers in Texas. For example, the Mexican government **outlawed** slavery in 1829. Although the government did not enforce this law in Texas, Texas slaveholders were afraid that it would. The Mexican government also placed taxes on goods that people imported into Texas. In addition, the government sent **troops** to Texas and built new **forts** there. The Mexican government was afraid that Texas would try to become part of the United States. Therefore, in 1830, it stopped American immigration to Texas.

Many Americans didn't like the Mexican government's control over Texas. This led to a period of political conflict.

In 1833, an army general named Antonio López de Santa Anna **came to power** in Mexico. Santa Anna wanted the American settlers to obey Mexican laws, so he sent more soldiers to Texas to enforce them.

▲ Antonio López de Santa Anna (1794–1876)

cotton, plant that produces material used for making cloth
worship, pray
outlawed, made illegal
troops, soldiers
forts, buildings that soldiers use to protect important places
came to power, became a leader

BEFORE YOU GO ON . . .

1. When did Mexico become independent from Spain?
2. What did the American settlers agree to do to get land at a low price?

HOW ABOUT YOU?

- Why do you think the settlers in Texas still considered themselves Americans?

▲ Siege of the Alamo

Austin tried to **settle conflicts** between the settlers and the Mexican government. However, he was put in prison in 1834. When he was freed, Austin thought that war with Mexico was certain.

The American settlers didn't like the Mexican laws or the soldiers who enforced them. Furthermore, they had no **representation** in Mexican government. They missed the rights and freedoms that they had enjoyed as U.S. citizens.

Many American settlers in Texas began to organize **volunteer** armies to fight for their independence from Mexico. They had the support of some Tejanos—Mexicans who lived in Texas. Not all Tejanos wanted independence from Mexico, but some didn't like Santa Anna. In 1834, Santa Anna **abolished** the Mexican constitution and became a **dictator**. As a dictator, he had complete control over Mexico and the Texas colony. This made him even more unpopular.

Texas Troops Take Action

In October 1835, Texas troops fought with Mexican troops in Gonzales. The troops forced the Mexicans to **retreat**. In the same month, Texas forces fought against

---

settle conflicts, end arguments
representation, people acting on their behalf
volunteer, made up of people who offer to join
abolished, ended
dictator, leader of a country who controls everything himself or herself
    and generally does not consider the opinions of others in decisions
retreat, move away from a place

184

Mexican troops at San Antonio. The Texas soldiers began a siege that lasted for seven weeks. Then, on December 5, the Texas troops attacked the Mexican troops. The attack ended on December 10, when the Mexican soldiers **surrendered**.

Santa Anna was determined to stop the Texas rebellion. He marched toward San Antonio with several thousand soldiers. By the time Santa Anna's army reached San Antonio, many Texans had left the city, including **General** Sam Houston and some of his troops. Fewer than 200 Texans remained. They gathered at a fort that the Texans called the Alamo.

The Siege of the Alamo

J. C. Neill was the first commander of the Alamo. When Neill left to take care of sick family members, he appointed William Travis to take charge. The famous frontiersmen Jim Bowie and Davy Crockett arrived with volunteer soldiers from other places.

On February 23, 1836, Mexican troops began a siege of the Alamo. They surrounded it and then attacked. The Texans fought bravely. However, Travis knew that his troops needed help. He sent a messenger past the Mexican soldiers with a letter addressed to the people of Texas and to all Americans:

> The enemy have demanded a surrender. . . . I have answered the demand with a cannon shot and our flag still waves proudly from the walls.
>
> I shall never surrender or retreat.
>
> I call on you in the name of **Liberty**, of patriotism, and of everything dear to the American character to come to our aid **with all dispatch**. . . .
>
> **Victory** or death!

▲ The Republic of Texas, 1836, showing movement of Mexican and Texas forces during Texas Revolution

---

surrendered, gave up
general, high-ranking officer in the army
liberty, freedom
with all dispatch, as quickly as possible
victory, success; act of winning

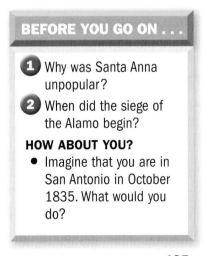

BEFORE YOU GO ON . . .

1 Why was Santa Anna unpopular?

2 When did the siege of the Alamo begin?

HOW ABOUT YOU?

- Imagine that you are in San Antonio in October 1835. What would you do?

Thirty-two men from Gonzales sneaked past the Mexican soldiers to fight in the Alamo. However, no large group of soldiers ever arrived in response to Travis's plea.

For twelve days, the people in the Alamo fought the Mexican soldiers. Then, on March 6, thousands of Mexican soldiers broke through the walls and entered the Alamo. When the battle was over, most fighters in the Alamo were dead. Male survivors were killed shortly afterward. However, Santa Anna spared the women and children.

Texas Declares Independence

At the same time as soldiers were fighting at the Alamo, a group of Texans in a small town called Washington-on-the-Brazos declared independence. On March 2, 1836, they created a nation. They called it the Republic of Texas and appointed Sam Houston commander of the Texas army. Volunteers of many nationalities continued to join the growing fight for Texas independence.

Less than three weeks later, Mexican soldiers killed several hundred Texans in the village of Goliad. The Texans had surrendered before they were killed.

The defeat at Goliad—as well as the fall of the Alamo and Houston's later retreat from Gonzales—terrified some Texans. Many people took their possessions and ran away from their homes to find a safer place.

Not all Texans were afraid or ran away. Some were angry and joined Sam Houston's army.

On April 21, 1836, Houston attacked Santa Anna and his army while they were camped near the San Jacinto River. The Texans waited until the afternoon, when the Mexican soldiers were resting. With cries of "Remember the Alamo!" and "Remember Goliad!" the Texans began fighting the Mexicans.

The Battle of San Jacinto lasted only about eighteen minutes. Although the Mexican army was bigger, the Texas

▲ Texans celebrate declaring independence on March 2, 1836.

▲ Sam Houston (lying against tree), who was injured during the Battle of San Jacinto, accepts Santa Anna's surrender.

army won. The next day, the Texans captured Santa Anna and forced him to sign a **treaty** giving Texas independence.

The Lone Star Republic

The new Republic of Texas adopted a constitution based on the U.S. Constitution and elected Houston president. Because they had carried a flag with a white star in battle, they **nicknamed** their nation the Lone Star Republic.

Houston realized that Texas couldn't survive as an independent country because it was poor and had few factories. Most Texans believed Texas should become part of the United States.

At first, the U.S. government refused to make Texas a state. Texas **was in debt**, and the United States didn't want to take over that debt. Many American leaders also wanted to avoid war with Mexico over Texas. In addition, many Texans were slaveholders, and people in the North were against slavery. But finally, the U.S. government and Texas reached a **compromise**, and Texas became the twenty-eighth state in 1845.

---

treaty, written agreement between two or more countries
nicknamed, gave an informal name
was in debt, owed money
compromise, an agreement in which both sides accept less than what they wanted at first

BEFORE YOU GO ON . . .

1 Why did Texans nickname their new nation the Lone Star Republic?

2 Why didn't the U.S. government want Texas to become a state?

HOW ABOUT YOU?
- Why do you think the Texans shouted, "Remember the Alamo"?

Review and Practice

Work in small groups. Copy the timeline onto poster paper. Use your notes to complete the timeline with important dates and events. Compare timelines as a class.

1820
—*Mexico wins independence from Spain (1821).*

1830

1840

1850

The inside of a pioneer's log cabin in Texas shows a spinning wheel (left), a bed, a trunk (right), and a ladder (behind trunk) to an attic. ▶

EXTENSION

Reread "The Road to Texas Independence." Note that the text discusses several events in terms of a cause-and-effect relationship. Copy the chart into your notebook. Complete it with information from the reading. Then compare charts in small groups.

Cause	Effect
Stephen Austin arranged for several hundred Americans to move to Texas.	*The colony of American settlers grew quickly.*
Most settlers still considered themselves Americans and felt no loyalty to Mexico.	
	In 1830, the Mexican government stopped American immigration to Texas.
Santa Anna wanted the American settlers to obey Mexican laws.	
	American settlers organized volunteer armies to fight for independence from Mexico.
Santa Anna was determined to stop the Texas rebellion.	
	Some Texans left their settlements to find a safer place to live.

DISCUSSION

Discuss in pairs or small groups.

1. Look at the chart you made in your notebook before you read the article. (See page 180.) How are your answers different now?

2. The land that is now Texas was part of Mexico in 1821. Imagine that you lived in the eastern United States in 1821. Would you move to Texas to join Stephen Austin's colony? Why or why not?

Historical Fiction

These journal entries are historical fiction. They are from the fictional diary of a thirteen-year-old girl, Lucinda Lawrence. She lived with her mother, father, and older brother, Willis, in Gonzales, Texas, in 1835. Lucinda is not a real person, but her journal entries contain factual information about Texas in 1835.

from

A Line in the Sand

Sherry Garland

Wednesday, September 16

A man from San Felipe, in Austin's Colony, rode through town today. San Felipe is over a hundred miles northeast of here, on the Brazos River, and is the **hub** of the Texas colonies. It even has a printing press. The rider dropped off letters and a stack of the *Telegraph and Texas Register* newspaper. How I love reading those wrinkled, inky-smelling pages.

We received a letter from Mama's brother, Henry, who lives with his wife, Nancy, and five children in San Felipe. Uncle Henry has decided to move to DeWitt's Colony next spring. When Papa heard the news, he didn't say a word. He just walked out onto the **gallery** and washed his face. Papa's never admitted it out loud, but I don't think he likes Uncle Henry much. Uncle Henry belongs to the War **Party**—he wants Texas to declare her independence from Mexico. Papa belongs to the Peace Party—he wants Texas to stay part of Mexico and **urge** a **democratic** constitution. Papa hates war. He says he saw enough killing in the War of 1812, serving under Andrew Jackson, who is now President of the United States.

Later That Day—

After supper Papa looked up from the newspaper and said, "It's just a **handful of slick lawyers** and **fool agitators** causing all

LITERARY ELEMENT

The *setting* is the time and place of a story—for example, the 1940s in Paris, France. What is the setting of this story?

this talk about war. Most of the colonists are farmers like me who want to live out their lives and raise their families and not get involved in politics."

Says Willis, "I've heard there are thirty thousand Americans settled in Texas now, and only four thousand Mexicans. If this were a democracy, the **majority** would rule. But this isn't America, it's Mexico, and Texians have no say in government affairs. That ain't right." Willis is just seventeen, but he talks like he knows everything.

Says Papa, "The Mexican army is one of the biggest in the world. Even if the Texians fought a war and won, it would be a costly victory."

Willis jumped up from the table and said, "But Papa, we can't just stand by and give up our freedoms. Grandpa Lawrence fought in the American Revolution, didn't he? And you fought the British at Horseshoe Bend. When it comes my turn to fight for freedom, I'll not **turn my back**."

BEFORE YOU GO ON . . .

1. How does Willis feel about war? Why?
2. How does Papa feel about war? Why?

HOW ABOUT YOU?
- Do you agree with Willis or Papa? Explain.

Papa shook his head as Willis left the room. Mama looked up from poking the fire logs and said, "Now, don't those words sound mighty familiar, Mr. Lawrence? I **recollect** you getting **all fired up** **twenty-nigh** years ago and running off to join the Georgia volunteers."

Papa **snorted**, then got quiet, lost in his memories.

Thursday, September 17

Talk of war has been going on all summer. Sometimes it scares me, but I think it is just talk. I don't believe war will really come. We are American born, but now we are Mexican citizens, for Texas is part of the Republic of Mexico. We came for the **fertile**, cheap land and the chance to farm and make a **decent** living.

Those early times were hard; some gave up, but not Papa. He says our roots are sunk too deep into Texas soil to **pull up** now. I think the worst is behind us and only good **looms on the horizon**. Our cotton crop is the grandest we've ever had, the town is growing, and a schoolhouse is to be built next spring. And the land is so unspoiled and beautiful—sometimes my

heart fills up with so much joy and freedom, I have to **whoop** and run across the **prairie** like a wild **mustang**. I pray we never, never leave this place.

---

whoop, shout
prairie, large area of land in North America covered with grass
mustang, small wild horse

About the Author
Sherry Garland

Sherry Garland's family has lived in Texas for many years. Her great-great-grandfather settled in Texas while it was still a republic. Garland decided to become an author after she won a high school essay contest on "Why I Love Texas." Many of Garland's books are about other times or cultures. She has written, "I believe that although our clothes, language, and foods are different, inside our hearts, humans are the same everywhere—and have been throughout time."

---

recollect, remember
all fired up, very excited
twenty-nigh, almost twenty
snorted, noisily forced air out through his nose, to express anger
fertile, good for farming
decent, good enough
pull up, move away
looms on the horizon, will happen in the future

BEFORE YOU GO ON . . .

1 Why did Lucinda's family move to Texas?

2 How does she feel about the future?

HOW ABOUT YOU?
- How do you feel about your future? What good things do you feel are ahead?

Link the Readings

Both "The Road to Texas Independence" and the excerpt from *A Line in the Sand* are about Texas history. Look at the readings again. Copy the chart into your notebook and complete it.

Title of Selection	Genre	Fiction or Nonfiction	Purpose of Selection	Setting
"The Road to Texas Independence"				
From *A Line in the Sand*				

DISCUSSION

Discuss in pairs or small groups.

1. Where did the events in each reading take place? Find the places on a map.

2. When did the events in each reading take place? How long a time does each reading describe?

3. Compare "The Road to Texas Independence" and the passage from *A Line in the Sand*. Which text gave you more of a feeling about life on the frontier? Which did you like better? Explain.

The San Jacinto Monument marks the place where Texas forces defeated Santa Anna and won independence from Mexico. ▶

Connect to Writing

GRAMMAR

Comparative and Superlative Adjectives

Use **comparative adjectives** to compare two things. Use **superlative adjectives** to compare three or more things.

> Comparative: Sara **is taller than** Jorge.
> Superlative: Laura is **the tallest** of the three.

Most one-syllable adjectives and some two-syllable adjectives add **-er** for comparatives and **-est** for superlatives, like this:

Adjective	Comparative	Superlative
young	young**er than**	**the** young**est**
big	bigg**er than**	**the** bigg**est**
busy	busi**er than**	**the** busi**est**

Most adjectives of two or more syllables use *more* for comparatives and *the most* for superlatives:

Adjective	Comparative	Superlative
famous	**more** famous **than**	**the most** famous
talkative	**more** talkative **than**	**the most** talkative

Some adjectives have irregular comparative and superlative forms:

Adjective	Comparative	Superlative
good	**better than**	**the best**
bad	**worse than**	**the worst**
far	**farther than**	**the farthest**

Practice
Copy these sentences into your notebook. Use the correct adjective form.

1. Texas is ____ ____ state in the Southwest. (larger than, the largest)

2. Land in Texas was ____ ____ land in Ohio. (cheaper than, the cheapest)

3. Texas's army was ____ ____ Mexico's army. (smaller than, the smallest)

4. Those soldiers were ____ ____ of all. (braver than, the bravest)

194

SKILLS FOR WRITING

Taking Notes for a Research Report

In a research report, a writer examines and presents important information about a topic. To gather that information, a writer first reads about the topic in a variety of sources. Sources might include reference books (such as encyclopedias), other books (such as biographies and histories), newspapers, magazines, and the Internet. Writers usually take careful notes to help them remember and organize the information they find. They often start by listing a few important questions they want to answer about their topic. Then they take notes on information that helps answer those questions. The questions are often called subtopics, or parts of the main topic. Here is an example of a note card for a report on Sam Houston.

Sam Houston, Life before Texas ← Write one subtopic at the top of each card.

1. Houston was born in Virginia on March 2, 1793. (p. 9) When Houston was 13, his dad died, and his family moved to Tennessee. (p. 10) In Tennessee, he ran away and lived with Cherokee Indians, who adopted him. (p. 11)

2. He joined the U.S. Army in 1813. (p. 12) At age 25, he resigned from the army. (p. 20) After that, he was elected Nashville's district attorney and then to the U.S. House of Representatives. His personality impressed people. (p. 22)

Source: Fritz, Jean. *Make Way for Sam Houston.* New York: G.P. Putnam's Sons, 1986.

3. In 1827, Houston was elected governor of Tennessee but resigned in 1829. In 1832, he moved to Texas. (p. 399)

Source: "Houston, Sam," *World Book 2001.*

Write information about the subtopic in your own words. To avoid borrowing a source's language, don't look at the source while writing notes.

Sources of information

1. What subtopic is the note card about?
2. How many sources did the writer use? What are the sources?

WRITING ASSIGNMENT

Notes

You will do research and take notes for a report on a topic about Texas history that interests you.

1. **Brainstorm** Reread "The Road to Texas Independence," on pages 182–187. Then think of a topic you would like to write about, such as the Battle of San Jacinto or Antonio López de Santa Anna.

Writing Strategy: Subtopic Web

After you choose a research report topic, decide what important questions, or subtopics, you need to answer for your report. Write your main topic at the top of your page. Then write some subtopics in circles below the topic. As you read, list two or three points you want to make about each subtopic under that subtopic. Look at this subtopic web about Santa Anna.

Santa Anna

personal qualities

important actions as president of Mexico

why he lost Texas

experiences that helped him lead
- He joined the Spanish army and learned to be a soldier.
- He changed sides and fought for Mexico's freedom.
- He became governor of Veracruz, Mexico.

---

2. **Make a subtopic web** When you have picked a topic, make a subtopic web in your notebook. Narrow your web to three or four subtopics.

3. **Write** Write at least one note card for each subtopic. As you read from sources and write your note cards, go back to your subtopic web. Add to the web the main points you have found out about each subtopic.

EDITING CHECKLIST

Did you . . .

▶ look for important and interesting information about three or four subtopics?

▶ write your notes in your own words?

▶ write a subtopic at the top of each card?

▶ write the source information for each note card?

Check Your Knowledge

Language Development

1. What is a good way to organize the notes you take on a history text?

2. What is a diary?

3. What is a story's setting? What is the setting of the excerpt you read from *A Line in the Sand*?

4. When do you use a comparative adjective? A superlative adjective?

5. What are the comparative forms of *grand, busy,* and *successful*? The superlative forms? Use them in sentences.

6. How can you use a subtopic web to organize information?

Academic Content

1. What new social studies vocabulary did you learn in Part 1? What do the words mean?

2. What events led to Texas's independence?

3. Who was elected president of the Republic of Texas?

Prepare to Read

BACKGROUND

Pecos Bill: The Greatest Cowboy of All Time is a tall tale. A tall tale is a humorous fictional story. Tall tales usually have characters with abilities and qualities that are exaggerated— enlarged beyond the truth. Many tall tales exaggerate things that happened on the American frontier. In the excerpt you are about to read, the main character is a young boy who gets lost on the Texas frontier. He meets a coyote, a wild animal that looks like a dog. He later meets some other wild animals.

Make connections Work in pairs or small groups. List wild animals that might have been common on the Texas frontier. Then compare lists as a class.

▲ Puma (also called a mountain lion or cougar)

◄ Porcupine

LEARN KEY WORDS

affection
cowboy
curious
den
pack
promise

VOCABULARY

Read these sentences. Use the context to figure out the meaning of the **red** words. Use a dictionary to check your answers. Write each word and its meaning in your notebook.

1. The two sisters show their **affection** for each other by hugging.
2. The job of a **cowboy** is to take care of the cows and horses on a farm.
3. The **curious** child was always opening things to see what was inside.
4. The bears went into their **den** to sleep through the winter.
5. Several wolves hunt together in a **pack**.
6. When you make a **promise** to do something, you must do it.

READING STRATEGY

Summarizing

Summarizing means restating the main ideas of a text in shorter form. It helps you identify and remember the most important points. It also helps you focus on your purpose for reading the text.

Use these steps to summarize a text.

- Read the text.
- Reread each paragraph or section. Then close your book and write the main ideas in one or two sentences. Use your own words.
- Read all your sentences. These sentences summarize the text.

Tall Tale

Skim this excerpt from Pecos Bill: The Greatest Cowboy of All Time. *Then reread it more carefully. Write one or two sentences summarizing the main ideas on each page. Then read all your sentences. This is your story summary. You may not understand every word of the story, but your summary will give you the main ideas.*

from

PECOS BILL:
The Greatest Cowboy of All Time

James Cloyd Bowman

▲ Pecos Bill falls out of the wagon.

Pecos Bill had the strangest and most exciting experience any boy ever had. He became a member of a pack of wild Coyotes, and until he was a grown man, believed that his name was **Cropear**, and that he was a **full-blooded Coyote**. Later he discovered that he was a human being and very shortly thereafter became the greatest cowboy of all time. This is how it all came about.

Pecos Bill's family was migrating westward through Texas in the early days, in an old covered wagon with wheels made from cross sections of a sycamore log. His father and mother were riding in the front seat, and his father was driving a **wall-eyed**, **spavined roan** horse and a red and white spotted **milch cow** hitched side by side. The eighteen children in the back of the wagon were making such a medley of noises that their mother said it wasn't possible even to hear the **thunder**.

Just as the wagon was rattling down to the **ford** across the Pecos River, the rear left wheel bounced over a great piece of rock, and Bill, his red hair bristling like **porcupine quills**, rolled out of the rear of the wagon, and landed, up to his neck, in a pile of loose sand. He was only four years old at the time, and he lay **dazed** until the wagon had crossed the river and disappeared into the sagebrush. It wasn't until his mother rounded up the family for the noonday meal that Bill was missed. The last anyone remembered seeing him was just before they had forded the river.

The mother and eight or ten of the older children hurried back to the river and hunted everywhere, but they could find no trace of the lost boy. When evening came, they were forced to go back to the covered wagon, and later, to continue their journey without him. Ever after, when they thought of Bill, they remembered the river, and so they naturally came to speak of him as Pecos Bill.

What had happened to Bill was this. He had strayed off into the **mesquite**, and a few hours later was found by a wise old Coyote, who was the **undisputed leader** of the Loyal and Approved Packs of the Pecos and Rio Grande Valleys. He was, in fact, the Granddaddy of the entire race of Coyotes, and so his followers, out of affection to him, called him Grandy.

---

mesquite, common trees or bushes in the southwestern United States
undisputed leader, someone everybody agrees is the leader

Cropear, animal with short, or cropped, ears
full-blooded Coyote, 100 percent coyote
wall-eyed, having eyes that turn outward
spavined, old and weak
roan, reddish brown mixed with white
milch cow, cow that gives milk
thunder, loud noise that you hear during a storm
ford, shallow place where you cross a river
porcupine quills, sharp needles on the back of a porcupine
dazed, shocked

BEFORE YOU GO ON . . .

1. How did Pecos Bill get separated from his family?
2. Who found Pecos Bill?

HOW ABOUT YOU?
- Have you ever been lost? If so, describe the experience. Who found you?

When he accidentally met Bill, Grandy was curious, but shy. He sniffed and he **yelped**, and he ran this way and that, the better to get the **scent**, and to make sure there was no danger. After a while he came quite near, sat up on his **haunches**, and waited to see what the boy would do. Bill trotted up to Grandy and began running his hands through the long shaggy hair.

"What a nice doggy you are," he repeated again and again.

"Yes, and what a nice Cropear you are," yelped Grandy joyously.

And so, ever after, the Coyotes called the child Cropear.

Grandy was much pleased with his find and so, by running ahead and stopping and barking softly, he led the boy to the jagged side of Cabezon, or the Big Head, as it was called. This was a **towering** mass of mountain that rose **abruptly**, as if by magic, from the prairie. Around the base of this mountain the various families of the Loyal and Approved Packs had **burrowed** out their dens.

Here, far away from the nearest human dwelling, Grandy made a home for Cropear, and taught him all the knowledge of the wild out-of-doors. He led Cropear to the berries that were good to eat, and dug up roots that were sweet and spicy. He showed the boy how to break open the small nuts from the piñon. . . .

Grandy became his teacher and schooled him in the knowledge that had been handed down through thousands of generations of the Pack's life. He taught Cropear the many **signal** calls, and the

---

yelped, made a sharp, high bark
scent, smell that animals or human beings leave
    behind
haunches, back legs

towering, very tall
abruptly, suddenly; steeply
burrowed, dug
signal, movement or sound telling someone something

▲ Pecos Bill meets Grandy.

▲ Pecos Bill learns from Grandy.

code of right and wrong, and the gentle art of **loyalty** to the leader. He also trained him to leap long distances and to dance; and to flip-flop and to twirl his body so fast that the eye could not follow his movements. And most important of all, he instructed him in the silent, **rigid pose of invisibility**, so that he could see all that was going on around him without being seen.

LITERARY ELEMENT

Hyperbole is a way of describing something by exaggerating on purpose—saying that it is much bigger, smaller, faster, slower, or in some other way more than it really is. For example, Grandy teaches Cropear "to twirl his body so fast that the eye could not follow his movements."

loyalty, support; faithfulness
rigid pose of invisibility, keeping one's body still so
   that others do not see it

As Cropear grew tall and strong, he became the pet of the Pack. The Coyotes were always bringing him what they thought he would like to eat, and were ever showing him the many secrets of the fine art of hunting. They taught him where the Field-mouse nested, where the Song Thrush hid her eggs, where the Squirrel stored his nuts; and where the Mountain Sheep concealed their young among the towering rocks. . . .

BEFORE YOU GO ON . . .

1 What does Grandy teach Bill?

2 How does the Pack feel about Bill?

HOW ABOUT YOU?
● Why do you think Grandy calls Bill Cropear?

203

▲ Grandy introduces Pecos Bill to the Mountain Lion, the Grizzly Bear, the Skunk, the Porcupine, and the Bull Rattlesnake.

Grandy **took pains** to introduce Cropear to each of the animals and made every one of them promise he would not harm the growing man-child. "Au-g-gh!" growled the Mountain Lion. "I will be as careful as I can. But be sure to tell your child to be careful, too!"

"Gr-r-r!" growled the fierce Grizzly Bear. "I have crunched many a **marrow** bone, but I will not harm your boy. Gr-r-r!"

"Yes, we'll keep our perfumery and our quills in our vest pockets," mumbled the silly Skunk and Porcupine, as if suffering from **adenoids**.

But when Grandy talked things over with the Bull Rattlesnake, he was met with the **defiance** of hissing rattles. "Nobody will ever make me promise to protect anybody or anything! S-s-s-s-ss! I'll do just as I please!"

"Be careful of your **wicked** tongue," warned Grandy, "or you'll be very sorry."

But when Grandy met the Wouser, things were even worse. The Wouser was a cross between the Mountain Lion and the Grizzly Bear, and was ten times larger than either. Besides that, he was the **nastiest** creature in the world. "I can only give you fair warning," yowled the Wouser, "and if you prize your man-child, as you say you do, you will have to keep him out of harm's way!" And as the Wouser continued, he stalked back and

---

took pains, was very careful
marrow, the soft substance in the hollow center of a bone
adenoids, growths in the throat that sometimes make breathing difficult

defiance, disobedient or disrespectful behavior
wicked, very bad
nastiest, meanest

forth, lashing his tail and gnashing his jaws, and acting as if he were ready to snap somebody's head off. "What's more, you know that nobody treats me as a friend. Everybody runs around behind my back spreading lies about me. Everybody says I carry **hydrophobia**—the deadly poison—about on my person, and because of all these lies, I am **shunned** like a **leper**. Now you come sneaking around asking me to help you. Get out of my sight before I do something I will be sorry for!"

---

hydrophobia, rabies (a deadly disease that people can get from animals)
shunned, avoided
leper, someone who has leprosy (a serious infectious skin disease)

"I'm not sneaking," barked Grandy in defiance, "and besides, you're the one who will be sorry in the end."

So it happened that all the animals, save only the Bull Rattlesnake and the Wouser, promised to help Cropear bear a charmed life so that no harm should come near him. And by good fortune, the boy was never sick. The **vigorous** exercise and the fresh air and the constant sunlight helped him to become the healthiest, strongest, most active boy in the world.

---

vigorous, active and energetic

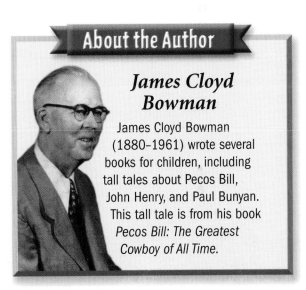

About the Author

James Cloyd Bowman

James Cloyd Bowman (1880–1961) wrote several books for children, including tall tales about Pecos Bill, John Henry, and Paul Bunyan. This tall tale is from his book *Pecos Bill: The Greatest Cowboy of All Time.*

BEFORE YOU GO ON . . .

1. Why does Grandy introduce Cropear to the other animals?
2. Which two animals refuse to promise not to harm Cropear? Why?

HOW ABOUT YOU?
- Do you believe that this story is true? Why or why not?

▲ Grandy introduces Pecos Bill to the Wouser.

Review and Practice

1. Look at the summary you prepared as you read the excerpt from *Pecos Bill: The Greatest Cowboy of All Time*. Compare your summaries in pairs or small groups. Do you have the same information? Reread the story and revise your summary if needed.

2. These events are from the story about Pecos Bill. Copy them into your notebook. Then number the events so that they are in chronological order.

   ___1___ Bill's family is traveling west in a covered wagon.
   _____ Grandy asks other animals not to harm Cropear.
   _____ Cropear becomes the strongest and most active boy in the world.
   _____ Grandy finds Bill and calls him Cropear.
   _____ Bill gets separated from his family.
   _____ Most of the animals promise that they won't harm Cropear.
   _____ Grandy teaches Cropear all the knowledge of the Pack.

Use your list of events to retell the story to a partner.

Copy the word webs into your notebook. Complete the webs with words that describe each character. Use information from the story. Then compare word webs in small groups.

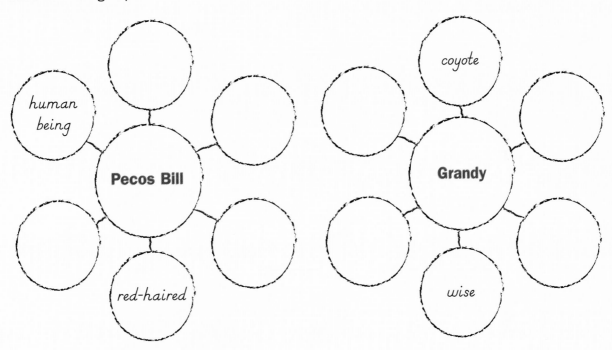

Discuss in pairs or small groups.

1. What parts of the story are believable? Explain.
2. What parts of the story are unbelievable? Explain.
3. What is hyperbole? Give an example from the story. Why is it hyperbole?

This is a social studies article. It gives historical information about the lives of cowboys. After you read, summarize the main ideas of each section in one or two sentences. Use the section heads to help you. Then reread your summary.

The Cowboy Era

Cotton and Cattle

Both cotton and **cattle** were important to the Texas **economy** when Texas became a state in 1845. Growing cotton was a lot of work. Most farmers planted, harvested, and picked their own cotton. Others were slaveholders, and enslaved Africans did much of the work. After the Civil War (1861–1865), the slaves were free. Many former slaves became **sharecroppers**. Others joined the growing number of Texans who became cowboys. They **herded** cattle on the large, open grasslands, called ranges.

▼ Texas cattle drive

Why were cattle important to the Texas economy? Beef was a popular food among Americans. In 1865, people in the northern and eastern United States didn't raise many cattle. Cattle there cost up to forty dollars **a head**. However, there were more than 4 million longhorn cattle in southern Texas. Cattle in Texas were worth only about four dollars a head. **Ranchers** quickly realized that they could make a lot of money by selling their cattle elsewhere. First, they could drive the cattle to Kansas or Missouri. There they could ship them to the northern or eastern United States by train. This idea led to the first cattle **drives**.

---

cattle, cows raised on a ranch
economy, a state's or nation's business and money system
sharecroppers, people who farm land that other people own; sharecroppers get part of the crop as pay
herded, animals made to move together as a group by humans on horseback and by their dogs
a head, each animal
ranchers, people who own or work on large cattle farms
drives, acts of herding large groups of animals to another place

The Great Cattle Drives

In 1866, the great cattle drives began. In that year, cowboys drove more than a quarter of a million Texas cattle through what is now Oklahoma to Kansas and Missouri. This was a journey of about 1,609 to 2,414 kilometers (1,000 to 1,500 mi.), and it took from three to six months to complete. The cowboys and cattle usually traveled on trails that already existed. About 2 million cattle were driven up the Chisholm Trail to Kansas between 1867 and 1871.

▲ Three trails on which cowboys drove cattle north from Texas

Cowboy Life

Cowboys did not have an easy job. Cattle drives were difficult and sometimes dangerous. Cowboys got little pay, worked long days, and got little sleep. River crossings and **stampedes** were particularly dangerous. Cowboys and cattle might drown crossing a river or get trampled to death in a stampede. Cowboys sometimes had to fight rustlers who tried to steal their cattle.

Some days were scorching hot, and some nights were freezing cold. Cowboys wore **practical** clothes to help them withstand these temperatures.

---

stampedes, sudden movements of large groups of running animals
practical, useful and sensible

BEFORE YOU GO ON . . .

1. Why did Texas ranchers want to move their cattle north?
2. What were some dangers on a cattle drive?

HOW ABOUT YOU?

- Would you like to be a cowboy? Why or why not?

Cowboy hats had to be strong and long lasting. On hot days, the high top part of the hat kept the head cool, while the broad brim shaded the eyes and neck. On rainy or snowy days, the hats worked as umbrellas. The hats also protected cowboys from thorns and low-hanging branches. Cowboys even used them to carry water, to fan or put out fires, and as pillows.

The cowboys' other clothing was also practical. Their shirts and pants were made of strong material. They lasted a long time and **protected** the cowboys' skin. When it was dusty, cowboys covered their noses and mouths with the bandannas they wore around their necks.

When riding horses, they could rest the high heels of their boots in the **stirrups**. When **roping** cattle, they could dig their boot heels into the ground.

Many cowboys were native Texans. Others came from the South, East, and Midwest. Some were African American, Native American, and Mexican. They all had excellent riding skills, enabling them to herd cattle on long drives.

End of the Cowboy Era

The cowboy era lasted only about twenty years. During that time, thousands of cowboys worked on cattle drives. What caused the end of the cowboy era? Until the 1870s, the ranges were open; there were no fences to stop the movement of cattle. However, in 1874, **barbed wire** was invented. Farmers and ranchers began **fencing** their land with barbed wire, so the ranges became closed. In addition, many railroads were built in Texas in the 1880s. Then ranchers could send their cattle to market directly by train, so cattle drives became **unnecessary**.

crown
brim
bandanna
lasso
cuff
belt
chaps
cowboy boots
spurs

▲ A cowboy's clothing and gear

---

protected, kept safe from damage
stirrups, metal rings where you put your feet when you ride a horse
roping, catching an animal with a circle of rope (lasso)
barbed wire, wire with short, sharp points on it
fencing, building wood or wire structures to stop people or animals from entering or leaving an area
unnecessary, not needed

BEFORE YOU GO ON . . .

1 How did a cowboy's clothing and boots help him?

2 Why did the cowboy era end?

HOW ABOUT YOU?

• Have you ever seen a cowboy? If so, where?

Link the Readings

Reread the *Pecos Bill* excerpt and "The Cowboy Era." Then copy the chart into your notebook and complete it.

Title of Selection	Genre	Fiction or Nonfiction	Purpose of Selection	Most Interesting Part
From *Pecos Bill: The Greatest Cowboy of All Time*				
"The Cowboy Era"				

DISCUSSION

Discuss in pairs or small groups.

1. The *Pecos Bill* excerpt and "The Cowboy Era" both tell about animals. List all the animals mentioned in both readings. What do you know about them?

2. Pecos Bill and the cowboys described in "The Cowboy Era" had to face dangers. Compare the danger of meeting the Wouser with that of being in a cattle stampede.

3. What did you learn about life in Texas in the 1800s from the two texts you read in Part 2? Would you want to have lived in Texas during that time? Why or why not?

Nat Love (1854–1921) was probably the most famous African-American cowboy. His autobiography, *The Life and Adventures of Nat Love,* was published in 1907. ▶

Connect to Writing

GRAMMAR

Using Possessive Adjectives and Possessive Pronouns

A **possessive adjective** is a form of a personal pronoun that modifies a noun (*my, your, his, her, its, our, their*).

A **possessive pronoun** takes the place of a possessive adjective + a noun. Possessive pronouns include *mine, yours, his, hers, ours,* and *theirs.*

Possessive Adjective + Noun	Possessive Pronoun
These are not **my gloves**.	These are not **mine**.
This is not **your saddle**.	This is not **yours**.
His boots are in the barn.	**His** are in the barn.
Her hat is brown.	**Hers** is brown.
Our horse is black and white.	**Ours** is black and white.
Their ranch is near the Pecos River.	**Theirs** is near the Pecos River.
Its name is Grandy.	No possessive pronoun replaces the possessive adjective **its**.

Practice

Copy the sentences into your notebook. Use the correct words in parentheses.

1. This is (my / mine). (Your / Yours) bandanna is blue.

2. This is (our / ours) covered wagon. (Their / Theirs) is across the river.

3. (Him / His) horse can run fast. (Her / Hers) is slow.

4. This hat isn't (my / mine). It is (your / yours).

5. (Their / Theirs) cattle are forty dollars a head. (Our / Ours) are four dollars a head.

212

SKILLS FOR WRITING

Writing Summaries and Reponses

As you have learned, a **summary** gives the most important ideas of a text in short form. A summary does not include your opinion about the text. A **response** gives your personal reaction to a text. It includes your thoughts and feelings about it.

Read the summary of and response to *Paul Bunyan*, another tall tale. Then answer the questions.

Melissa Gee

Summary

Paul Bunyan is a tall tale about a giant lumberjack who had incredible strength and helped create the natural wonders of the United States. According to one story, young Paul found a blue ox calf, which he adopted and named Babe. As Paul and Babe grew older and larger, they gained fame for their fantastic logging abilities.

Response

Paul Bunyan is my favorite tall tale because it is so funny and fantastic. A funny part was the description of Paul as such a big baby that his baby carriage was a wagon pulled by oxen. My favorite part is where Paul's big ax fell and cut the Grand Canyon. Paul and his blue ox do fantastic things like that all across the country.

---

1. What information is in the summary?
2. What information is in the response?
3. How is the response different from the summary?

WRITING ASSIGNMENT

Outline

You will write a sentence outline of the text "The Cowboy Era" on pages 208–210. In a sentence outline, you write a sentence that summarizes each important subtopic. Then, under each subtopic, you list each point you want to make about that subtopic. Write each point in the form of a sentence, too.

1. Read Review page 196 on how to make a subtopic web. What is the main topic of "The Cowboy Era"? What are the three or four main subtopics?

Writing Strategy: Outline

Follow this outline to organize the information in "The Cowboy Era." Notice that there are at least two main points under each subtopic. Each subtopic is numbered with a roman numeral. The main points under each subtopic are indented and listed as A, B, C, and so forth.

> Main Topic
> I. Subtopic
>   A.
>   B.
>   C.
> II. Subtopic
>   A.
>   B.
> III. Subtopic
>   A.
>   B.
>   C.

1. How many subtopics would be examined in the report outlined above?
2. How many main points for each subtopic would be examined in the report?

---

2. Make an outline Use the outline above and the subtopic web on page 196 as models. Make a subtopic web for "The Cowboy Era."

3. Write Write your outline, using a roman numeral for each subtopic and A, B, and so forth for the most important points under each subtopic.

EDITING CHECKLIST

Did you . . .

▶ list the main topic at the top?

▶ find the subtopics?

▶ find at least two important points for each subtopic?

▶ indent the points under the subtopics?

Check Your Knowledge

Language Development

1. Why is it helpful to summarize an article? A story?

2. What is a tall tale?

3. What is hyperbole? Give an example.

4. What is a possessive adjective? Give three examples and use them in sentences.

5. What is a possessive pronoun? Give three examples and use them in sentences.

6. How is a response different from a summary?

7. How does making an outline help you write a research paper?

Academic Content

1. What new social studies vocabulary did you learn in Part 2? What do the words mean?

2. What did you learn about cowboys in Part 2? What kind of work did they do? What was their clothing like?

3. What were some things that were happening in U.S. history during the cowboy era?

▲ Cowboys drive Texas longhorn cattle to Dodge City, Kansas.

Put It All Together

OBJECTIVES

Integrate Skills
- Listening/
  Speaking:
  Speech
- Writing:
  *Research
  report*

**Investigate
Themes**
- Projects
- Further
  reading

LISTENING and SPEAKING WORKSHOP

SPEECH

You will give a speech telling about an important event in your state's history. Your speech will be from the point of view of a person who played an important part in the event.

1 **Think about it** As a class, discuss these questions: What are some important events in your state's history? Who played an important part in each event? List the events and the people who influenced them. Use books or the Internet to help you find information, if necessary.

2 **Organize** Each student will choose one person from the list to research, using the library and the Internet. Make notes about an event in your state's history that he or she played an important part in. Then use your notes to write a speech in which the person describes the event from his or her point of view. Remember to use the personal pronouns *I* and *we* in your speech.

3 **Practice** Practice giving your speech in small groups. Ask your group to suggest ways to improve your speech. Revise your speech, if necessary.

4 **Present and evaluate** Present your speech to the class. After each person finishes, evaluate the presentation. What did you like best about the speech? Do you have suggestions for improvement?

SPEAKING TIPS

- Try to find out some personal characteristics of your historical person. For example, if he or she spoke in a loud voice, you might give your speech in a loud voice.
- Use active, colorful verbs and adjectives in your speech to describe the historical event.

LISTENING TIP

Listen to the verbs and adjectives the speaker uses. Try to visualize, or picture in your mind, the event that the speaker is describing.

RESEARCH REPORT

For a research report, a writer uses a variety of sources to gather information about a topic. Sources might include reference books, biography and history books, newspapers, magazines, and the Internet. The writer's purpose is to examine and present important, detailed information about a topic.

Your research report should include the following:

- a main topic and a few important supporting questions, or subtopics, that you answer or explain

- an introduction that presents the main points you want to make

- clearly organized information about your subtopics, gathered from a variety of sources, that supports your main idea and is written in your own words

- a conclusion that restates the most important points about your topic

- a list of your sources

You will write a research report about an important event in your state's history. Use the model on pages 218–219 to help you.

1 **Prewrite** Work in small groups. List important events in your state's history. Each student chooses one event to research. Use reference books, the Internet, and other sources for your research. Take notes about your event on note cards. Review how to make note cards on pages 195–196, if needed.

Organize your note cards by important subtopics. Then use the cards to write a sentence outline for your report. Review how to make an outline on page 214.

WRITING TIPS

- Don't copy information from a source. Restate the ideas in your own words.
- Make sure your information is accurate. If you aren't sure that something is correct, check it in another book, article, or encyclopedia. Don't assume that all the information in a book or an article on the Internet is correct.

Before you write a first draft of your report, read the following model. Notice the characteristics of a research report.

Jennifer Rosario

"Remember the Alamo"

In Texas's struggle for independence from Mexico, the siege of the Alamo in 1836 was a key event. Although the Alamo's defenders were all killed, their bravery made other Texans even more determined to win independence. ← **Introduction**

The Alamo began as a Spanish mission in about 1718. Located in what is now San Antonio, the mission included a church and monastery surrounded by high walls. After the mission closed, some Mexican soldiers used it as a fort. It became known as the Alamo, after the Mexican town the soldiers came from, Álamo de Parras.

In 1835, the American settlers in Texas began a revolt against the Mexican government. The Texans did not like being ruled by Mexico and wanted to form an independent country. Several important events and battles happened during 1835 and 1836, a period called the Texas Revolution.

In December 1835, Texas soldiers defeated Mexican troops at San Antonio. The victory alarmed General Antonio López de Santa Anna so much that he led a Mexican army of several thousand soldiers to San Antonio. The Texans withdrew to the Alamo. ← **Body of report, including subtopics supporting main idea**

The Mexican army attacked the group of fewer than 200 soldiers in the Alamo on February 23, 1836. Greatly outnumbered, the Alamo's defenders lasted until March 6. When they ran out of ammunition, the men fought with knives, sticks, and fists until they were all killed.

Although the Texas Revolution suffered more setbacks after that, the fierce Alamo battle inspired other Texans. At the Battle of San Jacinto on April 21, 1836, Texas soldiers shouted, "Remember the Alamo!" as they defeated Santa Anna's troops.

2

The Alamo siege shows how one historic event can
influence the outcome of a larger event—in this
case, the independence of Texas.

← Conclusion

Sources

"Alamo, The." <u>Microsoft Encarta Online Encyclopedia</u>.
©1997–2002. Microsoft Corp. Sept. 9, 2002.
<u>http://encarta.msn.com</u>.

Burgan, Michael. <u>The Alamo</u>. Minneapolis: Compass
Point Books, 2001.

Fisher, Leonard Everett. <u>The Alamo</u>. New York:
Holiday House, 1987.

← Sources

2 **Draft** Use the model and your outline to write your report.

3 **Edit** Work in pairs. Trade papers and read each other's reports. Use the editing checklist to evaluate each other's work.

EDITING CHECKLIST

Did you . . .

▶ state the main idea of your report in the first paragraph?

▶ clearly organize your subtopics?

▶ use several sources?

▶ present the information in your own words?

▶ check your facts, grammar, and punctuation?

▶ use possessive adjectives and pronouns correctly?

▶ use comparative and superlative adjectives correctly?

▲ An artist's depiction of the last fight for the Alamo

4 **Revise** Revise your report. Add details and correct mistakes, if necessary.

5 **Publish** Share your report with your teacher and classmates.

PROJECTS

Work in pairs or small groups. Choose one of these projects.

1 Use the library or Internet to research information about a historical place in your state. Then share the information with the class.

2 Read a tall tale about Pecos Bill, Paul Bunyan, Johnny Appleseed, John Henry, or another character. Then retell the story to the class.

3 Write a short play about how Pecos Bill becomes a coyote. You can use the dialogue in the story on pages 200–205 or your own words. One student can be the narrator and the others can be the main characters. Practice acting out the play. Then perform your play for the class.

4 Imagine that you are a teenager living during another time. Write daily diary entries to represent one week in your life.

5 Make up a new tall tale about Pecos Bill or another character. Include hyperbole. Create illustrations for your tall tale.

6 Play "Match the Word and Definition." Use index cards to make two sets of playing cards. Write each key word on one index card in one set. On cards in the other set, write a simple definition for each key word. Place each set of cards facedown. Take turns turning over two cards. When a player turns over two matching cards (word and definition), he or she removes the cards from the table and gets one point. The player with the greater number of points at the end of the game wins. You can add key words and definitions from other units.

Further Reading

To find out more about the theme of this unit, choose from these reading suggestions.

***The Jungle Book*, Rudyard Kipling** A family of wolves takes a young boy into its home in the jungle and names him Mowgli. The child plays with the wolf cubs and makes friends with Bagheera the panther and Baloo the bear. But can Mowgli, a man-cub, live in the jungle and learn how to speak and hunt the way the animals do? And will the tiger called Shere Khan catch him?

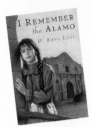

***I Remember the Alamo*, D. Anne Love** Jessie's family moves to Texas during the Texas rebellion. The family ends up in San Antonio, where Jessie makes friends with a Mexican girl. Jessie, her mother, and the younger children seek safety in the Alamo before the siege. Her father and older brother join the Texas soldiers at Goliad. After the Alamo falls, Santa Anna tells the women and children to leave Texas. But they still don't know the fate of Jessie's father and brother.

***The Great Turkey Walk*, Kathleen Karr** Teenager Simon Green decides to drive 1,000 turkeys from Missouri to Denver, Colorado, in 1860. Although Simon is not a good student, he is clever at business. He can buy turkeys for $.25 apiece in Missouri and sell them for $5.00 apiece in Denver. So he borrows money and accidentally finds some partners to help him walk his turkey herd to Denver.

***In the Days of the Vaqueros*, Russell Freedman** During the 1500s, Spanish colonists settling in Mexico brought along cattle and horses. They had to round up their cattle once or twice a year to brand and count them. The vaqueros, or cowherds, who rounded up the cattle were greatly admired for their horseback-riding and cattle-roping skills. Later, vaqueros taught their skills to settlers on the American frontier.

***The Longest Ride*, Denise Lewis Patrick** Midnight Son is a fifteen-year-old African-American cowboy and runaway slave. He and his best friend are caught in a blizzard in Colorado. When Midnight Son gets lost and injured, some Arapaho take him to their village. Although Midnight Son wants to search for his family, he decides he must first help his new Arapaho friends. While helping them and searching for his family, Midnight Son learns truths about life.

Observing the Universe

PART 1

- "Earth's Orbit"
- "How Glooskap Found the Summer"
- "Persephone and the Pomegranate Seeds"

PART 2

- *The Great Bear,* Pamela Gerke
- "Telescopes"

Since people first noticed the movement of the stars and the changing seasons, they have looked for explanations for those events. Long ago, many groups of people created stories, which we now call myths, to explain natural events. Later, people looked for scientific explanations.

In Part 1, you will read a science article about how Earth's movement in space causes the seasons. Then you will read a Native American myth and an ancient Greek myth explaining why the seasons change.

In Part 2, you will read a play about the creation of a constellation, or group of stars, known as the Great Bear. The play is based on a Mongolian myth. Then you will read about how to make a telescope so that you can observe planets and stars on your own.

Prepare to Read

BACKGROUND

"Earth's Orbit" is a science article. It contains factual information about how Earth moves around the sun. It also contains information about the seasons and how different cultures created calendars.

Make connections Think about and discuss these questions.

1. What do you know about Earth's movement around the sun?
2. What causes day and night?
3. Why is it hot in some places and cold in others?
4. What causes the seasons?

▲ An Aztec calendar stone, which the Aztec people of Mexico made more than 500 years ago, shows their ideas about creation, time, and space.

axis
equator
Northern Hemisphere
Southern Hemisphere
North Pole
South Pole
orbit
rotation

VOCABULARY

Look at the diagram of Earth. Read the labels. Use the diagram to figure out the meaning of the labels. Use a dictionary to check your answers. Write each word and its meaning in your notebook.

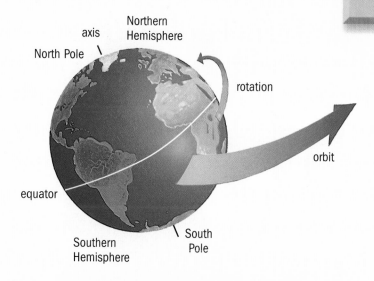

axis
Northern Hemisphere
North Pole
rotation
orbit
equator
Southern Hemisphere
South Pole

READING STRATEGY

Studying Diagrams

Studying diagrams can help you understand a text better. Science texts often include diagrams. When you read a text with diagrams, follow these steps.

- Read each section of the text.
- Look for a diagram that illustrates the section.
- Study the diagram.
- Read any labels on the diagram.
- Reread the section of the text.

As part of your previewing process, look at the diagrams throughout the article. After you read each section, look at the diagrams more carefully and read the labels. Then reread the section. How do the diagrams help you understand the text better?

Earth's Orbit

Earth's Rotation: Measuring Day and Night

The study of the planets, stars, and other objects in space is called astronomy. The word *astronomy* comes from two Greek words: *ástron*, which means "star," and *nomos*, which means "a system of knowledge about a subject." An astronomer is someone who studies the stars.

Ancient astronomers also studied the movements of the sun and moon. They thought that the sun and moon were moving around Earth. In fact, the sun and moon seem to move across the sky each day because Earth is rotating, or turning, on its axis. Earth's axis is the **imaginary** line that goes through Earth's center and the North Pole and South Pole. The turning of Earth on its axis is called its rotation.

23.5° North Pole

Sun's rays

Equator

Sun's rays

South Pole

▲ Earth rotates on its axis every 24 hours. Earth's rotational axis tilts at a 23.5 degree angle in relation to the sun.

---

imaginary, not real; in your mind

226

Earth's rotation on its axis causes day and night. As Earth rotates to the east, the sun appears to move to the west across the sky. It is day on the side of Earth that **faces** the sun. As Earth continues to rotate to the east, the sun appears to set in the west. Sunlight can't reach the side of Earth that faces away from the sun, so it is dark (night) there. It takes Earth 24 hours to rotate one complete turn on its axis. This 24-hour **cycle** is called a day.

Earth's Revolution: Measuring a Year

As well as rotating on its axis, Earth is traveling around the sun. The movement of one object around another object is called a revolution. Earth's path as it **revolves** around the sun is called its orbit. Earth's orbit is not really a circle. It is actually an oval, or egg, shape.

▲ Earth revolves around the sun in an oval orbit.

Earth's orbit around the sun takes about 365 days. In measuring four years of Earth's orbit, three years have 365 days and the fourth year has 366 days. This fourth year with an extra day is known as a leap year. During a leap year, February has 29 days instead of the usual 28 days.

Long ago, people tried to divide the year into smaller parts. They used moon cycles—the time between **full moons**—as a kind of calendar. There are about 29.5 days between full moons. However, a year of 12 moon cycles, or months, adds up to only 354 days. The ancient Egyptians created a calendar that had 12 months of 30 days each, with 5 days left over. The ancient Romans borrowed this calendar and made changes to it. With more changes, the Roman calendar finally became the calendar we use today. It consists of 11 months of 30 or 31 days each, plus 1 month of 28 or 29 days.

---

faces, points or looks toward
cycle, series of events that happen again and again in a repeating pattern
as well as, in addition to
revolves, moves in a circle around something
full moons, times when the moon looks completely round

BEFORE YOU GO ON . . .

1 How long does Earth take to rotate on its axis?

2 How long does Earth take to revolve around the sun?

HOW ABOUT YOU?

• When is the next full moon? Find it on a calendar.

How Sunlight Hits Earth

The equator is an imaginary line around Earth, halfway between the North and South poles. The equator divides Earth into two parts—the Northern Hemisphere and the Southern Hemisphere. It is always cold around the North and South poles and hot around the equator. The warm area around the equator is sometimes called the tropics. Most places outside the tropics have four seasons: winter, spring, summer, and autumn (also called fall).

Why are there different temperatures in different places on Earth? In the tropics, sunlight travels to Earth's surface most **directly**. As a result, the sun's energy—in the form of heat—is very strong. Closer to the North and South poles, sunlight hits Earth's surface more **indirectly**—**at an angle**. Near the poles, sunlight is spread out over a greater area. Therefore, its energy and heat are less strong, and the temperatures are much colder.

---

directly, in a straight line or path
indirectly, not directly
at an angle, not upright or straight

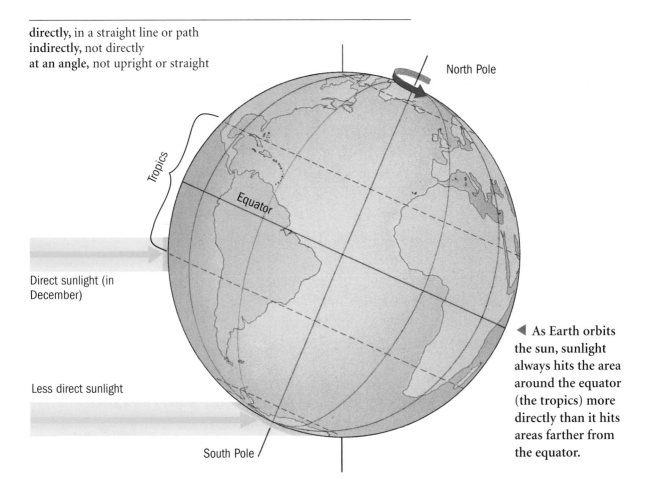

North Pole

Tropics

Equator

Direct sunlight (in December)

Less direct sunlight

South Pole

◀ As Earth orbits the sun, sunlight always hits the area around the equator (the tropics) more directly than it hits areas farther from the equator.

JUNE

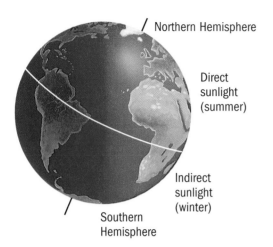

Northern Hemisphere

Direct
sunlight
(summer)

Indirect
sunlight
(winter)

Southern
Hemisphere

◀ JUNE
In June, the Northern Hemisphere is tilted toward
the sun. The sun's energy hits the Northern
Hemisphere more directly, so it is summer there.
The sun's energy hits the Southern Hemisphere
less directly, so it is winter there.

DECEMBER

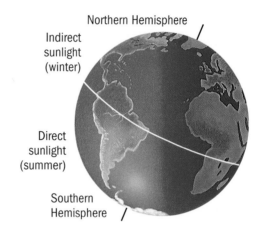

Northern Hemisphere

Indirect
sunlight
(winter)

Direct
sunlight
(summer)

Southern
Hemisphere

Why Earth Has Seasons

Why do temperatures around the world change with
the seasons? Earth's axis is **tilted** as it revolves around the
sun. The axis always points in the same direction. For part
of the year, Earth's axis is tilted away from the sun. For
another part of the year, the axis is tilted toward the sun.
When the north part of Earth's axis is tilted toward the
sun, it is summer in the Northern Hemisphere and winter
in the Southern Hemisphere. When the south part of
Earth's axis is tilted toward the sun, it is summer in the
Southern Hemisphere and winter in the Northern
Hemisphere.

Summer and Winter in the Northern and Southern Hemispheres

In June, the north part of Earth's axis is tilted toward
the sun. The hemisphere that is tilted toward the sun has
more hours of daylight than the hemisphere tilted away

▲ DECEMBER
In December, the Southern
Hemisphere is tilted toward the
sun. The sun's energy hits the
Southern Hemisphere more
directly, so it is summer there.
The sun's energy hits the
Northern Hemisphere less
directly, so it is winter there.

BEFORE YOU GO ON . . .

1 Why is the area near the
equator hot?

2 When is it summer in the
Northern Hemisphere? In
the Southern Hemisphere?

HOW ABOUT YOU?
• Describe the seasons in
your region.

---

tilted, with one side higher than the other, leaning

from the sun. The combination of direct sunlight and more hours of daylight creates summer in the Northern Hemisphere. At the same time, the Southern Hemisphere has fewer hours of daylight and indirect sunlight. The combination of indirect sunlight and fewer hours of daylight creates winter in the Southern Hemisphere.

In December, the Southern Hemisphere has more direct sunlight, so it is summer there. At the same time, the Northern Hemisphere has indirect sunlight and fewer hours of daylight. It is winter there.

Latitude and Solstices

Latitude is a measurement of distance north or south from the equator. Latitude is measured in degrees (°) north or south. For example, the equator is at latitude 0°, and the North Pole is at 90° north latitude. On two days each year, the noon sun is **overhead** at either 23.5° south latitude or 23.5° north latitude. Each of these days is called a solstice.

---

overhead, above your head

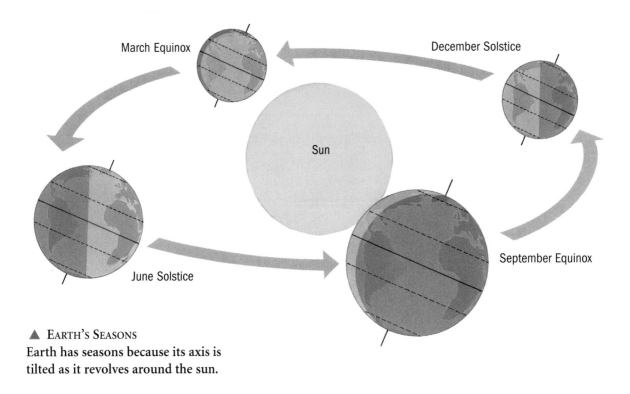

March Equinox

December Solstice

Sun

September Equinox

June Solstice

▲ EARTH'S SEASONS
Earth has seasons because its axis is tilted as it revolves around the sun.

▲ STONEHENGE
In about 1500 B.C.E., ancient peoples in what is now England completed Stonehenge, a giant stone monument. It is thought that they arranged the stones to record the sun's movements, such as the summer and winter solstices and the spring and autumnal equinoxes.

Each year on about December 21, the noon sun is overhead at 23.5° south latitude. This is the winter solstice in the Northern Hemisphere and the summer solstice in the Southern Hemisphere. It is the shortest day of the year in the Northern Hemisphere and the longest day of the year in the Southern Hemisphere. Similarly, on about June 21, the noon sun is overhead at 23.5° north latitude. This is the summer solstice in the Northern Hemisphere and the winter solstice in the Southern Hemisphere.

Equinoxes

On two days each year, the noon sun is directly overhead at the equator. **Neither** hemisphere is closer to or farther from the sun. Each of these days is called an equinox, which means "equal night." During an equinox, night and day are about the same length of time. The vernal equinox (spring equinox) occurs on about March 21 and marks the beginning of spring in the Northern Hemisphere. The **autumnal** equinox occurs on about September 23. It marks the beginning of autumn (fall) in the Northern Hemisphere.

---

neither, not one and not the other
autumnal, related to autumn, or fall

BEFORE YOU GO ON . . .

1 What is a solstice?

2 What is an equinox?

HOW ABOUT YOU?
- What is the latitude of your city or town? Find it on a map.

231

Review and Practice

Reread "Earth's Orbit." Copy the cause-and-effect chart into your notebook.
Use the words and phrases below to complete the chart.

summer	vernal equinox	summer solstice in Southern Hemisphere
winter	hot temperatures	autumnal equinox
day and night	cold temperatures	summer solstice in Northern Hemisphere

Cause	Effect
1. noon sun overhead at 23.5° north	*summer solstice in Northern Hemisphere*
2. indirect sunlight and fewer daylight hours	
3. noon sun directly over equator on about September 23	
4. noon sun overhead at 23.5° south	
5. noon sun directly over the equator on about March 21	
6. Earth's 24-hour rotation	
7. sun shines indirectly on an area	
8. direct sunlight and more daylight hours	
9. sun shines directly on an area	

EXTENSION

Copy the chart into your notebook. Complete it with holidays or celebrations that take place during each season. Then compare charts.

Spring	Summer	Autumn	Winter

DISCUSSION

Discuss in pairs or small groups.

1. In which season does your region get the most daylight? The least daylight?

2. Which month is the hottest where you live? The coldest?

3. Why doesn't it usually get as cold in Buenos Aires, Argentina, in the winter as it does in New York City in the winter?

4. Do you know about any calendars other than the one we use today? If so, describe them.

◄ New Yorkers ice-skate in Central Park in Manhattan during the winter.

Myths

Myths are fictional stories that often attempt to explain something about nature. "How Glooskap Found the Summer" is a Native American myth of the Algonquin people. "Persephone and the Pomegranate Seeds" is an ancient Greek myth. Both myths explain why Earth has seasons.

HOW GLOOSKAP FOUND THE SUMMER

Long ago, the Wawaniki people lived in the northeastern part of North America. Their leader's name was Glooskap.

One time, it grew very cold. Snow and ice were everywhere, and plants could not grow. The Wawaniki began to die from the cold and **famine**. Glooskap traveled far north, where the land was all ice. He came to a **wigwam**, where he found Winter. Winter was a **giant** with icy breath. Winter's breath was so cold, it had frozen all the land. Glooskap entered Winter's wigwam and sat down. Winter told him stories of the old times, when he, Winter, ruled Earth, when all the land was white and beautiful. As Winter talked, Glooskap fell asleep. Winter **put a charm on** Glooskap, and he slept for six months.

---

famine, time when there is not enough food
wigwam, a home Native Americans often made by
  covering a frame with bark or animal skins
giant, very large, strong person (in myths and
  children's stories)
put a charm on, used his power on

LITERARY ELEMENT

A *hero* or *heroine* is a character in a story whose actions are inspiring or noble. Heroes and heroines often struggle to solve or overcome a problem. The word *hero* was originally used only for heroic male characters, and *heroine* for heroic female characters. Today, however, the word *hero* can be used for either a male or a female character. Who is the hero or heroine in this story?

Finally, Glooskap woke up. A wild bird named Tatler the Loon came and told him about a country in the south that was always warm. The bird said that a queen lived there who could make Winter go away. "I must save my people," Glooskap thought. So he decided to go south and find the queen.

Glooskap traveled south until he came to a warm forest with many flowers and trees. There he found Summer, the fairy queen. Glooskap knew that Summer could make Winter go away, so he said to her, "Come with me to the land in the far north." Summer agreed to go with Glooskap.

When they reached Winter's wigwam, Winter welcomed them. "I'll make them fall asleep," Winter thought. But this time, Glooskap's power was stronger because Summer was with him. First, Glooskap and Summer made **sweat** run down Winter's face. Winter started to cry because he was losing his power. Next, Winter's icy wigwam **melted**. Then Summer used her power, and everything woke up: The grass and flowers grew, leaves appeared on trees, and the snow ran down the rivers. "My power is gone!" Winter cried.

Then Summer said, "I have proved that I am stronger than you. So now I will give you all the country to the far north. Six months of every year you may come back to Glooskap's country. During the other six months, I will come back to his land."

"I accept your offer," Winter whispered sadly. So every autumn, Winter returns to Glooskap's country and brings cold and snow. When he comes, Summer runs home to her land in the south. But at the end of six months, Summer always returns to **drive Winter away** and bring back the grass, leaves, and flowers.

---

drive Winter away, make Winter go away

---

sweat, liquid that comes out of your skin when you are hot
melted, ice changed to water by heat

BEFORE YOU GO ON . . .

1 What problem do the Wawaniki people have?
2 How does Summer help Glooskap?

HOW ABOUT YOU?

• In this story, Winter puts a charm on Glooskap. Do you know of another story like this one? If so, describe it.

Persephone and the Pomegranate Seeds

▲ **Pomegranate seeds and fruit**

Long ago, Demeter, the goddess of **agriculture**, had a beautiful daughter named Persephone. Demeter helped trees and plants grow on Earth. Pluto, the god of the **underworld**, lived under Earth, where it was always dark and cold. Pluto wanted a wife, but no one wanted to leave the sunshine to live in Pluto's dark world underground.

One day Pluto saw Persephone while she was picking flowers. He wanted to marry her, but he knew that Demeter would say no. So he rode a **chariot** and took Persephone to the underworld. As they were crossing a river, Persephone dropped her flowers into the water.

The river took the flowers to Demeter. Demeter asked Zeus, the king of the gods, to help her get Persephone back. Zeus answered, "I'll send my **messenger**, Hermes, to the underworld. But if Persephone eats anything there, she cannot return to Earth."

Pluto knew that if Persephone ate anything, she must stay with him. So he gave her twelve pomegranate seeds. She was very hungry and started to eat. While she was eating, Hermes arrived.

---

agriculture, farming, especially growing crops
underworld, place where the spirits of the dead lived
   (in ancient Greek mythology)
chariot, ancient vehicle that horses pulled
messenger, someone who takes information from one
   person to another

LITERARY ELEMENT

Conflict is a struggle between opposing, or opposite, forces. Conflict is important in stories because it causes action. Conflict can be between characters or between groups of people. It can also be between a character and a force of nature or can take place in a character's mind. What is the conflict in this story?

"Persephone, did you eat the twelve seeds?" he inquired.

"I ate only six," she replied. Hermes didn't know what to do, so he returned to Zeus.

Zeus said, "Persephone ate six seeds, so she must stay in the underworld six months a year. She can spend the other six months on Earth with Demeter."

And that is why there are six cold months of autumn and winter each year, and six warm months of spring and summer.

BEFORE YOU GO ON . . .

1 What does Pluto give Persephone? Why?

2 What does Zeus decide?

HOW ABOUT YOU?
- How many months of cold weather do you have in your city or town? How many months of warm weather?

Link the Readings

REFLECTION

Reread the article and stories. Copy the chart into your notebook and complete it. Then compare your charts in small groups.

Title of Selection	Genre	Fiction or Nonfiction	Purpose of Selection	How It Explains the Seasons
"Earth's Orbit"				
"How Glooskap Found the Summer"				
"Persephone and the Pomegranate Seeds"				

DISCUSSION

Discuss in pairs or small groups.

1. Which season do you like the best? The least? Explain.

2. Do you know any other myths about the seasons? If so, what are they?

3. At first, Zeus says that Persephone cannot return to Earth if she eats anything in the underworld. Later, Zeus decides to make Persephone stay in the underworld for six months and spend the other six months on Earth. Do you think Zeus's decision is fair? Explain. If you were Zeus, what would you do?

▲ *Demeter Mourning for Persephone*
(Evelyn de Morgan)

237

Connect to Writing

GRAMMAR

Using Quotations

A **quotation** is a speaker's exact words repeated in a text. The speaker's exact words are written between quotation marks. A subject and a reporting verb usually introduce the quotation. Use a comma after the reporting verb. Look at the examples.

Zeus said, "Persephone must stay in the underworld six months a year."

subject	reporting verb	quotation
Zeus	said,	"Persephone must stay in the underworld six months a year."

The subject and reporting verb can also come after the quotation. In statements, use a comma instead of a period at the end of a quotation that is followed by the subject and reporting verb. Put a question mark at the end of a question quotation.

"Persephone, did you eat the twelve seeds?" he inquired.
"I ate only six," she replied.

quotation	subject	reporting verb
"Persephone, did you eat the twelve seeds?"	he	inquired.
"I ate only six,"	she	replied.

Practice

Copy these sentences into your notebook. Add quotation marks and correct punctuation to show the speakers' exact words. Underline the reporting verbs.

1. Tatler the Loon said There is a country that is always warm.

2. Where is this country? asked Glooskap.

3. It's in the south Tatler answered.

4. Winter cried My power is gone!

5. Summer said You may come back for six months of every year.

6. I accept your offer Winter whispered sadly.

SKILLS FOR WRITING

Writing Dialogue

Dialogue is conversation between characters in a story. Dialogue can make the story more entertaining. In a story, use quotation marks to show dialogue.

Good writers use a variety of reporting verbs to make dialogue more interesting. Some reporting verbs show different purposes for speaking.

DIALOGUE TIPS

- Use quotation marks to show each character's exact words.
- Make your dialogue sound natural—the way people really talk.
- Use a variety of reporting verbs.

- *asked* or *inquired* (reporting a question)
- *responded* or *replied* (reporting an answer)
- *said* or *stated* (reporting an idea or opinion)
- *thought* (reporting a thought)

Other verbs describe the manner, or way, of speaking.

- *whispered* or *murmured* (describing quiet or soft speaking)
- *yelled, shouted,* or *cried* (describing loud or excited speaking)

Reread the myths "How Glooskap Found the Summer" and "Persephone and the Pomegranate Seeds." Then answer these questions.

1. Which characters have dialogue in the myths?

2. What reporting verbs do the writers use?

3. Which reporting verbs show the purpose for speaking? Which reporting verbs show the manner of speaking?

Sundial on a cathedral in France ▶

239

WRITING ASSIGNMENT

Myth

You will write a short myth to explain a natural event.

1. **Read** Review "How Glooskap Found the Summer" on pages 234–235 and "Persephone and the Pomegranate Seeds" on page 236. Who are the characters? What are the settings, problems or conflicts, and solutions?

Writing Strategy: Story Chart

A story chart can help you write your myth. Look at the story chart for the myth "How Glooskap Found the Summer."

Characters	Setting (Time and Place)
• *Glooskap (leader of Wawaniki people)* • *Winter (giant with icy breath)* • *Tatler the Loon (wild bird who knows many things)* • *Summer (fairy queen with great power)*	• *Long ago* • *Glooskap's land (northeastern part of North America)* • *Winter's land (far north, where land is all ice)* • *Summer's land (warm, in the south)*

Problem or Conflict	Solution
The Wawaniki people are dying from cold and famine. Glooskap finds out that Winter has frozen the land.	*Glooskap travels to Summer's land. Glooskap and Summer make Winter sweat and cry. His wigwam melts. Summer and Winter agree to stay in Glooskap's country for six months each.*

2. **Make a story chart** Think of an idea for your own myth. For example, why does the sun rise and set every day? Make a story chart for the myth in your notebook. Describe the characters, setting, problem or conflict, and solution.

3. **Write a myth** Use your story chart to help you write a short myth. Include dialogue.

EDITING CHECKLIST

Did you . . .

▶ write a myth about a natural event?

▶ include characters, a setting, a problem or conflict, and a solution?

▶ include dialogue and reporting verbs?

▶ use natural language in the dialogue?

Check Your Knowledge

Language Development

1. How can a diagram help you learn new words? How else can diagrams help you understand a text?

2. In what other ways can you use diagrams?

3. What is a myth? How can a story chart help you write a myth?

4. What is dialogue?

5. What do quotation marks show?

Academic Content

1. What new science vocabulary did you learn in Part 1? What do the words mean?

2. Why do temperatures around the world change with the seasons? Why is it hot near the equator and cold near the North and South poles?

3. What are some similarities and differences between the Greek myth and the Native American myth you read in Part 1?

OBJECTIVES

LANGUAGE DEVELOPMENT

Reading:
- Vocabulary building: *Context, dictionary skills*
- Reading strategy: *Reading plays aloud*
- Text types: *Play, science article*
- Literary elements: *Narrator, stage directions*

Writing:
- Story map
- Skit with dialogue and stage directions

Listening/Speaking:
- Read a play aloud
- Retell a story
- Identifying with a character

Grammar:
- Prepositional phrases

Viewing/Representing:
- Diagrams

ACADEMIC CONTENT
- Science vocabulary
- Constellations
- Telescopes

BACKGROUND

The Great Bear is a short play, or story that actors perform in a theater. This play is based on a myth of the Mongol people in the Ordos Desert region of northern China. The myth explains the creation of a constellation, or group of stars, called Ursa Major—the Great Bear.

Make connections Look at the constellation called Ursa Major. Seven bright stars called the Big Dipper form part of the bear's body and the tail. (A dipper is a cup with a long handle used for dipping.) Less bright stars form the bear's head and legs. Why do you think people called this constellation Ursa Major, or the Great Bear?

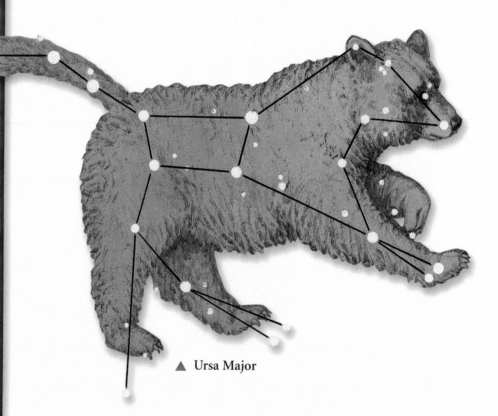

▲ Ursa Major

adventurers
conquer
contest
match
palace
realm

VOCABULARY

Read these sentences. Use the context to figure out the meaning of the **red** words. Use a dictionary to check your answers. Write each word and its meaning in your notebook.

1. **Adventurers** always look for exciting things to do and new places to discover.

2. The king's army is trying to **conquer** his enemies and end the fighting.

3. We had a **contest** to find the fastest swimmer.

4. The tennis **match** took more than an hour, but I finally won.

5. The queen's **palace** is the largest building in the country.

6. The queen has ruled over her **realm** for many years.

READING STRATEGY

Reading Plays Aloud

Reading a play aloud brings the story and characters to life. It allows the actors (the people performing) and the audience (the people watching) to participate in and enjoy the story.

To read a play aloud, follow these steps.

1. Read the list of characters. Choose one person (actor) to be each character. Each actor will speak a character's lines, or words.

2. Read the play to yourself. Pay special attention to your lines and the stage directions. Stage directions tell actors how to look, move, and speak when they read their lines.

3. Read the play aloud as a group. Listen carefully to the other actors so you know when to say your lines.

A boy uses a telescope to look at stars. ▶

243

Plays are usually divided into parts, called scenes. The Great Bear has six scenes. When you read your lines, try to sound like the character you are playing. The stage directions will tell you more about your part. (You read stage directions silently, not out loud.) Read the play aloud as a class.

The Great Bear

Pamela Gerke

CHARACTERS: Narrator, Two Hunters, Sky Shooter, Great Listener, Mountain Lifter, Swift Runner, Sea Swallower, Khan's son, Khan, Chief Archer, Warriors, Chief Wrestler, Old Woman Runner, Warrior

SCENE 1

(Setting: The Ordos Desert region of China)

NARRATOR: Long ago, in the Ordos Desert region of the land we now call China, between the Yellow River, the **Hwang Ho**, and the Great Wall of China, two young adventurers went hunting.
(HUNTERS enter, possibly carrying bows and arrows.)

NARRATOR: They soon met a young man who carried a bow and arrows.
(SKY SHOOTER enters, gazing up at the sky.)

HUNTERS: What are you doing?

Hwang Ho, another name for the Yellow River

SKY SHOOTER: This morning I shot a bird flying in **heaven** and now I'm waiting for it to fall.

(SOUND: Slide whistle. Bird with arrow in it falls from the sky.)

HUNTERS: *(To each other:)* And we thought *we* were good hunters! *(To Sky Shooter:)* Will you be our **blood brother** and travel with us?

SKY SHOOTER: Okay!

(They travel to the top of a mountain as GREAT LISTENER enters there and places her ear to the ground.)

NARRATOR: On top of the next mountain they saw a woman lying down with her ear to the ground.

---

heaven, the sky
blood brother/blood sister, a very good friend, who is like a brother or sister but isn't related to you

HUNTERS and **SKY SHOOTER:** What are you doing?

GREAT LISTENER: I'm listening to the earth and sky. I can hear everything that people are saying in both worlds.

HUNTERS and **SKY SHOOTER:** *(To each other:)* And we thought *we* had good ears! *(To GREAT LISTENER:)* Will you be our **blood sister** and travel with us?

GREAT LISTENER: Okay!

(They continue to travel as MOUNTAIN LIFTER enters and moves around two mountains.)

NARRATOR: Soon they came to a man standing between two mountains, which he kept moving about.

HUNTERS, SKY SHOOTER, and **GREAT LISTENER:** What are you doing?

MOUNTAIN LIFTER: I'm just exercising, to cure the rheumatism in my arms.

HUNTERS, SKY SHOOTER, and **GREAT LISTENER:** And we thought *we* were strong! *(To MOUNTAIN LIFTER:)* Will you be our blood brother and travel with us?

MOUNTAIN LIFTER: Okay!
(They continue to travel as SWIFT RUNNER and GAZELLES enter. SWIFT RUNNER chases the GAZELLES, captures them one by one, and then lets them loose.)

NARRATOR: On an open plain they saw a woman chasing gazelles, capturing them one by one, then letting them loose.

HUNTERS, SKY SHOOTER, GREAT LISTENER, and **MOUNTAIN LIFTER:** What are you doing?

SWIFT RUNNER: I'm just playing with these gazelles.

HUNTERS, SKY SHOOTER, GREAT LISTENER, and **MOUNTAIN LIFTER:** And we thought *we* were fast! *(To SWIFT RUNNER:)* Will you be our blood sister and travel with us?

SWIFT RUNNER: Okay!
(They continue to travel.)

NARRATOR: As the adventurers traveled, they wondered what they should do to earn their living. They asked Great Listener to put her ear to the ground and

find out what was happening on earth.
(GREAT LISTENER does so.)

GREAT LISTENER: Beyond the great sea a khan named Sadzaghai is making plans to conquer our empire. Let's stop him!

ALL OTHERS: Great idea!

NARRATOR: They set off at once for the realm of Khan Sadzaghai.
(They travel to the sea while SEA SWALLOWER enters there.)

NARRATOR: Soon they came to the great sea and asked the woman sitting there how they could cross the water.

---

rheumatism, a condition that makes joints and
  muscles painful and stiff
swift, very fast
gazelles, very fast animals, similar to deer
chasing, running after and trying to catch
earn their living, make money to live on

khan, Mongolian king
empire, group of countries that one king or queen
  controls

SEA SWALLOWER: That's easy!

(*SEA SWALLOWER "swallows" all the water—actor actually stuffs a blue cloth in her shirt while pretending to swallow it.*)

SEA SWALLOWER: Now you can cross!

ALL OTHERS: And we thought *we* had big mouths! (*To SEA SWALLOWER:*) Will you be our blood sister and travel with us?

SEA SWALLOWER: Okay!

(*They travel across the **seabed**. When they get to the other side, SEA SWALLOWER "spits" out the water. They continue to travel. KHAN'S SON enters.*)

NARRATOR: After a while they met a handsome young man carrying a bow and arrow. They told him they were going to the city of Khan Sadzaghai.

KHAN'S SON: Why are you going there?

ALL OTHERS: We would like to serve the khan.

KHAN'S SON: Then let's go to his palace. I am the khan's son!

(*All exit.*)

---

seabed, land at the bottom of the ocean

SCENE 2

(*Setting: The khan's palace. The KHAN'S SON and ADVENTURERS enter near the palace gate.*)

NARRATOR: The khan's son **escorted** them to a **magnificent** city. He left them at the gate to the palace while he went to tell his father of their arrival. (*KHAN'S SON goes into the palace as KHAN enters there.*)

KHAN'S SON: Father, today I met seven young adventurers who want to **serve** you.

KHAN: Are they worthy? Tomorrow we'll test them and see! Here's my plan. (*KHAN and KHAN'S SON **pantomime** talking together. Meanwhile, GREAT LISTENER puts her ear to the ground.*)

GREAT LISTENER: (*To the others:*) They say that tomorrow we'll have an **archery** contest.

SKY SHOOTER: Don't worry, I'll take care of it!

---

escorted, took someone from one place to another
magnificent, very beautiful and big
serve, do a helpful job for
pantomime, act without using words
archery, sport of shooting arrows from a bow at a target

BEFORE YOU GO ON . . .

1 How does Sea Swallower help the group cross the water?

2 What do the adventurers say they want to do in the khan's city?

HOW ABOUT YOU?

- Why do you think the khan wants to test the adventurers?

SCENE 3

(Setting: The same, next morning.)

NARRATOR: The next day the adventurers met with the khan, his chief archer, and some of his best warriors.
(CHIEF ARCHER and OTHER WARRIORS enter. All meet center stage.)

SKY SHOOTER: *(To CHIEF ARCHER:)* You can go first.
*(CHIEF ARCHER pantomimes shooting an arrow. SKY SHOOTER shoots, and the arrow goes farther. The ADVENTURERS **cheer** while KHAN and **CO.** are angry.)*

NARRATOR: Sky Shooter easily **defeated** the khan's chief archer, and the khan was **outraged**. He gathered his warriors together to plan the next contest.

---

cheer, shout in encouragement
CO., abbreviation for *company* (group of people that you work with or spend time with)
defeated, won against
outraged, very angry

*(KHAN, KHAN'S SON, and WARRIORS **huddle** together and pantomime talking, while in another area of the stage the ADVENTURERS gather around GREAT LISTENER while she puts her ear to the ground.)*

GREAT LISTENER: *(To the ADVENTURERS:)* They say that tomorrow we'll have a **wrestling** match.

MOUNTAIN LIFTER: Don't worry, I'll take care of it!
(ADVENTURERS go to the area by the palace gate, lie down, and go to sleep.)

NARRATOR: The adventurers found a place to sleep outside the palace gate. Meanwhile, the khan and his warriors went out into a field where there were trees growing at one end. They pulled some of the trees out by their roots and then stuck them in the ground at the other end.

*(WARRIORS pick up some of the trees and place them on the other side of the stage, **downstage**.)*

SCENE 4

(Setting: The same, next morning.)

NARRATOR: The next morning, they all gathered on the field.
(The ADVENTURERS wake up and go to center stage, where they meet the others.)

NARRATOR: The khan explained the rules of the wrestling contest.

---

huddle, move close together in a small group
wrestling, fighting by holding and trying to push or pull someone down
downstage, toward the front of a stage

KHAN: Our chief wrestler will start at this end *(points to end with the **uprooted** trees)*, and your wrestler will start at the other end *(points to other trees)*. They must pull out the trees as they move toward each other.

(CHIEF WRESTLER goes to the side with the uprooted trees. MOUNTAIN LIFTER goes to the other side. As the contest begins, the wrestlers pull up the trees and fling them aside as they come toward each other. CHIEF WRESTLER has trouble lifting trees, while MOUNTAIN LIFTER lifts trees fast and easily. They meet in the center and wrestle. MOUNTAIN LIFTER wins easily. The ADVENTURERS cheer; KHAN and CO. are angry.)

NARRATOR: Mountain Lifter easily won. The khan was terribly angry—being beaten once was bad enough, but *twice* was **intolerable**. He and his warriors huddled to choose a contest that would surely **destroy** the seven strangers.
(KHAN, KHAN'S SON, and WARRIORS huddle and pantomime talking, while in another area of the stage, GREAT LISTENER puts her ear to the ground.)

GREAT LISTENER: *(To the others:)* They say that tomorrow we'll have a footrace.

SWIFT RUNNER: Don't worry, I'll take care of it!

---

uprooted, taken out of the ground by the roots
intolerable, too difficult or unpleasant to accept
destroy, beat; defeat

SCENE 5

(Setting: The same, the next morning.)

NARRATOR: The next morning, Swift Runner met her **opponent**: an old woman with very long legs who had never been beaten at racing.
(SWIFT RUNNER goes to the starting point for the race. OLD WOMAN RUNNER enters and stands next to her.)

---

opponent, someone you compete with in a contest or game

249

NARRATOR: The khan gave the signal to begin the race around two mountains. *(SWIFT RUNNER and OLD WOMAN RUNNER race around the stage and audience. Eventually, OLD WOMAN RUNNER faints and falls, and SWIFT RUNNER wins the race. The ADVENTURERS cheer, while KHAN and CO. are angry.)*

NARRATOR: By now, the khan **had had it** with these adventurers. Some of his most **bloodthirsty** warriors had ideas about how to destroy them once and for all.

(KHAN, KHAN'S SON, and WARRIORS gather, while in another area of the stage, GREAT LISTENER puts her ear to the ground.)

GREAT LISTENER: They say that tomorrow they'll burn us to death in a **banquet** room.

SEA SWALLOWER: Don't worry, I'll take care of it!
(SEA SWALLOWER goes to the sea, "swallows" it and comes back to where the ADVENTURERS are.)

---

faints, becomes unconscious (unable to feel, see, move) for a short time
had had it, had become very angry
bloodthirsty, wanting to kill

banquet, formal dinner

SCENE 6

(Setting: The same.)

NARRATOR: The khan sent a messenger to the adventurers.

WARRIOR: The great Khan Sadzaghai is so impressed with your great skills that he would like to invite you to a **royal** banquet!

ADVENTURERS: We'd **be honored**!
(They give each other sly smiles and follow the WARRIOR to the banquet room, where they sit or stand at the table. KHAN and CO. spread coals around the room and then pantomime lighting them. The ADVENTURERS pantomime getting very hot.)

ALL: It sure is getting HOT in here!

SEA SWALLOWER: Don't worry—I told you I'd take care of it! *(SEA SWALLOWER "spits" out the sea and quenches the fire.)*

KHAN and CO.: *(Vexed.)* AAARRGGHH!!!
(They exit, running and screaming.)

MOUNTAIN LIFTER: Well, now that we've destroyed the khan, what shall we do next?

SWIFT RUNNER: Let's go home!
(The ADVENTURERS move into position to form the constellation onstage. Each holds up a large star.)

---

royal, belonging to kings or queens
be honored, feel very proud and pleased
quenches the fire, makes the fire stop burning
vexed, very angry

NARRATOR: They **ascended** into heaven and became the seven stars of the constellation Ursa Major, the Great Bear. There they live very happily and peacefully.

---

ascended, went up

About the Playwright

Pamela Gerke

Pamela Gerke is artistic director and playwright for Kids Action Theater in Seattle, Washington. Since founding the program in 1988, she has written and directed more than thirty children's plays. Gerke is also the author of several books about children's theater.

BEFORE YOU GO ON . . .

1. Who saves the adventurers?

2. What happens to the seven adventurers at the end of the play?

HOW ABOUT YOU?

- Who is your favorite character in *The Great Bear*? Explain.

COMPREHENSION

Reread *The Great Bear*. Copy the chart into your notebook. Complete it with information from the story.

Adventurers	Special Skill	How Character Helps Others in Group
Hunters	hunting	They ask others to join them and be their blood brother or blood sister.
Sky Shooter		
Great Listener		
Mountain Lifter		
Swift Runner		
Sea Swallower		

Work in pairs or small groups. Take turns using your charts to retell the play.

EXTENSION

1. Do you think the khan is a good ruler? Support your answer with information from the story.

2. If you could meet one of the adventurers, who would you like to meet? Why?

3. Have you ever seen other constellations? If so, which ones? Write a short description of each.

4. If you could have one special skill, what would it be? Why?

DISCUSSION

Discuss in pairs or small groups.

1. Would you like to be an adventurer? Explain.

2. Have you ever seen the Great Bear? If so, describe the constellation.

3. Which adventurer is most like you? Which one is least like you? Compare your answers.

4. Do you know a myth that explains how any other constellation was formed? If so, tell the myth to your group.

▲ Scorpius (the Scorpion)

"Telescopes" is a science article about how telescopes work. It also tells how to make and use a telescope. As you read, look at the diagrams to help you understand the article.

TELESCOPES

Light from the sky gives astronomers most of their information about the planets and stars. Astronomers use telescopes to collect and use this light. The more light a telescope collects, the more information it gives astronomers. There are two main kinds of telescopes that use visible light: refracting telescopes and reflecting telescopes.

Refracting Telescopes

The simplest telescope is a refracting telescope, or refractor. A refracting telescope uses a large **convex lens** to collect and focus a large amount of light onto a small area. A convex lens is a piece of **transparent** glass. It is curved so that the middle is thicker than the edges. A refracting telescope also has a smaller eyepiece lens that **magnifies** the images. A person uses the eyepiece lens to look through the telescope.

Reflecting Telescopes

Reflecting telescopes collect light using a curved mirror. The mirror focuses a large amount of light onto a small area. The larger the mirror, the more light the telescope can collect. Most modern **professional** telescopes are reflecting

▲ A refracting telescope uses a convex lens to focus light. The light rays refract, or bend, as they pass though the lens.

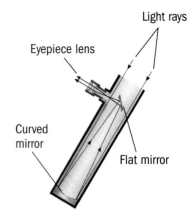

▲ A reflecting telescope uses a curved mirror instead of a convex lens. The light rays reflect, or bounce, off the curved mirror and travel to a small flat mirror so that the rays can be focused.

---

convex lens, piece of glass curved outward (like the surface of your eye), which makes something look bigger
transparent, clear; see-through
magnifies, makes something look larger
professional, used by people with special training

telescopes, with mirrors many meters wide. They are usually located in **observatories** on mountaintops.

Making a Refracting Telescope

To make a simple refracting telescope, you will need the following materials.

- 2 paper towel tubes of slightly different **diameters**
- plastic convex lens (43 mm [1.7 in.] diameter, 400 mm [16 in.] focal length)
- plastic eyepiece lens (17.5 mm [0.7 in.] diameter, 25 mm [1 in.] focal length)
- foam holder for the eyepiece, slightly larger than the diameter of the smaller tube
- transparent tape
- **meterstick** or **yardstick**

Use the following steps to make your telescope.

1. Put the smaller paper towel tube inside the other tube.
2. Place the convex lens flat against the end of the outer tube. Tape the lens in place. Try not to cover the lens with the tape.
3. Put the eyepiece lens in the middle of the foam holder. Draw a circle around the lens on the foam holder. Carefully cut the circle out of the foam holder. Put the eyepiece lens in the holder opening.
4. Trim the edge of the foam holder so that it will fit into the inner tube at the end of the telescope opposite the convex lens.
5. Tape a meterstick or yardstick to the wall. Stand 4.5 meters (5 yd.) from the wall. Look through the eyepiece. Slide the outer tube in and out to focus the telescope. Stop when you can read the numbers on the meterstick or yardstick.

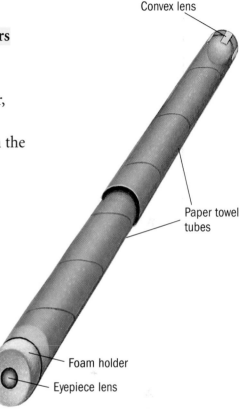

Convex lens

Paper towel tubes

Foam holder

Eyepiece lens

---

observatories, buildings where astronomers watch the sky
diameters, widths of circles, measured from side to side through the center
meterstick, measuring stick 1 meter long
yardstick, measuring stick 1 yard, or 3 feet, long

BEFORE YOU GO ON . . .

1 What is the simplest kind of telescope?

2 What kind of telescope uses mirrors?

HOW ABOUT YOU?

- Have you ever used a telescope? If so, what did you look at?

Using a Telescope

You can use your telescope to look at objects in the classroom and outside. *CAUTION: Do **not** look at the sun. You will damage your eyes.*

You can also use your telescope to observe the sky at night. Before you go outside, prepare carefully for your observations. First, decide which planets or stars you want to observe. Then make sure to take the following items.

- notebook
- pen or pencil
- **accurate** watch
- flashlight covered with red **cellophane**
- telescope or **binoculars**
- something to sit on
- books and star maps
- small table

If the weather is cold where you live, be sure to wear warm clothing, including a warm hat and **waterproof** shoes. It can take up to 30 minutes for your eyes to **become accustomed to** the dark and to get full **night vision**.

Outside, the flashlight covered with red cellophane gives off a reddish light. This reddish light makes it easier to read books or star maps and to take notes. Record the time, date, and location of your observations. You can make a chart like this in your notebook:

▲ Photograph of the moon taken through a telescope in 1863 by Henry Draper. © Hastings Historical Society, Hastings-on-Hudson, New York

Planets or stars observed:	
Time:	Date:
Location:	
Observations:	

accurate, correct
cellophane, thin, clear material used for wrapping things
binoculars, pair of glasses that you use to look at distant objects
waterproof, not allowing water to go through
become accustomed to, get comfortable with; adjust to
night vision, ability to see things at night

BEFORE YOU GO ON . . .

1 How long can it take to get full night vision?

2 Why should you cover a flashlight with red cellophane?

HOW ABOUT YOU?

- Do you know a good place to view the night sky? If so, where is it?

Link the Readings

REFLECTION

Reread *The Great Bear* and "Telescopes." Then copy the chart into your notebook and complete it. Compare your charts in small groups.

Title of Selection	Genre	Fiction or Nonfiction	Purpose of Selection	Main Idea
The Great Bear				
"Telescopes"				

DISCUSSION

Discuss in pairs or small groups.

1. Describe the Great Bear constellation.

2. Why is it helpful to use a telescope when you look at stars?

3. Imagine an adventurer with eyes like a telescope. How would such eyes be helpful?

4. Why do you think observatories are often located on mountaintops?

The Hubble Space Telescope orbits Earth. ▶

Connect to Writing

GRAMMAR

Using Prepositional Phrases

A **prepositional phrase** is a **preposition** + a **noun** or **pronoun**. Prepositional phrases often provide location, time, or description.

Prepositional phrases of location tell where.

	preposition	noun
The Wawaniki people lived	**in**	the **Northeast**.
We sat	**under**	the **stars**.
Khan and his son were	**at**	the **palace**.

Prepositional phrases of time tell when.

	preposition	noun
The summer solstice is	**on**	**June 21** this year.
The North Pole is tilted toward the sun	**in**	**June**.
School starts	**at**	**noon**.

Descriptive prepositional phrases usually answer the question Which one? or What kind of?

	preposition	noun
Great Listener is the woman	**with**	big **ears**.
This is an article	**about**	**telescopes**.
The museum has an exhibit	**of**	Chinese **art**.

Practice

Copy these sentences into your notebook. Underline each prepositional phrase. Circle each preposition. Write *L* (location), *T* (time), or *D* (description) to show the type of phrase.

Example: My brother hit the baseball (over) the fence. *L*

1. I like to play tennis in the evening.
2. The teacher gave a talk about American poetry.
3. We never go to school on Saturday.
4. The Big Dipper is a constellation with seven stars.
5. Tape a yardstick to the wall.
6. An observatory is a building with a large telescope.
7. You can observe many stars at night.

258

SKILLS FOR WRITING

Writing a Skit

A skit is a short play. The dialogue follows the character's name and a colon (:).
The dialogue has no quotation marks. Read this skit and answer the questions.

Jason Preston

Why the Sun and Moon Live in the Sky

Characters: Narrator, Sun, Moon, and Water; setting: Africa

NARRATOR: Long ago, Sun and Moon lived in a house on Earth. They were friends with Water. They visited Water often, but Water never visited them. One day, Sun asked why.

SUN: Why don't you ever come to see Moon and me?

WATER: Your house is too small. If I go into your small house, I will kick you out.

NARRATOR: To get Water to visit, Sun and Moon built a bigger house. When they finished, Moon spoke to Water.

MOON: We have built a huge house. Now will you visit us?

NARRATOR: Water said he would come the next day.

WATER: Here I am. May I come in?

SUN: Yes, please come inside.

NARRATOR: So Water poured into the house. When Water reached the ceiling, Sun and Moon climbed onto the roof. When Water covered the roof, Sun and Moon flew to the sky. They still live there.

1. What is the setting? Who are the characters?
2. How does the writer show dialogue?

WRITING ASSIGNMENT

Skit

You will write a skit telling a myth that explains something in nature or the universe.

1. Read Reread *The Great Bear* on pages 244–251. Who are the characters? What is the setting? What are the main events? What does the story explain?

Writing Strategy: Story Map

A story map can help you organize ideas. Look at the story map for the skit on page 259.

> *Title: Why the Sun and Moon Live in the Sky*

> *Characters: Narrator, Sun, Moon, Water*

> *Question: Why are the sun and moon in the sky?*

Events:

Long ago, Sun and Moon lived on Earth.

Sun and Moon were friends with Water.

They visited Water, but Water never visited them.

Water said their house was too small, so they built a big house.

Water visited their house.

The house began to fill with Water.

> *Explanation: When Water covered the roof, Sun and Moon flew to the sky.*

2. Make a story map Work in small groups. Choose or create a myth. Make a story map on a piece of paper. Write the title, characters, question, and explanation in your map. Then write the main events of the story in the map.

3. Write a skit Use your story map and the model to write a skit. Include stage directions and dialogue.

EDITING CHECKLIST

Did you . . .

▶ include a question, the main events, and an explanation?

▶ include two or more characters?

▶ add dialogue?

▶ include the setting and any necessary stage directions?

Check Your Knowledge

Language Development

1. How are plays different from other works of fiction, such as short stories? What is the main difference between a skit and a play?

2. What is the purpose of reading a play aloud?

3. What does a narrator do? Why do plays and skits have stage directions?

4. What is a prepositional phrase? Give examples of prepositional phrases that tell where, when, which one, or what kind.

5. How can a story map help you write a skit?

Academic Content

1. What new science vocabulary did you learn in Part 2? What do the words mean?

2. What is Ursa Major?

3. How are refracting telescopes and reflecting telescopes alike? How are they different?

▲ The sun sets over the Nile River.

Put It All Together

OBJECTIVES

Integrate Skills
- Listening/ Speaking: *Skit*
- Writing: *Short story*

Investigate Themes
- Projects
- Further reading

LISTENING and SPEAKING WORKSHOP

SKIT

You will perform a skit with a small group.

1 **Think about it** Return to the groups in which you wrote your skits. (See page 260.) Reread your group's skit. What supplies will you need to perform it? Discuss whether you will need costumes (special clothes) and, if so, what the costume should be for each character. Discuss whether you will need props— items that actors use in a skit or play. Plan how to show the setting. Would sound effects (special sounds) make your skit seem more realistic? Make notes about your ideas.

2 **Organize** Decide who will play each character. Find or create whatever costumes and props you plan to use.

3 **Practice** Act out your skit in your group. Memorize your lines, if possible.

4 **Present and evaluate** Perform your skit for the class. After each group presents its skit, evaluate the performance. What things did you like about each group's skit? Do you have suggestions for improvement?

SPEAKING TIP

Face toward the audience when you speak to the other actors. Speak clearly and loudly. If you turn away from the audience too much, people may not be able to hear or understand you.

LISTENING TIP

Listen carefully to the other actors so that you know when to say your lines. Watch the actors and listen for cues—words or actions that signal it is your turn to speak.

SHORT STORY

A short story is a work of fiction shorter than a novel. The writer usually presents a short sequence of events, or plot. One or more characters usually experience a problem or conflict. (A story about a myth usually presents a question and an explanation.) A short story usually has a clear beginning, middle, and end. The writer's purpose is to entertain and to present a message about life.

A short story usually includes the following:

- a setting
- a series of events that includes a problem, conflict, or question and a solution or explanation
- dialogue in quotation marks
- a beginning, middle, and end

You will write a short story based on the skit your group wrote and performed. Use the following steps to help you.

 Prewrite Return to the group in which you wrote your skit. Compare the skit on page 259 with the story map on the next page. How is the skit different from the story map?

Reread the skit your group wrote. Review the myths on pages 234–236 and look at the story chart on page 240. Then, together, plan your short story. Make a story map or story chart to help you organize your story.

WRITING TIP

When writing dialogue in a short story, you can sometimes use adverbs or other words to show how the characters feel or speak. For example, adding the adverb *sadly* shows how the character Winter feels in the myth on pages 234-235:

"I accept your offer," Winter whispered sadly.

Some other adverbs are *angrily, quietly, happily, loudly.*

In a skit or play, stage directions often tell how characters feel or speak.

Before your group writes a first draft of the story, read the following model story, based on the skit on page 259. Notice the characteristics of a short story. Notice also that the student includes more details and builds up more suspense.

Jason Preston

Why Sun and Moon Live in the Sky

Long ago, Sun and Moon lived in a house on Earth. Sun and Moon were friends with Water. They visited Water often, but Water never came to see them.

Setting (beginning)

One day, Sun asked Water, "Why don't you ever visit Moon and me?"

"Your house is too small!" Water exclaimed. "If I go into your house, I will kick you out."

Problem, conflict, or question

Sun and Moon built a bigger house so that Water could visit them. When they finished, Moon went to see Water.

"We have built a huge house," Moon said proudly. "Now will you come to see us?"

"Yes, I will," Water said eagerly.

Dialogue in quotation marks

The next day Water came to their house and called out loudly, "Here I am. May I come in?"

"Yes, please come inside," Sun answered happily.

So Water started to pour into the house. Soon it was half full of Water.

"Is it still okay for me to come in?" Water asked.

Series of events (middle)

"Yes, please come in," Sun and Moon replied.

More Water poured in. When Water reached the ceiling, Sun and Moon climbed onto the roof.

"Do you still want me to come in?" Water asked.

"Yes, we do. Please come in!" Sun and Moon replied.

When Water covered the roof of the house, Sun and Moon flew into the sky. And they still live there today.

Solution or explanation (end)

2 **Draft** As a group, use the model, your skit, and your story map or story chart to help you write your short story.

3 **Edit** Work with another group. Trade papers and read each other's stories. Use the questions in the editing checklist to evaluate each other's stories.

EDITING CHECKLIST

Does your story . . .

▶ have a beginning, middle, and end?

▶ include a problem, conflict, or question and a solution or explanation?

▶ use dialogue in quotation marks?

▶ start new paragraphs when different characters speak?

▶ use prepositional phrases correctly?

▶ use correct spelling and punctuation?

4 **Revise** As a group, revise your story. Add details or dialogue and correct mistakes, if necessary.

5 **Publish** Share your stories with your teacher and classmates.

PROJECTS

Work in pairs or small groups. Choose one of these projects.

1 Use the library or Internet to research an astronomer or astronaut. Make a poster about the person. Then share the poster with the class.

2 Write a poem about the sun, moon, stars, or planets. Read the poem to the class.

3 Make a calendar for the year. Include the winter and summer solstices and the vernal and autumnal equinoxes for this year. Ask classmates, teachers, and friends about holidays that they celebrate. Add these holidays to your calendar. Then share your calendar with the class.

4 Find a picture of Vincent van Gogh's painting *The Starry Night*. Then make a drawing or painting of the night sky where you live. Compare your picture with van Gogh's painting. Share your picture with the class.

5 From the library or from a friend, borrow a CD of *The Planets*, a musical work composed by Gustav Holst. The music has seven parts, each about a different planet: Mercury, Venus, Mars, Jupiter, Saturn, Uranus, and Neptune. In the music, Holst tried to express the spirit of the ancient god that each planet was named for. The music called "Mars," for example, is violent and loud, full of clashing war sounds. Pick one of the planets Holst wrote music about. Research the ancient Greek or Roman god and listen to the music. Then write a paragraph telling how the music shows the spirit of that god.

▲ Apollo 13 space mission emblem showing the Greek sun god, Apollo

Further Reading

To find out more about the theme of this unit, choose from these reading suggestions.

***Gus Grissom: A Space Biography,* Carmen Bredeson** Astronaut "Gus" Grissom's biography is also about the early U.S. spaceflight program. In 1959, NASA chose Grissom and six other pilots to be the first U.S. astronauts. Two years later, Grissom became the second American to fly in space. He flew in space again in 1965. But while practicing for a third flight in 1967, Grissom and two others died in a fire aboard the spacecraft *Apollo I.*

***How Night Came from the Sea: A Story from Brazil,* Mary-Joan Gerson** This Brazilian myth is about the daughter of an ancient African sea goddess. The story tells how the goddess, Lemanjá, sent the gift of night to her daughter, who was living in a world where there was only sunlight, brightness, and heat. Carla Golembe created the bold, colorful illustrations for the story.

***The Stargazer's Guide to the Galaxy,* Q.L. Pearce** This book tells about many objects in the universe and who discovered them. You'll read about the sun, the moon, and the planets and find out what asteroids, comets, meteoroids, black holes, white dwarfs, and neutron stars are. The book includes maps of the night sky at different times of the year and pictures to help you spot constellations. There are also myths and legends about the constellations.

***Hubble Space Telescope: New Views of the Universe,* Mark Voit** Gorgeous images of the universe taken by the Hubble Space Telescope dominate this book. The huge, powerful telescope orbits Earth every 97 minutes at a height of 600 kilometers, or 370 miles, above Earth. You'll see pictures of seven planets (including a cyclone on Mars), time-lapse images of pieces of a comet bombarding Jupiter, images of a star's death, and views of galaxies colliding.

***When Jaguars Ate the Moon,* María Cristina Brusca and Tona Wilson** Thirty myths explain how various animals and plants of North and South America came to be the way they are. The stories come from places as far apart as northeastern Canada and southern Argentina.

Glossary

ACTIVE VOICE /ak′tiv vois/
A verb is in the active voice when its subject is the performer of the action: *The firefighters rescue people from the building.*

ADJECTIVE /aj′ik tiv/
An adjective describes nouns (people, places, and things) or pronouns. In the sentence *I have a blue car,* the word *blue* is an adjective.

ADVERB /ad′vûrb/
An adverb usually describes the action of a verb, such as how an action happens: *The boy runs quickly.* The adverb *quickly* describes the verb *runs.* Several adverbs, such as *always, usually, often, sometimes,* and *never,* are called frequency adverbs: *She never found her necklace.*

ALLITERATION /ə lit′ə rā′shən/
Alliteration is the poetic use of two or more words that begin with the same sound. Writers use alliteration to draw attention to certain words or ideas, to imitate sounds, and to create musical effects.

ARTICLE /är′ti kəl/
An article is a piece of nonfictional writing that is usually part of a newspaper or magazine.

AUTOBIOGRAPHY /ȯ′tə bī og′rə fē/
An autobiography is the story of the writer's own life, told by the writer, usually in the first person. It may tell about the person's whole life or only a part of it. Because autobiographies are about real people and events, they are nonfictional.

BASE FORM /bās fôrm/
The base form, or simple form, of a verb has no added ending (*-s, -ing, -ed*). *Talk* is the base form of the verb *talk.* (Other forms of *talk* are *talks, talking,* and *talked.*)

BIOGRAPHY /bī og′rə fē/
A biography is the nonfictional story of a person's life told by another person. Biographies are often about famous or admirable people.

CAUSE-AND-EFFECT ORGANIZATION
/kȯz and ə fekt′ ôr′gə nə zā′shən/
Science and social studies texts often have cause-and-effect organization, in which the writer discusses an effect, or problem (such as pollution), and its causes (such as the reasons for pollution). The text sometimes includes a discussion of a solution and its benefits.

CHARACTER /kar′ik tər/
A character is a person or an animal that takes part in the action of a literary work.

CHARACTERIZATION /kar′ik tər ə zā′shən/
Characterization is the creation and development of a character in a story. Writers sometimes show what a character is like by describing what the character says and does.

COMPARATIVE /kəm par′ə tiv/
A comparative is an adjective or adverb used to compare two things. Most one-syllable adjectives and some two-syllable adjectives add *-er* for comparatives: *Bigger* is the comparative form of *big.* Most adjectives of two or more syllables use *more* for comparatives: *This rose is more fragrant than that one.* (*See also* Superlative.)

COMPLEX SENTENCE
/kom pleks′ sen′təns/
A complex sentence contains an independent clause and a dependent clause. The dependent clause usually begins with a subordinating conjunction. (*See also* Independent clause, Dependent clause, Subordinating conjunction.)

COMPOUND SENTENCE
/kom′pound sen′təns/
A compound sentence contains two or more independent clauses (sentences) joined by a coordinating conjunction, such as *and, but, so, for,* and *or.* (*See also* Coordinating conjunction.)

CONFLICT /kon′flikt/
A conflict is a struggle between opposing forces. Conflict is one of the most important elements of most stories, novels, and plays because it causes the action. Conflict can be between characters or between groups of people. Conflict can also be a struggle between a character and a force of nature or can take place in the mind of a character.

CONJUNCTION /kən jungk′shən/
A conjunction connects subjects, verbs, or objects in sentences that have more than one subject, verb, or object. The words *and, but, so, or, nor, for,* and *yet* are conjunctions.

CONTRACTION /kən trak′shən/
A contraction is a short form used to join two words. For example, the contraction of *I am* (the verb *am* and the subject pronoun *I*) is *I'm.* The contraction of *you are* is *you're.* In a contraction, an apostrophe replaces one or more letters. Contractions are used in speaking and informal writing.

COORDINATING CONJUNCTION
/kō ôr′dn āt ing kən jungk′shən/
A coordinating conjunction joins two independent clauses. Coordinating conjunctions include *and, but, so, or, nor, for,* and *yet.*

DEPENDENT CLAUSE /di pen′dənt klòz/
A dependent clause has a subject and a verb, but it does not express a complete thought. It cannot stand alone as a complete sentence. A dependent clause usually begins with a subordinating conjunction, such as *because, before, after, when, while, although,* and *if.*

DESCRIPTIVE ESSAY /di skrip′tiv es′ā/
In a descriptive essay, descriptive details are used to help the reader visualize what a person, place, or thing is like.

DIALOGUE /dī′ə lòg/
Dialogue is conversation between two or more persons. In poems, novels, and short stories, dialogue is between characters and usually appears in quotation marks (" ") to indicate a speaker's exact words. In plays and skits, dialogue follows the names of characters, usually after a colon (:). No quotation marks are used for dialogue in a skit or play.

DIARY /dī′ə rē/
A diary is a book in which a person writes each day about personal thoughts, things that happened, or things that he or she did.

ESSAY /es′ā/
An essay is a group of paragraphs about one topic. All the information in an essay supports one main idea.

EXCERPT /ek′sėrpt/
An excerpt is a passage or section taken from a book, article, letter, speech, film, or the like.

EXPOSITORY PARAGRAPH
/ek spoz′ə tôr′ē par′ə graf/
An expository paragraph is a paragraph that explains something by presenting factual information.

FABLE /fā′bəl/
A fable is a brief story or poem, usually with animal characters, that teaches a moral, or lesson. The moral is usually stated at the end of the fable.

FACT /fakt/
A fact is something that can be proved. It is a truth known through experience or observation to exist or to have happened.

FICTION /fik′shən/
Fiction is prose writing that tells about imaginary characters and events. Short stories and novels are works of fiction. (*See also* Historical fiction.)

FLASHBACK /flash′bak′/
A flashback is an interruption of the sequence of events in a story to tell about something that happened in the past.

GENRE /jän′rə/
A genre is a division or type of literature. Literature is commonly divided into three major genres: poetry, prose (fiction and nonfiction), and drama (plays, skits, etc.).

HERO/HEROINE /hir′ō /her′ō ən/
A hero or heroine is a character in a story whose actions are inspiring or noble. A hero or heroine often struggles to solve or overcome a problem.

HISTORICAL FICTION
/hi stôr′ə kəl fik′shən/
Historical fiction, such as a historical novel, combines imaginary elements (fiction) with real people, events, or settings (history).

HYPERBOLE /hī pėr′bə lē/
Hyperbole is a way of describing something by exaggerating on purpose—saying that it is much bigger, smaller, faster, or in some other way more than it really is: *I'm so hungry, I could eat a horse.* (*See also* Tall tale.)

INDEPENDENT CLAUSE
/in′di pen′dənt klōz/
An independent clause is a complete sentence. It has a subject and a verb and expresses a complete thought.

INFORMATIONAL TEXT
/in′fər mā′shən əl tekst/
An informational text is a nonfictional text. Its purpose is to present facts and other information about real people, events, places, and situations.

INTERVIEW /in′tər vyü/
An interview is a meeting or conversation in which a writer or reporter asks a person about his or her life, ideas, and feelings. The interviewer uses that information in an article for a newspaper, a radio or TV broadcast, or an online publication.

LETTER /let′ər/
A letter is a written communication from one person or group to another person or group. Letters can be formal or informal. Sometimes people write formal persuasive letters to newspapers to express their opinions and try to persuade readers to support their position. One type of informal persuasive letter is an e-mail message.

MAKING INFERENCES
/mā′king in′fər ən səz/
Figuring out a writer's meaning when the writer suggests something rather than presenting information directly is called making an inference.

MONITORING COMPREHENSION
/mon′ə tər ing kom′pri hen′shən/
Monitoring comprehension means that a reader checks his or her comprehension while reading a text. A reader monitors comprehension by rereading the text, trying to put the important information in his or her own words, writing questions about information that isn't understood, and looking for answers in the text or asking the teacher.

MOOD /müd/
Mood, or atmosphere, is the feeling that a literary work or passage creates. The mood can be sad, funny, scary, tense, happy, hopeless, and the like.

MYTH /mith/
A myth is a fictional story. Long ago, many groups of people created myths to explain natural events or the actions of gods and heroes. Parents told such myths to their children, and the myths passed from generation to generation as part of a group's spoken tradition.

NARRATIVE /nar′ə tiv/
A narrative is a story. It can be either fiction or nonfiction. Novels and short stories are fictional narratives. Biographies and autobiographies are nonfictional narratives, or true stories. A personal narrative tells about an experience in the writer's life.

NARRATOR /nar′ā tər/
A narrator is a character or speaker who tells a story. The narrator sometimes takes part in the action while telling the story. At other times the narrator is outside the action and just speaks about it. Some plays have a narrator who introduces, comments on, and concludes the story.

NONFICTION /non fik′shən/
Nonfiction is prose writing that tells about real people, places, objects, or events. Biographies, reports, and newspaper articles are examples of nonfiction.

NOUN /noun/
A noun is the name of a person, place, or thing. Examples of common nouns are *plane, building,* and *child.* Examples of proper nouns are *Robert, Chicago,* and *Puerto Rico.*

NOVEL /nov′əl/
A novel is a long work of fiction. Novels contain such elements as characters, plot, conflict, and setting. The writer develops these elements.

OBJECT PRONOUN /ob′jikt prō′noun/
An object pronoun *(me, you, him, her, it, us, you, them)* is used as an object in a sentence: *John took the ball and gave it to me.*

PARAGRAPH /par′ə graf/
A paragraph is a group of sentences about one idea in a piece of writing.

PASSIVE VOICE /pas′iv vois/
In the passive voice, the subject of the sentence receives the action: *The ball was caught by the outfielder.*

PERSONIFICATION
/pər son′ə fə kā′shən/
Personification is the giving of human qualities to animals or things.

PLAY /plā/
A play is a story that actors usually perform in a theater. Although plays are meant to be performed, actors can also read aloud the written version, or script, and the action can be imagined. (*See also* Dialogue, Setting, Stage directions.)

PLAYWRIGHT /plā′rīt/
A playwright is a person who writes plays.

PLOT /plot/
A plot is a sequence of connected events in a fictional story. In most stories, the plot has characters and a main problem or conflict. The plot usually begins with information to help the reader understand the story. Then an event introduces the main problem. The problem grows until there is a turning point, or climax, when a character tries to solve the problem. The events after the climax lead to the end of the story.

POEM /pō′əm/
A poem is a piece of writing that expresses ideas, experiences, and emotions. The written lines of a poem are often short. Groups of these lines are called stanzas or verses. Sometimes words in poems rhyme. Poets—people who write poems—may choose words for the way they sound. (*See also* Alliteration, Rhyme.)

POINT OF VIEW /point ov vyü/
Point of view is the perspective, or position, from which a story is told. The point of view can be that of a narrator outside the story or of a character in the story. In the first-person point of view, a character tells the story using the first-person pronouns *I* and *my*.
In the third-person point of view, the narrator tells someone else's story using third-person pronouns.

POSSESSIVE ADJECTIVE
/pə zes′iv aj′ik tiv/
A possessive adjective is a form of a personal pronoun that modifies a noun *(my, your, his, her, its, our, their): Victoria wrote her report.*

POSSESSIVE PRONOUN
/pə zes′iv prō′noun/
A possessive pronoun takes the place of a possessive adjective + a noun. *Mine, yours, his, hers, ours,* and *theirs* are possessive pronouns: *Her key is in her purse. His is in the car.*

PREPOSITION /prep′ə zish′ən/
A preposition is a connecting word, such as *to, with, from, in, on, at, by, of,* and *for,* that is always followed by a noun or pronoun and often indicates location or time: *Amy's mother drives her to school. School starts at 8:30 a.m.*

PREPOSITIONAL PHRASE
/prep′ə zish′ə nəl frāz/
A prepositional phrase is a preposition + a noun or pronoun. Prepositional phrases are used to indicate location, time, or description: *My family lives on the corner* (location). *The movie starts on Tuesday* (time). *The boy in the green coat is Jim* (description).

PREVIEWING and PREDICTING
/prē′vyü′ing and pri dikt′ing/
Previewing a text is looking at the text to get some ideas about it before reading. Previewing includes thinking about what you already know about the subject; looking at the title, headings, photographs, and other graphic elements; and using that information to predict, or try to figure out in advance, what the text is about.

PROCESS PARAGRAPH
/pros′es par′ə graf/
A process is an event or activity with steps in a particular order. A process paragraph is a paragraph in which the steps of a process are presented clearly in the correct order.

PRONOUN /prō′noun/
A pronoun is a word used to replace a noun: *Carlos goes to school. He likes it. He* replaces the proper noun *Carlos*; *it* replaces the noun *school*.

PROSE /prōz/
Prose is the ordinary language people use in speaking and writing. Most writing that is not poetry, drama (such as plays), or song is considered prose. Prose is one of the major genres of literature and occurs in fiction and nonfiction.

PUNCTUATION /pungk′chü ā′shən/
Punctuation is the system of using certain signs or marks, such as periods and commas, to divide writing into phrases and sentences so that the meaning is clear. Besides periods and commas, common punctuation marks include exclamation points, question marks, hyphens, semicolons, and colons.

QUOTATION /kwō tā′shən/
A quotation is a speaker's exact words repeated in a text. The exact words are written between quotation marks. A subject and reporting verb generally introduce or come after the quotation: *Bill said, "I won't be going to school tomorrow." "Is your homework finished?" the teacher asked.*

REAL CONDITIONAL
/rē′əl kən dish′ə nəl/
A real conditional sentence includes an *if* clause and a main clause. A real conditional sentence tells a fact—something that is true. The *if* clause tells a condition, and the main clause tells the result or possible result of that condition: *If we ride bikes to school, we don't use fossil fuel.*

RHYME /rīm/
Words that rhyme have the same ending sounds but different beginning sounds. Many poems have words that rhyme at the ends of lines: *Little Jack Horner/Sat in a corner.*

SENTENCE /sen′təns/
A sentence is a group of words that has a subject and a verb and expresses a complete thought.

SEQUENCE OF EVENTS
/sē′kwəns ov i vents′/
A sequence, or order, of events is a series of related events or actions that has a particular result. In both fiction and nonfiction writing, the sequence of events is often in chronological (time) order.

SEQUENCE WORDS /sē′kwəns wėrdz/
Sequence words help make the order of steps or events clear. Some common sequence words are *first, second, next, then, after that,* and *finally: First, you should finish your homework. After that, you may go outside.*

SETTING /set′ing/
The setting is the time and place of action in a literary work, such as a story or play. The time might be the year, the season, the day, or the hour. The place might be a city, a forest, a garden, or a kitchen.

SHORT STORY /shôrt stôr′ē/
A short story is a work of fiction shorter than a novel. A short story usually presents a sequence of events, or plot, and has a clear beginning, middle, and end. One or more characters usually experience a problem or conflict. (A story about a myth usually includes a question and explanation.) A short story usually presents a message about life.

SIMILE /sim′ə lē/
A simile is a figure of speech that uses the word *like* or *as* to compare two different things in an unusual way: *She was pale as a ghost. The news spread like wildfire.*

SIMPLE PAST /sim′pəl past/
Verbs in the simple past tell about an action that happened in the past and is completed: *The boy ate the apple. The girl walked up the hill.*

SKIMMING /skim′ing/
Skimming a text is reading it very quickly to gain a general understanding of it. Skimming involves reading the first and second paragraphs quickly, reading only the first sentences of the following paragraphs, and reading the last paragraph quickly.

SKIT /skit/
A skit is a short play.

SONG /sȯng/
A song is a piece of music with words. It can also mean the act or art of singing.

STAGE DIRECTIONS /stāj də rek′shənz/
Stage directions are instructions for the director and actors in a play. Stage directions are usually printed in italics and enclosed in parentheses. Stage directions tell actors how to talk, how and where to move, and when to enter and exit the stage. They are not spoken out loud as part of the play.

STUDYING DIAGRAMS
/stud′ē ing dī′ə gramz/
Studying diagrams can help a reader understand a text better. Science texts often include diagrams, such as drawings showing relationships among objects or events. Social studies texts often include bar charts, pie charts, and other graphic organizers providing information in a visual form.

SUBJECT PRONOUN /sub′jikt prō′noun/
A subject pronoun is used as the subject of a sentence. It can be singular or plural. Singular pronouns *(I, you, he, she, it)* refer to singular nouns: *Roberto walks to school because it is only a block away.* Plural pronouns *(we, you, they)* refer to plural nouns: *Our parents went to the store. They will be back soon.*

SUBJECT-VERB AGREEMENT
/sub′jikt vėrb ə grē′mənt/
In the simple present, the subject (or subjects) and verb must agree in number (singular or plural). With a subject that is a singular noun (or with the subject pronoun *he, she,* or *it*), add *-s* or *-es*: *A man runs. She catches the ball. It stays inside.* With a subject that is a plural noun (or with the subject pronoun *I, we, you,* or *they*), do not add *-s* or *-es*: *The men run. You catch the ball. I stay inside.*

SUBORDINATING CONJUNCTION
/sə bôr′dn āt ing kən jungk′shən/
A subordinating conjunction connects a dependent clause to an independent clause. Some subordinating conjunctions are *because, before, after, when, while, although,* and *if.*

SUMMARIZING /sum′ə rīz′ing/
Summarizing is restating the main ideas of a text in a shorter form. A way of summarizing is to read a text, reread each paragraph or section, put the text aside, and write the main ideas in one's own words in a sentence or two.

SUMMARY /sum′ə rē/
A summary is a brief statement that gives the main ideas of an event or literary work.

SUPERLATIVE /sə pėr′lə tiv/
A superlative is the form of an adjective or adverb used to compare three or more things. Most one-syllable adjectives and some two-syllable adjectives add *-est* for superlatives: *Biggest* is the superlative form of *big.* Most adjectives of two or more syllables use *the most* for superlatives. (*See also* Comparative.)

SUSPENSE /sə spens′/
Suspense is the creation of a feeling of uncertainty or worry in a reader about the outcome of events in a story. Writers often create suspense by delaying letting readers know what is going to happen next or how a problem or conflict is going to be resolved.

TAKING NOTES /tāk′ing nōts/
Taking notes while reading often helps a reader organize and remember information in a text. One note-taking method is to create two columns in a notebook and write important dates and time periods in the left column and corresponding events in the right column. These notes can be used to review the chronology of events.

TALL TALE /tôl tāl/
A tall tale, like a myth, is often passed from generation to generation as part of a group's spoken tradition. Tall tales are usually about characters with very exaggerated abilities or qualities. Pecos Bill and Paul Bunyan are examples of characters in tall tales. Tall tales often use hyperbole. (*See also* Hyperbole.)

VERB /vėrb/
A verb is a word or words used in a sentence to express action *(swims, drives)* or being (for example, *is*): *Tom swims fast* (action). *Sally is very sick* (being).

VISUALIZING /vizh′ü ə līz′ing/
Visualizing is picturing something in your mind.

Index

Acknowledgments

Albert Whitman & Company. "Pecos Bill Becomes a Coyote," from *Pecos Bill: The Greatest Cowboy of All Time* by James Cloyd Bowman. Copyright © 1937, 1964 by Albert Whitman & Company. Excerpt reprinted by permission of Albert Whitman & Company. All rights reserved.

The Belknap Press. "The Snake," reprinted by permission of the publishers and the Trustees of Amherst College from *The Poems of Emily Dickinson,* Thomas H. Johnson, ed., Cambridge, Mass.: The Belknap Press of Harvard University Press, Copyright © 1951, 1955, 1979 by the President and Fellows of Harvard College.

Doubleday & Co., Inc. "The Bat," copyright © 1938 by Theodore Roethke, from *Collected Poems of Theodore Roethke* by Theodore Roethke. Used by permission of Doubleday, a division of Random House, Inc., and Faber & Faber Ltd.

Dutton Children's Books. Excerpt from *My Side of the Mountain* by Jean Craighead George. Used by permission of Dutton Children's Books, an imprint of Penguin Putnam Books for Young Readers, a division of Penguin Putnam, Inc. All rights reserved.

HarperCollins Publishers. "Come with Me," from *Come with Me: Poems for a Journey* by Naomi Shihab Nye. Text copyright © 2000 by Naomi Shihab Nye, Greenwillow Books. Used by permission of HarperCollins Publishers.

HarperCollins Publishers and Paul Fleischman. "Virgil," from *Seedfolks* by Paul Fleischman. Text copyright © 1997 by Paul Fleischman. Used by permission of HarperCollins Publishers and Paul Fleischman.

HarperCollins Publishers and The Firm. "China's Little Ambassador," from *In the Year of the Boar and Jackie Robinson* by Bette Bao Lord. Text copyright © 1984 by Bette Bao Lord. Used by permission of HarperCollins Publishers and The Firm.

Pearson Education, Inc. Adapted from *American Expressions: Changes* by Dina Anastasio © 1997 Globe Fearon. Used by permission of Pearson Education, Inc.

Pearson Education, Inc. "Telescopes" and "The Earth's Orbit," from Prentice Hall *Science Explorer: Earth Science* by Michael J. Padilla, Ioannis Miaoulis, and Martha Cyr © 2001 Pearson Education, Inc., publishing as Prentice Hall. Used by permission.

Rachel Barenblat. "Interview with Naomi Shihab Nye" by Rachel Barenblat. Reprinted by permission of the author.

Scholastic, Inc. From *A Line in the Sand: The Alamo Diary of Lucinda Lawrence* by Sherry Garland. Copyright © 1998 by Sherry Garland. Reprinted by permission of Scholastic, Inc.

Scott Treimel NY. *River to Tomorrow* by Ellen Levine. Copyright © 1990 by Ellen Levine. Reprinted by permission of Scott Treimel NY.

Smith & Kraus, Inc. *The Great Bear* by Pamela Gerke, adapted from *Multicultural Plays for Children: Volume 1: Grade K–3* by Pamela Gerke. Copyright © 1996 by Pamela Gerke. All rights reserved. Reprinted by permission of Smith & Kraus, Inc.

Credits

Illustrators: Stephan Daigle 235; **Mike DiGiorgio** 164, 165, 166; **Leslie Evans** 58-59, 60; **Inklink Firenze** 55, 77, 78, 121; **L. R. Galante** 4, 7, 22, 110; **John Hovell** 142-143, 169; **Tom Leonard** 146, 147, 225, 229, 255; **Todd Leonardo** 68-69, 71, 72; **Mapping Specialists** 33, 34, 185, 209; **John F. Martin** 24-25, 26-27, 28; **Craig Spearing** 200, 202, 203, 204, 205, 220; **Ron Tanovitz** 244-245, 246-247, 248, 249, 250, 252; **Jean & Monsien Tseng** 157, 159, 160-161; **Cornealis van Wright & Ying-Hwa Hu** 190; **Qi Wang** 112-113, 114-115, 117.

Photography:

COVER: Panel top, NASA; middle, Masahiro Sano/CORBIS; middle, Archivo Iconografico SA/CORBIS; bottom, Dorling Kindersley; background, Eyewire/Getty Images; inset left, National Museum of American History; inset right, Joseph Sohm/Chromosohm/ CORBIS.

UNIT 1: 2 top, Lewis and Clark Collection, Smithsonian Institution; 2 middle, American Philosophical Society; 2 bottom, Dartmouth College Library; 2 inset, Dartmouth College Library; 2 foreground, David Schultz 1995, Voorhis Collection, Missouri Historical Society, St. Louis; 2-3 © Willard Clay; 3 foreground, Wayne Mumford; 6 top, Dorling Kindersley; 6 bottom, Robert Frerck/Odyssey Chicago/Robert Harding Picture Library; 7 Dorling Kindersley; 8 Dorling Kindersley; 9 New York Public Library/Art Resource; 10 top, Gunter Marx/CORBIS; 10 bottom, Dorling Kindersley; 11 American Museum of Natural History; 13 Here Now & Always Gallery/Museum of Indian Art Culture; 15 inset left, Roda/Natural Selection; 15 inset right, Mark Heifner/Natural Selection; 14-15 Dave Reede/Natural Selection; 16 Hulton/Archive; 17 left, Wayne Mumford; 17 right, Wayne Mumford; 19 Dorling Kindersley; 21 Dorling Kindersley; 23 Dorling Kindersley; 29 Courtesy of A. P. Koedt; 32 Dorling Kindersley; 35 American Philosophical Society; 39 Dorling Kindersley; 40 Dorling Kindersley; 41 top, Photodisc/Getty Images; 41 bottom, Dorling Kindersley; 43 José Luis Pelaez/CORBIS; 44 all, Dorling Kindersley.

UNIT 2: 46 top, Dorling Kindersley; 46 middle, Dorling Kindersley; 46 bottom, Dorling Kindersley; 46 inset, Dorling Kindersley; 46 foreground, © Jerry Young; 46-47 Grant V. Faint/The Image Bank/Getty Images; 47 bottom left, Dorling Kindersley; 47 bottom right, Dorling Kindersley; 48 top left, Digital Vision/Getty Images; 48 top right, Nicholas Devore/Stone/Getty Images; 48 bottom left, Dorling Kindersley; 48 bottom right, G. Ochocki/Photo Researchers; 50 all, Dorling Kindersley; 51 top, Dorling Kindersley/Kim Taylor; 51 bottom, Dorling Kindersley; 52 top, Lester Lefkowitz/Taxi/Getty Images; 52 bottom, Ecoscene/CORBIS; 53 Dorling Kindersley; 54 all, Dorling Kindersley; 56 Getty Images/Taxi; 59 © Burt Glinn/Magnum Photos; 60 right, Bettmann/CORBIS; 61 Dorling Kindersley; 62 Dorling Kindersley; 63 Dorling Kindersley; 65 Dorling Kindersley; 66 top, David Ulmer/Stock Boston; 66 bottom, Pearson Education Digital Archive; 67 Dorling Kindersley; 73 Ellan Young Photography; 74 Dorling Kindersley; 75 Dorling Kindersley; 76 all, Dorling Kindersley; 79 Dorling Kindersley; 81 Dorling Kindersley; 83 Dorling Kindersley 84 Dorling Kindersley; 85 Dorling Kindersley; 87 Dorling Kindersley; 88 all, Dorling Kindersley.

UNIT 3: 90 top, Dorling Kindersley; 90 middle, Phil Schermeister/CORBIS; 90 bottom, Dimaggio/Kalish/CORBIS; 90 foreground, Stone/Getty Images; 90-91 Charles O'Rear/CORBIS; 91 top, Duomo/CORBIS; 91 bottom, Tom Stewart/CORBIS; 92 Bettmann/CORBIS; 93 NASA; 94 top, Albright-Knox Art Gallery. Buffalo, NY. Bequest of A. Conger Goodyear, 1966.; 94 bottom, Private Collection/The Bridgeman Art Library; 95 © James McGoon; 96 top, AP/Wide World Photos; 96 bottom, Jerry Ohlinger/CORBIS Sygma; 97 AP/Wide World Photos; 98 top, AP/Wide World Photos; 98 bottom, Roger Ressmeyer/CORBIS; 99 top, Owen Franken/CORBIS; 99 bottom, Bettmann/CORBIS; 100 left, Bettmann/CORBIS; 100 middle, Madison Nye; 100 right, AP/Wide World Photos; 101 left, Henry Horenstein/CORBIS; 101 middle, Roger Ressmeyer/CORBIS; 101 right, AP/Wide World Photos; 102 top, Amy Arbus; 102 bottom, Dorling Kindersley; 103 top left, Dorling Kindersley; 103 top right, George H.H. Huey/CORBIS; 103 bottom left, John & Dallas Heaton/CORBIS; 104 top, Stone/Getty Images; 104 bottom, Courtesy Rachel Barenblat; 105 Dorling Kindersley; 106 Dorling Kindersley; 109 left, Dorling Kindersley; 109 right, Gianfranco Gorgoni/Contact Press Images/PictureQuest; 116 Courtesy Candlewick Press; 118 Henry Doubleday Research Association/Dorling Kindersley; 119 Stone/Getty Images; 120 Dorling

Kindersley; 122 all, Dorling Kindersley; 123 Dorling Kindersley; 125 Dorling Kindersley; 127 Dorling Kindersley; 129 Jim Cummins/CORBIS; 131 Dorling Kindersley; 132 Dorling Kindersley; 132–133 Dorling Kindersley.

UNIT 4: 134 top, Peter Beck/CORBIS; 134 middle, Alan Schein/CORBIS; 134 bottom, Joseph Sohn/Chromosohm/ CORBIS; 134 top foreground, Owakikulla/CORBIS; 134–135 top, Matt Brown/CORBIS; 134–135 bottom, Richard Stockton/Index Stock Imagery; 135 inset, Todd Gipstein/CORBIS; 136 Dorling Kindersley; 137 Dorling Kindersley; 138 Superstock 139 Dorling Kindersley; 140 top, Dorling Kindersley 140 bottom, Richard Hamilton Smith/CORBIS; 141 bottom, Dorling Kindersley; 142 top, Dorling Kindersley; 143 top, John Mead/SPL/Photo Researchers; 144 Derek Trask/CORBIS; 145 left, Jules Frazier/Getty Images/Photodisc; 145 right, Ford Motor Company; 148 Ernest Anastasio; 149 Raymond Gehman/CORBIS; 150 Larry Williams & Associates/ CORBIS; 153 Underwood & Underwood/CORBIS 154 Kevin R. Morris/CORBIS; 155 Joseph Sohm/CORBIS; 156 Dorling Kindersley; 161 Jim Kalett/Harcourt, Inc.; 162 Dorling Kindersley; 163 Dorling Kindersley; 167 Spencer Grant/PhotoEdit; 168 Dorling Kindersley; 171 Edward Keating/The New York Times; 174 top, Chris Rogers/Index Stock Imagery; 174 inset top, Anne W. Krause/CORBIS; 174 inset left, Grafton Marshall Smith/CORBIS; 174 inset right, James L. Amos/CORBIS; 176 top, Dorling Kindersley; 176 bottom, Bill Bachmann/Photo Researchers, Inc.

UNIT 5: 178 top, Dorling Kindersley; 178 middle, Photodisc/Getty Images; 178 middle, Danny Lehman/CORBIS; 178 bottom, Dorling Kindersley; 178 foreground left, Dorling Kindersley; 178 foreground right, Dorling Kindersley; 178–179 Dan Coffey/The Image Bank/Getty Images; 179 inset, Jim Cummins/Taxi/Getty Images; 179 bottom, Dorling Kindersley; 180 all, Dorling Kindersley; 181 Dorling Kindersley; 182 top, Dorling Kindersley; 182 bottom, Texas State Library and Archives Commission; 183 Hulton/Archive; 184 Bettmann/CORBIS; 186 Bettmann/CORBIS; 187 Bettmann/CORBIS; 188 Bob Daemmrich/Stock Boston/ PictureQuest; 189 Dorling Kindersley; 192 Courtesy of Sherry Garland; 193 Craig Aurness/CORBIS; 197 Lake County Museum/ CORBIS; 198 all, Dorling Kindersley 199 Dorling Kindersley; 205 Courtesy Little Brown & Company; 206 Jan Butchofsky-Houser/CORBIS; 207 Dorling Kindersley; 208–209 CORBIS; 210 Dorling Kindersley; 211 Bettmann/CORBIS; 212 Dorling Kindersley; 215 Hulton/Archive; 219 Bettmann/CORBIS; 220 Dorling Kindersley.

UNIT 6: 222 top, NASA; 222 middle, Masahiro Sano/CORBIS; 222 middle, Archivo Iconografico SA/CORBIS; 222 bottom, Dorling Kindersley; 222 top right, NASA; 222–223 Matthias Kulka/CORBIS; 222 foreground left, Floyd Dean/Taxi/Getty Images; 222 foreground right, Dorling Kindersley; 223 inset, National Maritime Museum, London/Dorling Kindersley; 223 bottom, Dorling Kindersley; 224 Dorling Kindersley; 227 Dorling Kindersley; 226 & 228 Dorling Kindersley 230 Dorling Kindersley; 231 Yann Arthus-Bertrand/ CORBIS; 233 Dorling Kindersley; 234 Dorling Kindersley; 236 Dorling Kindersley; 237 The De Morgan Foundation, London/The Bridgeman Art Library; 239 Dorling Kindersley; 241 Dorling Kindersley; 242 Dorling Kindersley; 243 Tony Freeman/PhotoEdit; 251 Courtesy Kids Action Theater; 253 all, Dorling Kindersley; 254 all, Dorling Kindersley; 256 Hastings Historical Society; 257 NASA; 261 Dorling Kindersley; 262 Dorling Kindersley; 265 Dorling Kindersley; 266 all, NASA.